$c

PUBLIC POLICY OPINION
AND THE ELDERLY,
1952–1978

Recent Titles in
Contributions to the Study of Aging

Geriatric Medicine in the United States and Great Britain
David K. Carboni

Innovative Aging Programs Abroad: Implications for the United States
Charlotte Nusberg, with Mary Jo Gibson and Sheila Peace

The Extreme Aged in America: A Portrait of an Expanding Population
Ira Rosenwaike, with the assistance of Barbara Logue

Old Age in a Bureaucratic Society: The Elderly, the Experts, and
the State in American History
David Van Tassel and Peter N. Stearns, editors

The Aged in Rural America
John A. Krout

PUBLIC POLICY OPINION AND THE ELDERLY, 1952–1978

A KALEIDOSCOPE OF CULTURE

JOHN E. TROPMAN

CONTRIBUTIONS TO THE STUDY OF AGING, NUMBER 6

GREENWOOD PRESS

NEW YORK • WESTPORT, CONNECTICUT • LONDON

HQ
1064
.U5
T76
1987

Library of Congress Cataloging-in-Publication Data

Tropman, John E.
  Public policy opinion and the elderly, 1952-1978.

  (Contributions to the study of aging.
ISSN 0732-085X ; no. 6)
  Bibliography: p.
  Includes index.
  1. Aged—United States—Attitudes—Longitudinal
studies. 2. United States—Social policy—Public
opinion—Longitudinal studies. 3. United States—
Economic policy—Public opinion—Longitudinal studies.
4. Public opinion—United States—Longitudinal studies.
I. Title. II. Series.
HQ1064.U5T76   1987   305.2'6'0973   86-27150
ISBN 0-313-25432-X (lib. bdg. : alk. paper)

Library of Congress Catalog Card Number: 86-27150
ISBN: 0-313-25432-X
ISSN: 0732-085X

First published in 1987

Greenwood Press, Inc.
88 Post Road West
Westport, Connecticut 06881

Printed in the United States of America

The paper used in this book complies with the
Permanent Paper Standard issued by the National
Information Standards Organization (Z39.48-1984).

10 9 8 7 6 5 4 3 2 1

TO THE MEMORY OF MY GRANDPARENTS,
ARTHUR R. AND ANNA OVERFIELD,
AND JOSEPH M. AND KATHRYN TROPMAN,
AND TO THE MEMORY OF MY GREAT GRANDFATHER,
ANGUS MACDONALD, CAPTAIN OF THE *HUDSON*,
LOST AT SEA WITH ALL HANDS, OFF EAGLE RIVER,
KEWEEANAW POINT, LAKE SUPERIOR, SEPTEMBER 1901.

". . . every culture contains all the possible values. The contrasts are not between opposites, but between preferences and priorities. Tension arises over rank order, not complete negation of alternatives, in almost every instance."

C. Attneave, "American Indians and Alaska Native Families in Their Own Homeland."

"The ideologies of modern societies are a complex blend of contradictory themes, both meritocratic and egalitarian, individualistic and collectivistic; such ambivalence is built into the structure of modern life."

From the Foreword by Harold Wilensky in Richard M. Coughlin, *Ideology and Public Opinion and Welfare Policy.*

"Between the laughing and the weeping philosopher there is no opposition; *the same facts* that make one laugh make one weep. No whole-hearted man, no sane art, can be limited to either mood."

George Santayana, *Persons and Places.*

CONTENTS

Charts   xi

Figures   xiii

Tables   xv

Acknowledgments   xvii

Introduction   1

1.   Cultural Conflict, Cultural Change, and the Elderly   5

PART I.   A KALEIDOSCOPE OF CULTURE

2.   A Conflict Theory of Values   25

3.   Policy-Value Conflicts in American Society   35

PART II.   POLICY OPINION AND THE ELDERLY: 1952-1978

4.   The Eclipse of Public Function   61

5.   Righting Civil Wrongs   95

6.   The Wavering of Traditional Commitments   111

PART III.   PATTERNS IN THE STONES

7.   The Mosaic of Culture   127

8.   The Personal Roots of Commitment   145

9.   American Values and the Elderly   169

APPENDICES

Appendix A.   Frequency Data for Floating Bar Charts   186

Appendix B.   International Comparisons— Germany and Japan   203

Appendix C.   A List of Questions from the National Election
Study, University of Michigan, and the Gallup Poll   213

Appendix D.   Data and Method   223

Appendix E.   Factor Analysis Techniques   227

Bibliography   229

Index   243

CHARTS

1. Public Opinion Trends, 1950-1975   11

2. Policy-Relevant Questions from the National Election
Study and the Gallup Poll, 1952-1978   13

3. Policy Value Conflicts in American Society   30

4. Correspondence between Policy Opinion Questions
and Policy Value Dilemmas   36

5. The Distribution of Variables Included in the Factor
Analysis of Respondent Opinion   130

6. The Clustering of "Policy" Opinion, 1956-1978:
Factor Analysis by Year of Repeated Questions   132

7. The Clustering of "Policy" Opinion, 1956, 1964, and
1972: Factor Analysis by Year of Repeated Questions by
Age Groupings of under 30, 30-65, and Over 65   140

8. Factor Clustering of Policy Opinions by Age, 1978   142

9. Coding of Independent Variables Regression
Analysis of Repeated Policy Opinion Questions: 1952-1978   147

FIGURES

PUBLIC FUNCTION

1. Trust in Government, 1958-1978   64

2. Who Is the Government Run for the Benefit of? 1958-1978   67

3. People Like Me Don't Have Any Say About What the Government Does, 1952-1978   69

4. Voting Is the Only Way that People Like Me Can Have Any Say about How the Government Runs Things, 1952-1978   72

5. Public Attitudes towards Government Action to Insure Everyone a Job (and a Good Standard of Living), 1956-1978   77

6. Feeling Thermometers, 1964-1978   80

7. Public Support for Government Involvement in Health Care, 1956-1978   82

8. Opinion on Government Involvement in Electric Power and Housing, 1956-1964   85

9. Is the Government in Washington Getting Too Powerful? 1964-1978   88

CIVIL RIGHTS

10. Should Government See to It that Blacks Get Fair
    Treatment in Jobs and Housing? 1952-1972   97

11. Public Attitudes towards the Speed of the Civil
    Rights Movement, 1964-1976   100

12. Public Attitudes towards Change in the Position
    of Negroes (Blacks), 1964-1976   102

13. Public Attitudes towards Protecting the Rights of
    the Accused, 1970-1978   105

14. Public Attitudes towards Women's Rights, 1972-1978   107

TRADITIONAL COMMITMENTS

15. Frequency of Church Attendance, 1952-1978   113

16. Public Attitudes towards the Issue of Reducing the
    Hours in a Work Week, 1953-1965   116

17. Public Attitudes about the Ideal Number of
    Children in a Family, 1941-1978   118

TABLES

1. R² Values for Dependent Variables, Multiple
   Regression Analysis with 14 Independent Variables   149

2. Percentage of 14 Independent Variables Significant at
   .05 Level for Different Dependent Variables   152

3. Percentage of Times a Particular Variable Is Significant
   at .05 Level   153

4. Median Beta Weights over Time and Selected
   Independent Variables   156

5. Rank Order Comparisons of Independent Variables   157

6. Factor: Questionable Public Entitlements   160

7. Factor: Public Inadequacy   162

8. Factor: Privatism and Self-Reliance   164

9. Factor: Public Inequity   165

ACKNOWLEDGMENTS

As in all scholarly efforts, the help of many organizations and individuals is required to crystallize the results one calls a book. The original support for this research came from the Administration of Aging (90-A-1325). Additional support was provided through the Social Research on Applied Issues of Aging Project supported by the National Institute of Aging (A600117-03). Continuing support from the School of Social Work, the Institute of Gerontology, and the School of Business at the University of Michigan were crucial. Dean Harold Johnson of the School of Social Work has been especially supportive, both intellectually and personally; and I owe him a substantial debt. The original theoretical notions that inform this analysis were developed several years ago while I was a visiting faculty associate at the Joint Center for Urban Studies of MIT/Harvard and have been refined and developed in scholarly exchange since then. Henry J. Meyer, now professor Emeritus of the University of Michigan, was especially challenging and skeptical (and probably remains so), but his influence and demand for rigor improved this effort substantially. Shortly before his death, Talcott Parsons spent a day discussing these concepts and made penetrating and helpful comments. Andrew Achenbaum, Brian Gratton, Phyllis Day, William Birdsall, John Campbell, John Strate, John Peterson, Eric Rabkin, John Nesselroade, and Jane McClure are but a few of the individuals with whom I have shared parts of this approach and who have contributed ideas and perspectives. Bill Birdsall, especially, provided more support for the entire project than he is aware, and he deserves my special thanks.

The editorial assistance of Gersh Morningstar has been invaluable. As a critic and friend, he always refused to let bad enough alone and merits special recognition. He is as close as anyone I know to what I think Mark Twain must have been like; and, if one can imagine trying to explain and justify concepts to Twain, one can understand the improvements that would result.

Sharon Jablonski and David Crystal not only assisted in manuscript preparation with extreme care but made substantial intellectual contributions as well. John Strate did the original charts and convinced me to leave the numbers out (through they are mentioned in the text), arguing that they were more elegant without the "numeric junk." I think he was right. For those interested in numbers, however, the appendices provide specific values. Stannette Amy made careful editorial assessments and corrections, and Dan Madaj prepared the bibliography and tables.

This volume, of course, is one of secondary analysis. Thus, it is fitting and proper that I acknowledge all of the respondents and the interviewers, stretching as far back as 1942, who provided the pieces of this mosaic, and the archivists and data managers who kept the material in usable condition.

To all of these individuals, and to others who helped, I express my thanks.

Finally, to my wife, Penny, and to my children, Sarah, Jessica and Matthew, I want to express deep appreciation. They helped with this volume in so many ways—some big, some small—over the several years of its development that they are as much a part of it as I am. And beyond contributions to the volume itself, their tolerance and support of this application of my energy and effort made it all possible.

PUBLIC POLICY OPINION
AND THE ELDERLY,
1952-1978

INTRODUCTION

This book is about public policy opinion and older Americans in the period from 1952 to 1978. Because it involves many elements, let me lay out here something of the background and structure of the volume.

For many years the Inter-university Consortium on Political and Social Research (ICPSR) at the University of Michigan has maintained an archive of studies and made them available for scholarly research. In this presentation, one particular study series was used—the National Election Study—which has been completed every two years since 1950. From these surveys, questions were selected that had been asked in succeeding years; and, thus, a comparison is possible among a sequence of answers. The questions I selected were those that focused on policy matters; e.g., the role of government, the need for public programs, civil rights, and women's rights. There were also some questions on family structure and on work. In all, seventeen questions were repeated often enough to be included here: fifteen from the National Election Study and two from the Gallup Poll, provided by the Roper Center. (There is more detail in appendix D on method.) Because investigators in other countries repeated some of the National Election Study questions, examples of the same questions asked during the analysis period in Germany and in Japan are also available and are reported here.

My focal interests, right now, are the elderly (sixty-five years and older) and their public policy opinions during this time frame. It is necessary, of course, to look at all age groups in such an analysis in order to see the changes elderly respondents exhibit and to assess the extent to which such changes are the same as or different from those exhibited by younger adults. While special attention is paid to matters relating to the elderly, therefore, there is much information on middle-aged and young adults as well. Indeed, this volume presents a fairly clear picture of the structure of public policy opinion for the third quarter of the twentieth century in the United States.

The time frame is specific to the span of years reflected in the studies used. With so many samples from the public (each study being considered a sample), one can have some confidence that trends emerging over time continue today.

The results are instructive. The elderly are not, overall, greatly different from other citizens in their public policy expressions. In some specific areas (trust in government, rights of accused criminals, women's rights, and ideal family size), they do express differences from younger Americans; in some cases by a little, in others by a lot. But of the seventeen separate questions examined here, the large majority show consistency among the three age groups I looked at (18 to 30, 30 to 65, 65 plus).

This study is unusual for several reasons. To begin with, the multi-year, multi-question format provides an exceptionally broad base from which to assess changes in U.S. public policy opinion over the period studied. Data are not only presented descriptively, they are analyzed in some detail to seek for hidden patterns and to discern what personal characteristics are linked to what kinds of opinion patterns. In addition, the study presents a theoretical framework within which one can look at such a vast number of data points—the conflict theory of values. This perspective suggests that commitments (values, attitudes, beliefs—I am not discriminating here for the moment) come in linked pairs that are partially opposed to each other (e.g., adequacy and equity or public and private). These competing commitments fight for expression within us and within our society. Part of the way opinion changes over the years can be understood, I think is, as part of the process of adjustment from honoring one commitment to honoring another. The likelihood is that society will swing back, having swung from conservative times (the 1950s) to more liberal times (the 1960s and early 1970s) to more conservative times once again (the later 1970s and 1980s). The data in no way test this conflicting values perspective. Rather, that perspective provides a point of view through which one can gain a sense of the sweep of public policy opinion.

One final point needs to be mentioned. The multi-year focus presented some problems in data presentation. It was difficult to find a way to display the results such that a picture of change over the flow of years could be seen easily and quickly. For this purpose floating bar charts were selected. The shape of the charts over time gives a quick sense of what has been happening to opinion on each particular question. For elegance' sake, numbers were not included. Because some readers may wish to know the exact values for specific answers to specific questions, a complete set of tables is provided in appendix A, each table keyed to its own figure. Hence, both numbers and shape are available for inspection.

1

CULTURAL CONFLICT, CULTURAL CHANGE, AND THE ELDERLY

When viewed from the vantage point of today, the third quarter of the twentieth century has been a time of tremendous change and conflict within U.S. society. The 1950s were years of relative tranquillity. In the 1960s, however, we experienced a cataclysmic period of trouble and difficulty. Then the 1970s brought us both change and readjustment. For many it is difficult to believe that the same society was characterized by such conflicting and contrasting styles: massive changes in the role of government occurred during that period of time. The civil rights movement blossomed. Questions about traditional commitments to church and family were raised (Yankelovich, 1981). Indeed, the conflicts seemed to be characterized by an almost complete reversal of conventional commitments. Yankelovich's subtitle in his book *New Rules* is "Searching for Self-Fulfillment in a World Turned Upside Down." Almost the same phrase appears as a subtitle in J. M. Yinger's book, *Countercultures: The Promise and Peril of a World Turned Upside Down* (1982). Yinger sees counter-culture as a central concept that might define the period:

The term counterculture is appropriately used whenever the normative system of the group contains, as a primary element, a theme of conflict with the dominant values of society, where the tendencies, needs, and perceptions of the members of that group are directly involved in the development and maintenance of its values, and wherever its norms can be understood only by reference to the relationship of the group to the surrounding dominant society and its culture. (Pp. 22-23)

Most observers would agree with the conclusion of Lipset and Schneider (1983) who begin their study of public confidence with the observation: "The 1960s and 1970s were decades of introspection for Americans. Our political and economic systems were severely tested by the conflicts and reversals of those years" (p. 1). Among the many changes during this quarter was the rise in interest in the older American. The science and discipline of gerontology, just in its beginning phase in 1950, was in full flower by 1975. There had already been White House Conferences on the Aging. Major social-policy initiatives had been proposed, legislated, and put into practice.

Some thought the role of the elderly in American society was changing, too. Historian David Hackett Fischer (1978), for example, suggested that the nation was moving from a period of *gerontophobia*—"fear of the aged"—to *gerontofratria*—"a brotherly association."

Clearly, a change in the role and position of the elderly in U.S. society and their claims on it were part of the large-scale shifts that characterized the third quarter of the twentieth century. Little is known, however, about how the elderly felt during this period of time. No one knows for certain if the opinions of elderly Americans were changing or remaining constant throughout the sixties and seventies. If they were changing, we do not know if such opinions were leading or lagging those of other age groups. Those who have tried to chart opinion during that period (see, especially, Yankelovich, 1982; Lipset and Schneider, 1983) are relatively silent on the position of the elderly. The mission of this volume is to chart the changes in public views over the years 1952 through 1978, with a special eye on differences among varying age groups. In examining these changes and differences I shall also offer an interpretive framework to assist in understanding the changes and the constancies.

THE AXES OF CHANGE

So many changes and differences in public opinion occurred during the 1952-1978 period that it would be almost impossible to attempt to detail them all. The three areas mentioned here—public function, civil rights, and traditional commitments—seem to be among the most important for society as a whole. They also represent those that are of focal interest when considering elderly Americans and their commitments and interests. Certainly, these areas would be of great concern to the elderly and to those who desire to know about changes in the public views held by the elderly.

Public Function

In a society that emphasized privatism and self-reliance, the period between 1952 and 1978 was in the midstream of important social change. Governmental activity to achieve social purposes had been massive and successful since 1935. Starting with governmental social programs in the Depression and continuing through successful governmental activity in World War II, the nation seemed to have the view, as it came out of that period, that government could do things successfully and on a massive scale. The impetus generated by these earlier successes appeared to carry through until twin defeats in the same area—the War on Poverty and Vietnam.[1] Lipset and Schneider (1983) comment:

As it happened, the early 1960s turned out to be a high water mark in the history of the American public's attitudes toward their key social, political, and economic structures. The explosion of protest against U.S. participation in the Vietnam War, as well as other conflicts stemming from the rise of militant social movements concerned with the status of women and various minority groups—blacks, Hispanics, American Indians—apparently changed the prevailing perception that Americans had of their country. One public opinion survey after another registered a steady decline in the public's confidence in the country's institutions and in the people running them. (P. 15)

The current emphasis on privatism, the resurgence of voluntarism, and the defederalization of social policy back to state suggest an important trend away from behavioral patterns that were characteristic of the 1950-to-1975 period.

During the third quarter of this century, the elderly were among the beneficiaries of public policy, particularly in the area of pension benefits, improvements in Social Security and health care, and the passage of Medicare. The elderly gained arguably as much as and perhaps more than any other group in real dollar terms. How did they feel about the public weal? Did they share with their younger counterparts questions about the public emphasis that had characterized this later period of their lives? The theory of rational self-interest would suggest that those who benefit from a governmental program should continue to support it and, indeed, might even demand increments and augmentations. One might expect, therefore, the elderly group to exhibit continuing support of public programs while younger age groups were becoming more conservative. The converse hypothesis also sounds quite plausible. The elderly group, being more "traditional" as Shils (1983-1984) suggests, drawing on values and commitments of an older period, might well seek to return to the public-private balance of their younger days, while younger Americans would support the status quo. Although the data presented here will suggest some perspectives on these issues, it will not resolve them.

Civil Rights

Of commensurate importance to the body politic is the vigorous emergence of civil rights as a cause and concern. Minorities of color— especially blacks—were the focal point of an increasingly vocal protest movement. Within the period under consideration, I would earmark the 1954 court decision in *Brown* v. *The Topeka Board of Education* as a starting point, generating forces that culminated in the civil rights activism of the sixties and the march on Washington, spearheaded by Rev. Martin Luther King, Jr. With his death on April 4, 1968, a watershed was reached, at least with respect to more militant and activist postures.

But blacks were not the only group affected by the civil rights revolution. Racism was joined by sexism, ageism, and classism as positions to be abhorred. Gays, the handicapped, women—all groups whose rights had been truncated and circumscribed—began to demand those rights. In the case of women's activism, the issue achieved the status of a proposed constitutional guarantee of equality. Not since the 1860s and the Civil War, perhaps, had issues of equality been so much on the public's consciousness.

But how did the elderly feel? In 1965, everyone over sixty-five had been born in the nineteenth century. These were the individuals who had, by and large, contributed by agreement or acquiescence to the status quo we had known before the civil rights revolution. Were they joining as eagerly as the others? The data here should give us some clues.

TRADITIONAL COMMITMENTS

Traditional commitments and orientations are often thought of as the hallmark of the elderly. Edward Shils (1983-1984) expresses it well when he talks about age and tradition:

Numerous investigations in the United States, Great Britain, France, Western Germany, and other countries bear witness to this difference between generations. Although the proportion of persons with a "traditional" outlook in each age-group is often substantial, there is a more or less steady decrease as one moves downward from those persons sixty and over, through those between forty-five and fifty-nine years old and those between thirty and forty-four years old, toward those between fifteen and thirty years old. The decline in traditionality from the older to the younger age-groups does not, however, necessarily mean that the members of the younger age-group will retain their present relatively indifferent or hostile attitude toward traditional beliefs and conduct when they become older. (Pp. 28-29)

While Shils cites no studies to support this particular contention, its unchallenged publication in the *American Scholar* testifies to its wide acceptance. Shils not only suggests that the older individual is more traditional, but he implies in addition that the process of growing older is a process of traditionalization and attachment to more of the long-standing commitments.

Among these commitments, work, family, and religion certainly rank high. If Shils' contention is correct, one would expect to see among the elderly attitudinal manifestations of higher religious orientation, higher work orientation, and higher familial orientation. Accepting for a moment that operationalization is a decided difficulty here, it is in the area of these traditional realms that whatever differences exist might be most prominent. Shils himself comments on work: "Except for a few geniuses in the art of leisure and consumption, regularity of work and reasoned expenditures of income are indispensible to an ordered life" (p. 34). The emphasis on personal values and an ethos of self-development seems to have been the hallmark of the "Me" generation and the New Narcissists. Peggy Rosenthal (1984), in her book on words and values, talks about "the attractions of self" and "growth and development to realize your potential" but concludes on the more traditional note that relationships and emphasis on them are on the rise. She comments:

Today, carrying on both these sets of values, we seem to value *self* and *relations* about equally, although not usually at the same time. We switch back and forth between seeing *self* or seeing *relationship* as our central terms; but the switch is less like one between different slides projected on a screen than like a Gestalt switch between different ways of perceiving the same projection, different ways of focusing on the same picture of the world. (P. 248, emphasis in original)

Her conclusion is the same as Yankelovich's. Despite the fact that we are in a secular age (Rosenthal, p. 254), Yankelovich (1981) concludes:

But the overall judgment holds so that by the mid 70's a majority of the American people had reached a conclusion comparable to that reached by intellectual critics of industrial civilization in earlier years, namely, that our civilization is unbalanced, with excessive emphasis on the instrumental, and insufficient concern with the values of community, expressiveness, caring and with the domain of the sacred. (P. 232)

What of the elderly? Does Yankelovich suggest greater traditional emphasis? Not quite. He concludes that they are more likely to be "retreaters":

In 1970, my firm's surveys of cultural trends identified almost two out of five Americans as having a "sour grapes" outlook on life. These people believed in the American dream of "bettering oneself" by acquiring education, money possessions, recognition and status, but in their own lives the dream had failed. My associate, Florence Skelley, named these people "retreaters" because so many felt bitter, negative and withdrawn about their lives. Among the retreaters were many older Americans: their median age was fifty-three compared to twenty-eight for the population as a whole. (P. xvi)

But the elderly adult is no more cast in stone than the younger person. Yankelovich himself points out that by 1980, the number of retreaters—38 percent in 1970—had dropped substantially to about 18 percent. What was the elderly adult thinking during this period of change?

OPINION AND AGE

Given all this tumultuous development in the cultural system, what do elder adults feel or believe? Their opinions are increasingly important because of their actual and potential political weight *and* because of the amount of public resources they consume.

There are several ways one can ask this question. One of them, of course, is to look at the views of people over some particular age—we'll choose sixty-five for our purpose here—and at different times during the period under analysis. Alternatively, one can try to follow cohorts as they move through the system. A person who is forty in 1950 will be sixty-five by 1975. Hence, one cannot only consider the views of elderly adults at any moment in time, but—on a very tentative basis, to be sure—chart changes over the flow of time. In both cases one can look at the relationship between the elderly and younger adults either through time or at a moment in time. This process of investigation, this more detailed assessment, is one step in providing a more balanced picture of our pluralistic society. In such a heterogeneous culture as the United States, one would expect a heterogeneity of views. The particular heterogeneity ascribable to or attributable to the elderly has been largely ignored. It is the hope of this study to use *public opinion* data (that I call *policy opinion* for reasons to be mentioned shortly) to chart the position of the elderly during changing times.

The picture of what was happening during this third quarter of the twentieth century is an extremely complex one for a range of reasons. *Public Opinion* Magazine summarizes contradictory trends over three decades in their September-October 1978 issue. They point to trends toward conservatism on the one hand, trends toward liberalism on the other, and mixed signals. Their summary is displayed in chart 1.

Yankelovich finds the same thing. He comments: "In American life, continuity and far reaching change do coexist with each other. So variegated is American culture that an observer who wishes to highlight its continuity can easily do so; and conversely, an observer who wishes to document the changing nature of American life can also have his way" (p. xvii).

He refers to researchers who redid the famous Lynd study of Middletown to illustrate the same point:

The Middletown III researchers found abundant evidence of cultural change in the Muncie of the seventies: more divorce, pot smoking, overt pornography, greater tolerance. But what struck them most forcefully was not change, but continuity. In the midst of social upheaval, they were astonished to find that Muncie high school students gave the same answer to certain questions in 1977 that their grandparents had given to the Lynds in the 1920's: the same numbers reported disputes with parents over getting home late at night, and a majority said they still regard the Bible as a "sufficient guide to all the problems of modern life." (P. xvii)

Chart 1
PUBLIC OPINION TRENDS, 1950-1975
LEFT AND RIGHT ON THE ISSUES:
THREE DECADES OF CHANGE

Box Score on Ideological Shifts[1]

Shift Toward "Conservatism"	Shift Toward "Liberalism"	Mixed Signals
*Growing feeling that government is too powerful	*Growing support for government medical programs and employment guarantees	*Legalized abortion and easier divorces may be losing support after initial liberal shift in late 60's
*Rising opposition to taxes	*Recent growth in support for wage and price controls	*Wavering support for ERA
*Hardening attitude toward treatment of criminals	*Increasing support for legalized marijuana	*Mixed views of SALT and defense
*Increase in support for death penalty	*Growing feeling that premarital sex is not wrong	*Mixed views of government regulation: gone "too far" vs feeling that government should limit corporate profits
*Sustained widespread opposition to busing	*Increase in numbers who would vote for Black or woman president	
*Support for defense spending rises to pre-Vietnam war levels	*Rise in support for right of Blacks to live anywhere	
	*Growth in tolerance of "anti-establishment" figures like atheists and socialists	

1. Reported with permission from Public Opinion, September/October 1978, p.34

Thus, attention must be given not only to the areas of change but also of continuity. Hence, there is the need not only to look at key moments in time but at change over time. The National Election Study conducted by the University of Michigan's Institute for Social Research provides an excellent vehicle for this effort, supplemented in two particular cases by data from the Gallup Poll (public attitudes toward reducing hours in the work week and attitudes about the ideal number of children in the family). These particular data are ideal for providing a perspective on public opinion in American society over time because they are surveys of the public that have been administered over a number of years. The National Election Study, in fact, began around 1952. (There were some early attempts in survey work in 1948 and 1950.) The Gallup Poll has a similarly long tradition. Such data as these provide the opportunity to study historical periods where questions have been repeated enough times so that one can have a sense of whether the respondent group is changing and the ways in which responses are changing. Suffice it to say here that I sought questions that emerged repeatedly during the 1950-to-1975 period in the general areas that are the focus of our interest: public function, civil rights, and traditional commitments. In particular, the studies used began in 1952 and ended in 1978 for the National Election Study questions. The Gallup Poll questions begin somewhat earlier. In all, seventeen questions were found to be in the general area of interest and were repeated three or more times. Data for 1978, three years beyond 1975, the end of the third quarter, are included in order to answer the question that is sure to be asked when reading these kinds of results—where are people heading, particularly the elderly, as we approach contemporary times? The questions are displayed in chart 2.

The kinds of effects that are the result of "age" are not easy to anticipate. There is no acceptable theory now available to explain why age should make a difference in opinion, value, or belief, which complicates the matter. Riley, Johnson, and Foner (1972) talk about reference group activity. Miller, Gurin, and Gurin (1980) believe "common sense tells us that the perception of belonging to a particular age category may influence the way individuals organize, simplify and give meaning to their cognitions of themselves and their social environment" (p. 691). Unfortunately, common sense tells us little about the dynamics that are operating or about the processes of identification and the areas where common views are likely to emerge. No matter how this issue is approached, comparisons between the elderly and younger age groups are absolutely essential. Studies of the elderly *only* do not permit meaningful generalizations about age effects.

A more useful, appropriate, and scientific approach is to start with an examination of the null relationship; i.e., to investigate the idea that there is no difference between the elderly and younger respondents explainable on the basis of age. One begins such an investigation with the initial expectation that age makes little or no difference. (As I will show in chapter

Chart 2
POLICY-RELEVANT QUESTIONS FROM THE NATIONAL ELECTION STUDY AND THE GALLUP POLL, 1952-1978

PUBLIC FUNCTION

1. Trust in Government, 1958-1978

2. Who Is the Government Run for the Benefit of? 1958-1978

3. People Like Me Don't Have Any Say About What the Government Does, 1952-1978

4. Voting Is the Only Way that People Like Me Can Have Any Say about How the Government Runs Things, 1952-1978

5. Public Attitudes towards Government Action to Insure Everyone a Job (and a Good Standard of Living), 1956-1978

6. Feeling Thermometers (Democrats, Republicans, Liberals, Conservatives), 1956-1978

7. Public Support for Government Involvement in Health Care, 1956-1964

8. Opinion on Government Involvement in Electric Power and Housing, 1956-1964

9. Is the Government in Washington Getting Too Powerful? 1964-1978

CIVIL RIGHTS

10. Should Government See to It that Blacks Get Fair Treatment in Jobs and Housing? 1952-1972

11. Public Attitudes towards the Speed of the Civil Rights Movement, 1964-1976

12. Public Attitudes towards Change in the Position of Negroes (Blacks), 1964-1976

13. Public Attitudes towards Protecting the Rights of the Accused, 1970-1978

14. Public Attitudes towards Women's Rights, 1972-1978

TRADITIONAL COMMITMENTS

15. Frequency of Church Attendance, 1952-1978

16. Public Attitudes towards the Issue of Reducing the Hours in a Work Week, 1953-1965

17. Public Attitudes about the Ideal Number of Children in a Family, 1941-1978

Questions 1-15 come from the National Election Study; question 16 and 17 come from the Gallup Poll.

7 and 8, the null hypothesis is not correct. While not the *most* important predictor, age is *an* important predictor of policy opinion.) If differences do exist, it may well be because age groupings conceal concentrations of other social identifications (such as race, social class, or income), which might be more predictive of policy opinion. To the extent it can be shown that differential proportions of these important social identifications do exist within age groups and are associated with policy opinion, one can then argue that age effects have been incorrectly used as explanations (Miller, Gurin, and Gurin, 1980).

Another approach to assessing the impact of age is to look at the similarity or difference in policy opinion over the years, tracking individuals longitudinally by using panel data. Although less definitive, it is still useful to look at cohorts as they age, even though the individuals are not the same over time and different people are interviewed for different surveys. Nevertheless, one can get a sense of the direction and the extent to which the cohort changed. The expectation of no effect of age would predict similarity of response over the life span.

One might think of such a similarity of values over the age span as "consistency" (Palmore, 1981). Such continuity would obtain in measuring a group of individuals at time one, time two, time three, and so on, and finding no difference over time. Those concerned with maturity, growth, and development would probably argue against this kind of "continuity" (Lowenthal, Thurnher, Chiriboga, 1975). An examination of the mean response to policy opinion questions of the various groups is a useful measure in such a study.

On the other hand, one might expect to find greater variation of values among the elderly cohorts from among the younger because of their greater amount and variety of experience (heterogeneity). A comparison of relative change between the elderly and younger groups is a useful measure for this kind of investigation. The experience hypothesis is an alternative to the consistency or null hypothesis, and one set of expectations would thus be in conflict with the other.

There is, of course, the problem of distinguishing consistency from rigidity. One perspective might suggest that individuals become less adaptable to changing circumstances as they age. In this case, one would expect that correlations among question items would increase as the group surveyed becomes older. This result is embodied in the notion of rigidity; i.e., that experience has little effect. It sees greater homogeneity and less variability in elderly respondents than in younger ones. The difference between the consistency hypothesis and the rigidity hypothesis is, in part at least, the difference between looking *between* questions over time and *among* questions at a moment in time, with the former exemplifying consistency and the latter rigidity.

Conservatism often implies rigidity. Elderly adults are often thought to be conservative. (For a review, see Cutler, 1973, and Neuman, 1981.) It is frequently unclear what a conservative response is in any given case, but Campbell and Strate (1981) have used a range of assessment questions and conclude that differences between age groups are small. (As I will show in chapters 5 and 6, it is only on certain questions, notably those dealing with the rights of women and the rights of the accused, where marked "conservatism" appears.) Conservatism as an omnibus perspective, therefore, must be questioned. Such a perspective suggests little variation in response to the substance of questions. I did not find this to be true. There is also the matter of what it is that is actually changing. Do individuals in fact change with age, or, as Abramson (1976) suggests, do newer groups entering the system have different opinions?[2]

There are, of course, many reasons why the elderly might be more conservative. They may have, for example, more to conserve than younger adults—relative income, status, position, etc. Certainly, conservativism is one way of preserving their position. On the other hand, if they feel that some components of their position have been lost, they may exhibit "less conservative sociopolitical attitudes," as Cutler (1973, p. 72) suggests. The same factors, however, may also be true of younger people.

Overall, therefore, there is a range of perspectives, by age, that one might expect. At the moment, though, there is no specific expectation either in general or for the particular period examined in this study, the third quarter of the twentieth century. Indeed, contradictory expectations seem to be suggested. The ability to compare elderly and younger respondents over a span of years and questions gives a firmer footing than has been present in earlier research. The data suggest that the elderly are not a great deal different from younger adults. If conservatism is a trend, then we all share it. There are some differences that can be noted in particular policy areas, such as punishing criminals, women's rights, and ideal family size, among others. Empirically, age is found to be moderately important as an independent predictor (fourth in a list of fourteen variables). In chapter 8, I will offer a theoretical explanation for its importance. That explanation links age to unchangeable social position rather than to stratification variables. (See also Tropman and Strate, 1983.)

PUBLIC OPINION AND POLICY OPINION

The phrase policy opinion has been used to describe the sorts of questions dealt with here. Because it is a new concept, I will elaborate on the idea.

Public opinion focuses upon what the word *public* really refers to. There is some considerable question about who holds the opinion. As Bishop, Hamilton, and McConahay (1977)) comment: "Survey researchers and others who read the entrails [*sic*] of polls and election returns should be very cautious in interpreting a shift on a single issue (i.e., abortion or marijuana laws) or the outcome of a single election (especially a single issue election) as meaning a general shift in the electorate along the liberal-conservative continuum" (p. 22).

It is for this reason that I have included a range of questions in each of the sectors of interest. This will permit us to look at patterns of different questions at the same time and at the relationships of those patterns over time. I cannot answer completely the question of whether there is an attitude system or a belief system "out there" or not. Some analysts have argued that these kinds of results are not terribly stable and don't really represent any kind of pattern. (For a summary, see Converse, 1980.) Other analysts seem to believe there is a pattern. As Bishop, Hamilton, and McConahay (1977) suggest:

The general pattern of our findings was that both the college and non-college portions of our sample had relatively high test-retest correlations. While the stability correlations were slightly lower for the non-college sample than for the college sample, this difference was quite small and statistically nonsignificant. More importantly, the magnitude of the stability correlations of the non-college sample makes it difficult to argue that substantial portions of this group were responding randomly to the items. On the contrary, the present results suggest that respondents in both college and non-college groups had quite stable attitudes on specific issues. (P. 18)

Judd and Milburn (1980) also find stability in their study of "attitude systems in the general public." They do point out, however, that the specific issues are important, noting that "it is also true that there are systematic differences between respondents in the extent to which an underlying ideology is used to respond to a question on a *specific* attitude issue" (p. 642, emphasis in original).

The differences may be, in part at least, a matter of perspective. From a cultural structure point of view—the view taken here—one does seem to find the emergence of persuasive patterns of response to questions over time.[3] For more detailed analyses to be undertaken, however, with narrower questions and more detailed breakdowns of respondents, greater variability would certainly emerge. It probably goes back to the point made by Yankelovich (1982): that there is both stability and change, pattern and variability, in the belief systems of the general public. The task here is to outline the areas in which both occur and to try to understand a bit more about the underlying conditions.

It is this point that leads us to *policy opinion*. Policy opinion focuses on one particular realm of public opinion—questions that deal with policy-related values, principally aimed at governmental activity in the social-

policy and civil rights area (public functioning and civil rights) and changes
in the work patterns as manifested in changes in the work week.[4]

Two of the questions focus on personal behavior not tied explicitly to
policy matters: the ideal number of children in the family and reported
church attendance. These, nonetheless, are similar in character to other
policy opinions in that they talk about personal policy. (For a discussion of
personal policy, see Pierce, 1984; Tropman, 1984.)[5]

All of the questions don't fit the categories as well as one might like, but
they do begin to suggest or provide guidelines about things people would
like to do or have done, i.e., vectors of action that they would support.
Wohlenberg (1976), for example, comments about this relationship with
respect to welfare attitudes and policies: "A fundamental assumption
undergirding the final phase of this study is that public opinion does matter
in America, that statutes and administrative policy concerned with welfare
programs are molded to some extent by the desires of the general public"
(p. 502).

What was his conclusion? "With respect to public opinion, of the nine
census regions, the nonliberal segment comprises the largest proportion of
the adult population in two southern regions (East South Central and West
South Central) followed by two western regions (Mountain and Pacific).
The poor in these regions must suffer under more restrictive and penurious
welfare programs" (p. 503).

Monroe (1978) comes to the same conclusion in looking at public
preferences and policy outcomes in several areas (including social welfare
and civil rights and liberties). He observes: "Overall, about two-thirds of
the cases demonstrate consistency between public opinion and policy
outcomes. This suggests that the political process at the national level does
tend to respond to public preference, but in a decidedly imperfect way"
(p. 544).

The imperfections he has in mind are due to *salience*. The greater the
salience or relevance of a *particular* issue to *particular* individuals, the
greater the likelihood of conformity between public opinion (what I call
policy opinion) and policy. Olber (1979) comes to the same judgment and
urges more intensive study of evidence about public attitudes toward
specific policies.

Policy opinion, then, represents the respondent's disposition toward
decision areas. We would expect to see some links between policy opinion
and policy. It's not to be expected that these links are completely clear,
however. The words themselves are confusing. As Rosenthal (1984) notes:

This contemporary faith in *opinion* merges, in the characteristic wording of survey
instructions, with another dominant faith of our time: in *feelings*. Questionnaires
make no distinction between the two words, asking "what is your opinion of?"
interchangeably with "how do you feel about?" and typically slipping *opinion* and

feelings—as well as *belief* and *thought*—in place of each other randomly: "Some people *feel* that the government in Washington should see to it that every person has a job and a good standard of living. Others *think* that the government should let each person get ahead on his own. And, of course, other people *have opinions* somewhere in between. Suppose people who *believe* that the government in Washington should see to it that every person has a job and a good standard of living are at one end of this scale. . . . [italics Rosenthal's] Questionnaires' blurring of *thought, belief,* and *opinion* is another expression of the relativism we've been noting in surveys. (Pp. 158-159)

Most assuredly there is a lack of clarity and understanding here, and at least some of this is what Converse (1980) and his adherents pick up. There are also problems of social lag, however. Monroe (1978) observes:

First, one of the major barriers to consistency between public opinion and public policy is the fact that the institutional structure of the political process tends to inhibit change, and this lessens opinion policy consistency. Thus, policy decisions which do not have to run the usual course of full legislative action (as many foreign policy decisions do not) tend to have higher levels of consistency. (P. 545)

Social lag occurs when policy opinion (beliefs, opinions, feelings) have changed faster than the policy (or social structures, social opportunities, etc.) with which they are to be consistent. In this case, change in opinion runs ahead of change in policy. But the other path is possible, too. The sociologist William Ogburn calls this "cultural lag," and he had in mind situations where the social system (or policy itself) changes ahead of policy opinion and public opinion (Faris, 1968).

The point I wish to make is not that there is exact congruence at any moment in time between policy opinion and policy, between thought and action. Rather, they tend to operate as two mutually adjusting elements in the total social system, with now one ahead and then the other, in a dynamic equilibrium.

I must emphasize that the study of the relationship between policy opinion and policy is *not* the subject of this volume. At this moment I will try only to lay out the structure of policy opinion in the three subject areas I have mentioned and try to put the development of that opinion within the third quarter of the twentieth century into an understandable perspective. I have stressed the link, however tentative, between policy opinion and policy action in order to suggest the wider relevance of a study of policy opinion. To the scholar and gerontologist it may be interesting in and of itself, but those who have a sustaining interest in this alone are few. Most of us have the nagging belief that what people think affects what people do. We are none of us too clear on the ways in which those two worlds are traversed, and the maps of both are obscure. Nonetheless, it is the potential impact of ideas on action that inspirits the study of ideas; it is the potential change of ideas created by action that vivifies the study of social behavior.

POLICY OPINION: ITS ROOTS AND STRUCTURE

It might be sufficient in a study of this kind simply to report in a variety of tables and charts the policy opinions of elderly and younger Americans in the third quarter of the century. Certainly, the accomplishment of that task is part of my purpose here. However, this is essentially what Lipset and Schneider did in their fascinating volume, *The Confidence Gap* (1983). As interesting as those reports are, reviewers have found some flaws. William R. Keach (1984), reviewing that book in *Science,* writes:

The book's efforts to explain the causes and consequences of the declining confidence is perhaps inevitably less successful than the description of American belief systems which is the major achievement of Lipset and Schneider's work. There's little reason to doubt the authors' attribution of the decline to the policy failures and corruption of the 1960's and 70's, but the discussion of the consequences does not yield clear answers, and it suffers from the lack of theory in the area. (P. 43)

Actually, there is some reason to doubt that attribution. What Lipset and Schneider (1983) say is: "We suggest that the increase in political dissatisfaction was not a cognitive or ideological change; it was rather a response to events and to the perception of events, primarily in the political sphere" (p. 399).

But it seems equally plausible that some of the difficulties that Lipset and Schneider refer to as political failures might themselves have been the result of declining confidence, what I call the *eclipse of public function.* It's doubtful that the question will be settled here. It is at least possible, however, to provide an alternative perspective.

Following Keach, Knoke (1984) comments in his review that there is an "absence of a carefully articulated set of theoretical principles about how popular opinions are formed and changed" (p. 276). It is my hope in this volume to do more than look at the shift of public opinion by age, useful as that is. I will attempt to provide the necessary context or theoretical perspective that helps one understand the formation and change of policy opinion (and, perhaps, other opinion, beliefs, values, etc., as well) and the role of the elderly in that process. It is to this end that chapters 2 and 3 are aimed. A perspective is needed to help us understand the contrasting and, indeed, conflicting changes in policy opinion that seem to have gone on during the period under discussion. The contradictory tendencies outlined in chart 1 only serve to support the importance of this view. For those readers, however, who would like to get right into the charts and figures, I suggest that you skip chapters 2 and 3 and read them after you have finished the remainder of the book. They may serve better for you as an integrating perspective. My preference, of course, is for individuals to take a brief detour through those chapters to get a better picture of the theoretical context in which policy opinion exists. By way of anticipation, the theoretical perspective relies essentially on a dualistic conception of value orientations. Policy opinion and public opinion are seen as manifestations of linked but conflicting value commitments. As Erikson (1976) says:

Any list of "traits" seems to have a certain consistency when the items are laid out one after another in a written account, but human experience is not arranged in so linear a form. The items themselves are part of a continuous whole, an entire package; and, when one looks back over the list of traits and tries to imagine how they would appear fused into a single configuration, it becomes hard to avoid the conclusion that there is a good deal of contradiction and discrepancy there. (P. 77)

He is studying the mountain people of Appalachia and their response to a particular catastrophe that occurred in one of their communities. He comments on the contradictions that those he is studying exhibit:

The mountain people are warm and hospitable, yet they are deeply suspicious of others. They are fiercely independent, yet they are so reliant upon family and kin that they scarcely know who they are when separated from that familiar surround. They are capable of an almost heroic ferocity when betrayed, yet are passive in the face of misfortune and resigned to the inevitable futilities of existence. They are proud and resourceful and obdurate, yet they are often overwhelmed by their own vulnerability. They are profoundly individualistic, holding to a philosophy of life in which no one is beholden to the viewpoint of another, yet they are so bound by codes and so anxious to conform to the opinions of others that they are unwilling to stand apart even for the purposes of doing something out of the ordinary or enjoying an original thought. They are exuberant yet depressed, outgoing yet taciturn, steady yet impulsive, indulgent yet firm. (Pp. 77-78)

What Erikson talks about with respect to the mountain people is worthy of close attention. It could be a description of the U.S. policy-opinion system itself. Indeed, to look at the system of policy opinion through this prism is illuminating.

These points of contradiction can be regarded as stones in the kaleidoscope of culture. The same stones, when rearranged, can provide, as has been suggested, a very different picture. The elderly adult fits into that picture now similarly to others, now different from them. Before we look at how the elderly American, in particular, and the American people, in general, have changed in the third quarter of the twentieth century, attention needs to be given to the development of a perspective that will help put those changes into focus.

NOTES

1. Even though some may agree that the War on Poverty has had some successes, the stature of its programs does not compare to those of the Depression era.
2. Abramson (1979) points to differences in "formative socialization" as an

important cause of generational differences. But that socialization must have occurred by parents who were socializing their children in values and opinions different from their own. This problematic position can be understood using the dualistic theory of values discussed in chapters 2 and 3. If one assumes that values are held and taught in pairs of sets of competing perspectives, then new generations have a way to learn what seem to be contradictory values from their parents. The difference is not in the values and opinions but, rather, in what subset of values of values and opinions generations choose to emphasize. Choice may be dictated in part by reacting to parental emphasis.

3. By cultural structure, I mean the patterns of values, beliefs, attitudes, and opinions over time. Social structure is the patterns of behaviors, actions, laws, and so forth, over time. The social system is comprised of both the cultural structure and the social structure.

4. Policy opinion would include, of course, policy areas other than those considered here; e.g., defense, environmental quality, and so on.

5. Personal policy (Pierce, 1984; Tropman, 1984) includes those rules we personally live by and on the basis of which we make important life decisions. The last will and testament and the marriage contract are well-known examples of personal policy.

PART I

A KALEIDOSCOPE
OF CULTURE

2
A CONFLICT THEORY
OF VALUES

Policy opinion—that segment of public opinion that embodies orientations toward decisions in the three areas mentioned in chapter 1 (public function, civil rights, and traditional commitments) is itself a representation (or a mental manifestation) of enduring and more widespread values. For my purposes, it is essential to understanding policy opinion in particular and public opinion in general to see questions in this larger context. Without such understanding it becomes too tempting to get involved in their concrete manifestations: the specific question that is asked, the specific issue that is addressed. While these are not to be ignored, seeing the answers to the policy-opinion questions discussed here within the larger context of values helps to smooth the rough terrain of the mental map. An understanding of the particular pattern of policy opinion at some moment in time, then, and the shifts in the structure of policy opinion over time, require some sense of the value system from which that policy opinion is being sampled.

A value is an idea to which commitment is attached, William Lee Miller (1977) states:

[U]nderlying values need to be exposed, examined, and revised, however limited the range of choice in policy may be at any one moment. In the longer run the condition of moral understanding of the public will affect what choices the option people with their incremental changes are able to act upon. . . . There are settings in which one is not dealing with the marking up of a bill in Congress or the fine turning [sic] of policy but rather with the shape of public conviction. (Pp. 52, 51)

Values embody our fundamental assumptions about the goals and meaning of existence. They form the foundations of our behavior and of our opinions about appropriate terms for that behavior. A *value* can be described as a standard that discriminates the aims or actions that we perceive are important to pursue. This description is close to that of Bengtson's and Lovejoy's (1973), who define values as "conceptions of the desirable which orient toward action" (p. 880). This stated supposition, that values influence behavior, forms the conceptual link that helps us understand how people's values relate to their choices and positions within the larger society. Bengtson and Lovejoy add that values "represent an important conceptual link between social structure and personality" (p. 880).

THE GRAMMAR OF VALUES

Major perspectives on values tend to assume that values come in sets that are harmoniously ordered and to which orders of priority may be attached. Rarely is it stressed that there might be values that cannot be ordered in terms of priorities. Robin Williams (1960), in his work on American society, lists fifteen values, but does not rank them. Rokeach (1968, 1973, 1979) postulates sets of higher order and lower order values, but they remain in a hierarchical form. Hirschman (1982) discusses "the conventional assumption of economic theory in general and of consumption theory in particular, which conceives of its central actors as being 'decked in the glory of their *one* all purpose preference ordering' as Amartya Sen put it ironically" (p. 68). Hirschman agrees. He has not found this assumption helpful. He comments: "But the task I have set myself—the explanation of large scale changes in life style—can be eased by a substantial modification of the conventional postulates, leading to a more complex, but also more plausible, view of the process under study" (p. 68).

Hirschman's task in some fundamental sense is very similar to that undertaken here. The large-scale change that he talks about is one that we will see in the policy-opinion data and that can also be perceived in the operations of our political system at this moment. From my perspective, Hirschman's suggested "substantial modification" could be called the "conflict theory of values."

I believe it makes increasingly good sense to think of the value system as made up of conflicting values, each competing with the other for dominance and expression. I go a step further and argue that values come in linked sets that might be called in Erikson's (1976) terms, "counterpart values." The perspective offered here is that values are learned in paired sets. They are present in the individual, as Erikson suggests, but are learned from sets that have developed over time. This dualistic paradigm is quite different from the one that is more conventional and linear, but it will help us to understand policy opinion, its changes, and its likely direction.

The conflict theory of values derives in part from the observation that values are commonly seen as both complementary and in opposition to each other, and that, indeed, this is an accepted way of talking about them. In the literature of sociology, for example, authors write of "sacred and secular" (Main); *Gemeinschaft* and *Gesellschaft*" (Tönnies); "instrumental and expressive" (Parsons); "mechanical and organic solidarity" (Durkheim); "categoric and corporate groups" (Hawley).

Lynd's (1939) famous volume *Knowledge for What?* lists twenty paired assumptions and he points out that they involve systematic contradictions. For example:

5. Everyone should try to be successful.
   But: The kind of person you are is more important than how successful you are.
6. The family is our basic institution and the sacred core of our national life.
   But: Business is our most important institution, and, since national welfare depends upon it, other institutions must conform to its needs. (Pp. 60-62)

Merton and Barber (1963) pick up Lynd's discussion as one portion of an extended analysis of ambivalence in social affairs. Among the various kinds of ambivalent situations they mention are those presented by role definitions (concerning the roles of wife and mother, for example) and multiple roles occupied by the same person within a status (teaching versus research in the university, for example). Ambivalence is also particularly central to the studies of alcohol problems and policies. (See Tropman, 1983). The conflicts Merton and Barber pose tend to be structural ones, with one exception: "A fourth kind of sociological ambivalence is found in contradictory cultural values held by members of society. These values are not ascribed to particular statuses but are normatively expected of all in society (e.g., patriotism and honesty)" (p. 98).

Yet, theoretically, these conflicts and others appear to be viewed by some not as sets of value conflicts, adding up to a pattern of culture, but as total frameworks that the individual and the region or society either completely accept or reject. It seemed reasonable to exploit this gap between theory and practice, to consider that the value system itself may be made of conflicting values, and that this system is, in a variety of ways, present in the individual because of society.

Erikson (1976), however, took that step and developed a conflict theory of values as a perspective in his studies on the culture of Appalachia:

What I am proposing here, then, is that the identifying motifs of a culture are not just the *core values* to which people pay homage but also the *lines of point and counterpoint* along which they diverge. That is, the term "culture" refers not only to the customary ways in which a people induce conformity in behavior and outlook, but the customary ways in which they organize diversity. In this view, every human culture can be visualized, if only in part, as a kind of theater in which certain contradictory tendencies are played out. . . . These contrasting tendencies are reflected at many different levels within the social order. At the individual level, first of all, they are experienced as a form of *ambivalence*. . . . Whatever the outcome, though, both halves of the dilemma remain as active potentials in his consciousness, ready to assert themselves if conditions change.

At the societal level, these contrasting tendencies are experienced as a form of *differentiation*. (P. 82)

As Erikson suggests, then, it is reasonable to assume that the same structure of values, as it is present in society, will appear within the individual, although the balance and specifics of orientation will likely differ from person to person. Social values, those that can be identified on the macroscopic level, are also likely to emerge as personal ones.

Others have used such modes of approach in policy analysis. Geoffrey Vickers (1973), writing in *Policy Sciences,* comments that values appear to come in clustered pairs:

complementary . . . and partly inconsistent pairs, such as freedom and order, independence and interdependence, equality and self-development, justice and mercy. Each member of a pair is a compendious label for a number of "values" more or less inconsistent with those implied by the other. . . . They thus supply an indispensable means to discuss the always conflicting and disparate costs and benefits which can be anticipated as likely to flow from any deliberate human intervention in the course of affairs. (P. 106)

Edelman (1977) discusses the two assumptions (poverty as a result of personal inadequacy versus poverty as a result of system failures) that must pervade thinking about the poor, assumptions to which policies must pay tribute: "We find, then, a pair of opposing political myths for each of the conflicting cognitive patterns that define our attitudes toward social problems, the authorities who deal with them, and the people who suffer from them. Ambivalence is reflected in concomitant myths, each of them internally consistent, though they are inconsistent with each other" (p. 8). Edelman notes, too, "both patterns of belief are present in our culture and in our minds" (p. 8).

An analysis of value conflicts in poverty programs is presented in the work of S. M. Miller (1968). He had his own set of juxtaposed values:

1. fundamentalism vs incrementalism
2. universality vs selectivity
3. ambiguity vs specificity
4. continuity vs succession
5. equality of opportunity vs conditions
6. elite vs self-determination
7. centralization vs decentralization

These differ a bit from the list of policy values that I will be sharing in that they are more planning oriented; i.e., they focus not on the nature of the policy choices themselves, nor on the bases for those choices, but upon subsequenty design for carrying out policy.

While the distinctions made by Vickers, Edelman, and Miller are rather theoretical and abstract, concern for an understanding of the kinds of value conflicts I have been discussing here extend well beyond academia, pervading the thinking of a considerable segment of the general public. Ellen Goodman, a currently popular commentator and syndicated columnist, in her book *Turning Points* (1979), excerpts of which have been published in local newspapers, writes:

In many ways, the women's movement has pushed up to the surface some of the conflict latent in American society. The ones I see lie at the core of our history. Americans have always valued individual rights on the one hand and a sense of community on the other. We believe in independence of family members and the importance of the family unit. We value self-realization—the quest for individual growth—and self sacrifice—the virtue of doing for others. We need the warmth, safety and security of tradition on the one hand, and desire the excitement of risk, adventure and exploration on the other. We pursue material values, and condemn "materialism." These ambivalences provide the tension in our society which is both dynamic and unsettling. (P. 293)

There is little in this with which Lynd, Merton and Barber, Vickers, Edelman, or Miller would take exception. What is striking about her comments is that they appeared in the local, popular press; that they were designed for the general reading public; and that, presumably, they dealt with concepts, ideas, matters that were understandable by and of importance to that general public.

Others have touched upon ideas similar to this, as well. J. Milton Yinger, whose book *Countercultures* (1982) I have cited previously, observes:

Related to the presence of "subterranean" values is the fact that many societies, perhaps most, have more explicit contradictions and ambivalence built into their cultures. At least since Goethe there have been discussions of the "two Germanys." Similarly, from Toqueville's observations a century and a half ago down to the present, examination of the tension between the values of equality and of liberty in the United States has been crucial to cultural analysis. In *Childhood and Society*, Eric Erikson observed that a culture is much more richly defined by such point-counterpoint tensions than by a list of mutually consistent values. (Pp. 24-25)

Reamer (1983) has talked about the conflicts between paternalism and freedom. Barbour et al. (1982) talk about values and environmental policies as "social-political dilemmas." Jean Hardy (1981) titled her book on British social policy *Values in Social Policy: Nine Contradictions*. William Ryan

(1981) discusses the "equality dilemma—fair play or fair shares?" Ozawa (1974) introduced the ideas of individual equity and social adequacy, which are similar to these kinds of conflicts. And Cumming (1967) seems close to Yinger in her development of the concept of "anti-values" or negative values.

The idea, therefore, of a value conflict theory is developing. In my work, I have developed a series of seven policy-value conflicts that will be useful here (Tropman, 1978; Tropman and McClure, 1978, 1980-1981). Those policy-value conflicts are listed in chart 3.

The scheme of dual, juxtaposed values presented here, then, I shall call the *conflict theory of values*. As such, I shall attempt to reflect not only the nature of much recent academic thinking on values, but also the way people generally think about the problems that beset them. Choices are always present; solutions are rarely clear. We are more likely to have a leaning toward some value than to manifest complete certainty. In fact, people who have—or appear to have—complete certainty are often thought of as rigid and inflexible. While I know of no specific test for popular utility in such matters, it is interesting that aphorisms often appear in exactly this dual

Chart 3
POLICY VALUE CONFLICTS IN AMERICAN SOCIETY

Equity	vs	Adequacy
Private	vs	Public
Independence	vs	Interdependence
Struggle	vs	Entitlement
Work	vs	Leisure
Secular	vs	Religious
Personal	vs	Family

These are derived from the work of Tropman (1978) and Tropman and McClure (1978, 1980/1981). In the original list the names of two of the values were slightly different: Personal vs Family was called Individual vs Family; Independence vs Interdependence was Self-Reliance vs Dependence. These changes simply represent a clarification and specification of the original ideas.

form; for example, "he who hesitates is lost" is countered by "look before you leap," or "a fool and his money are soon parted" can be contrasted with "nothing ventured, nothing gained." Such dual pairings are common in our popular guides to living. They are not typically mentioned together, however. Instead, we tend to isolate them from each other as contrasting values within our overall value system. While we may be aware generally of some of the contradictions we encounter daily, we often seem to segregate them so that the conflict will not be too severe or too obvious. (See Edelman, 1977.) What we normally hide from ourselves, of course, comes up in policy decision-making, where the necessity to choose forces contradictions to the surface.

In summary, there is more conflict between two juxtaposed values or sets of values than may be apparent at first. Not only is there conflict within each pair, but there is also bound to be conflict among the dimensions themselves, for all seven dimensions cannot be maximized at the same time.

THE FUNCTIONING OF CONFLICT

In this approach conditions that suggest one value or set of values are seen necessarily to suggest another, often conflicting, set of conditions. Duality is a crucial feature of the system and gives a special flavor to the conflicts analyzed. To think about things public requires one to think also about things private; to think about family requires thinking about the individual; to think about self-reliance requires thinking about dependency. In every instance the values are locked together.

Such interlocking implies conflict but not necessarily opposition. That is why I use the term *juxtaposed*. Private is not simply the opposite of public; family is not simply the opposite of personal; independence is not simply the opposite of interdependence. The value elements stand in relationship to each other like supply and demand—they are independent, but each increment in one vector creates a tension to which the other must adjust. Rising demand may create shortages of supply. As family values increase, there is some sacrifice of individual ones. As work values increase, there is some sacrifice of leisure. As religious values increase, there is some sacrifice of secular beliefs. In each case an extension of one means an adjustment in the other. There is, thus, a continual tension in the value system, a tension that may be an essential mechanism for ideological pruning and self-correction within the structure of society as a whole. Certainly, to some extent at least, private activity, for example, could be extended without loss of public concerns; the reverse is also true. But at some point this extension can be expected to threaten public territories. The converse is also true for this value pair and for all the others. Benefits tend to become more adequate for all concerned as they depart from strict adherence to the equity principle—the principle that what someone receives should bear some proportionate relationship to what one contributes, whether it be income from Social Security or the grade one receives on a term paper. It is essential to an understanding of the U.S. value system and of its implications for the elderly that we see this juxtaposed, conflicting relationship among many of our most cherished beliefs. The constant crisis of values derives not simply from controversy between opposing values but, perhaps more significantly, from the threats that certain values we hold pose for other values *that we also hold*. Thus, the ever-present need for compromise is to be explained not only or always by the pressures of factions against each other, as James Madison anticipated in the tenth *Federalist Paper*, but by this insistent friction between highly cherished values held to some degree by all parties.

In this sense, the notion of value-behavior consistency, which has had such mixed scientific results, may in part have been looking in the wrong direction to the extent that it looks for *a* value system with which *the* behavior can be consistent. If one assumes that both individuals and society have a system of dual and juxtaposed values, then behavior can be consistent even with values that appear to be mutually contradictory. The key problem for behavior in a given instance may well be how to maximize what one value represents without detracting from—or by only minimally detracting from—what another value represents. Especially in the policy area, one can observe the plausibility of this line of argument as policymakers seek to balance demands for mutually contradictory lines of action, both of which often come from the same people and each of which has strong value support.

DOMINANT AND SUBDOMINANT VALUES:
INDIVIDUAL AND COLLECTIVE

The rule of dominance and subdominance is useful in keeping this elaborate picture straight. I argue that in American society one set of values tends to be more dominant than the other; that they are not completely symmetric; and that one set of values will, over time, be the more common or the more prominent. In cases of absolutely forced-choice condition, the more common/prominent one will be the usual winner. In chart 3 the values on the left side of the list seem at present to be the more dominant; those on the right, subdominant.

It is of crucial importance to realize that current programs and services for the elderly, if I am correct in my assessment of which values are dominant, tend to be based on subdominant values. This means that many policies and programs for elderly Americans have relatively fragile support and that the values that chiefly underlie them tend continually to threaten our society's more dominant values.

The concept of dominance must, however, be taken as a provisional hypothesis only. Williams (1969), although he does not have a paired value scheme, mentions this idea and gives the criteria of extensiveness, duration, and intensity as main elements. Both sides of the value pairs I am using display extensiveness and duration; i.e., they have been widely held over a long period of time. Perhaps, then, it is intensity that marks the chief difference between any two values. It is possible, for example, that dominance varies over the value set from only a slight to a substantial preference. It may be that the balances of preferences will vary over time and within groups. Edelman (1977), for example, comments about the explanations (value perspectives) that people use: "Though each person's social situation is likely to make one or the other of these perspectives his or her dominant one, everybody learns both of them, for they are stock explanations of a universal phenomenon" (p. 6).

In terms of my analysis, Edelman is right on target. He does not, however, go quite far enough. It is also necessary to explore *why* people think as they do and what these patterns mean.

A related feature has to do with the distinction between individuals and collective values. Those on the right side of my scheme are collective values. Williams (1960) observes that such values "not only are shared by a number of individuals but are regarded as matters of collective welfare by an effective consensus of the group" (p. 400). Williams calls these values "social values."

On the left side are individual values. The distinction is not simply between two morally correct positions, but between a kind of good that is more personal, that can be more enjoyed by the person, that is related to the individual and his or her orientation, and that increases the acquisitions that an individual has. This distinction contrasts with collective values, which are more communal, more related to the activity of the group as a whole. Religion, family, interdependence, entitlements, adequacy, and public evoke notions of collective well-being.

The distinction between collective and individual is sometimes characterized as patterns of values common within a given society. Individual values represent the pattern of values held by a particular individual within a society. Individual values are probably the dominant ones held in the United States. There are certainly cultures, however, in the Orient, for example, where the values of society are more social or collective in nature.

CONCLUSION

In a pluralistic society such as the United States, it would be, upon reflection, unusual to find a single set of values, a single standard to which people conform. In a sense, however, the very pluralism of our nation may have prevented us from seeing the pluralistic and multi-dimensional nature of our value system. While we recognized a pluralism of perspectives, it may also have been reasonable to think that different perspectives were associated with different groups. Each group, thus, has its own unitary system with a readily understood hierarchy of priorities. Indeed, it is probably true that there are different patterns of values manifested by different groups. I prefer to view these as different mixes of stones from the same kaleidoscope.

My argument, then, is that values come in juxtaposed sets. I have identified seven relevant value-policy conflicts. The notion of value dualism is not unique to my presentation. Others, studying similar kinds of complex phenomena, have come to the same conclusion. In fact, as the literature cited here suggests, a fairly large number of individuals have made suggestions that approximate the idea I offer here. Erikson (1976) comes closest to the point, but he is clearly not alone. What seems to have been missing is the crystallization of these various approaches into a single, coherent statement about the grammar of the value system—its pattern and structure—and the way in which this might then be used to analyze social change. It is in this connection that Erikson comes especially close to the effort here. While he was looking at community change under catastrophic conditions, and I am looking at shifts in policy opinion over time, we both attempt to use the dualistic values conception for purposes of analysis and understanding.

But most of the scholars' treatments of these matters are relatively brief and do not explain to any considerable degree the nature of the value conflict involved. I am attempting here to take that necessary additional step, particularly as such conflicts may be relevant to policy change in the third quarter of this century and as they may bear on understanding the role of the elderly as generators and recipients of those changes.

3
POLICY-VALUE CONFLICTS
IN AMERICAN SOCIETY

Interest in change and stability in three main policy-opinion sectors—public function, civil rights, and traditional commitments—occupy the attention of this book. More is needed, however, than simply to chart the flow of policy opinion over time. It is my hope to put that policy opinion into a perspective, and I have offered seven value conflicts as a way of approaching that goal. The purpose of this chapter is to discuss those conflicts in more detail, outlining in particular their relevance to the older adult and the concerns of the older adult. Still, the initial task is to link the policy-opinion questions with the policy-value conflicts. The fit is not exact, nor am I suggesting that there is one indicator for each value conflict. There is a correspondence, however, and that correspondence is reflected in chart 4.

The questions about public function focus on dilemmas of public vs private orientation in the United States today. But they also pick up on issues of fairness of social benefits vs the adequacy of those benefits. Questions of government involvement in the health needs and requirements of the nation, for example, always evoke concerns about independence vs interdependence. As I will suggest in the conclusion, the questions themselves are not always clear with respect to which of these value dimensions they seek to address. This is because the questions, as they have been formulated over the years, have lacked a particular theoretical guiding principle or point of view. Nonetheless, the questions do chart a course

Chart 4
CORRESPONDENCE BETWEEN POLICY OPINION QUESTIONS
AND POLICY VALUE DILEMMAS

Policy Opinion Questions   Policy Value Dilemmas

Public Function

1. Trust in government   Equity vs Adequacy
2. Who is government run for benefit of?   Private vs Public
3. People like me don't have any say about   Independence vs Interdependence
   what the government does
4. Voting is the only way that people like me
   can have any say about how the government
   runs things
5. Public attitudes towards government actions
   to insure everyone a job (and a good
   standard of living)
6. Feeling thermometers (Rep., Dem., Lib., Cons.)
7. Public support for government involvement in
   health care
8. Opinion on government involvement in electric
   power and housing
9. Is the government in Washington getting
   too powerful?

Civil Rights

10. Should government see to it that blacks   Struggle vs Entitlement
    get fair treatment in jobs and housing
    (Help Minorities in 1978)
11. Public attitudes towards the speed of the
    civil rights movement
12. Public attitudes towards change in the
    position of Negroes (blacks)
13. Public attitudes towards protecting the
    rights of the accused
14. Public attitudes towards women's rights

Traditional Commitments

15. Frequency of church attendance   Secular vs Religious
16. Public attitudes towards reducing the   Work vs Leisure
    hours in a work week   Personal vs Family
17. Public attitudes about the ideal number
    of children in a family

among competing value perspectives and between specific sets of commitments.

The issue of civil rights is clearly captured by the notion of struggle vs entitlement. It is certainly true that all kinds of rights are guaranteed by the Constitution. There is also much important legislation, such as the Voting Rights Act. It remains the case, nevertheless, that the operationalization of civil rights is far from being achieved. Indeed, in certain specific areas—especially with respect to minorities and women—egregious violations continue.

In terms of traditional commitments—work, religion, and family—we can get some measure of where the public is going, of what areas more traditional commitments are present, of who, if anyone, holds them. One might expect in these areas, for example, that the elderly respondent is most traditional. The extent to which such an expectation is fulfilled will become clear as we proceed.

It is probably true that the value system, much like our governmental form, is a system of checks and balances. That is the essential feature of the perspective I offer here. It is important, therefore, for us to see any particular set of measures that ask about things related to values—in this case, policy opinion—as being located within that type of context. As we think of one particular value, such as work, we are able to think of leisure as a competing value, at least to some extent. A consideration of adequacy presents the opportunity to ask about the counterpoint value, to use Erikson's (1976) term. If nothing else, a dualistic values framework will help keep a straighter, more self-correcting course than might be true with some other perspective. Let me now turn to a discussion of each of the value areas for more detailed consideration.

EQUITY VS ADEQUACY

One of the most cherished American values is that of "equity" or fair play. This policy value is one that is applied in a broad range of instances, from sporting events to classroom grades, even to the largest social policies, such as the Social Security Act (Ozawa, 1974). *Equity* refers to a sense of distributive justice in a system in which outcomes are, in some understandable way, related to contributions, in which there is some proportionate return to the individual for his or her investment. We think of policies as "unfair" that provide the same increments or decrements to people regardless of the contributions they might have made. This essential relationship between contribution and return is what Aristotle called "proportionate equality" (McKeon, 1947). In more modern times, the Walsters and Ellen Berscheid (1978) have considered the whole issue of equity in their book by that title. The application of the fairness principle, because of the element of contribution, is not synonymous with "equality" or sameness.

Essentially, fairness implies, and, indeed, requires, differential outcomes so long as those outcomes are based upon the application of the criterion of merit or contribution. The establishment of differential rewards based upon nepotism or favoritism or "brownnosing" is not an appropriate application of the equity principle. As in school, students not only tolerate but expect differences in grades that members of the class receive, based upon the presumed variation of the students in talent and work.[1]

The principle of adequacy is of an entirely different sort and stems from a different basis. While equity is guided by contribution, adequacy is guided by need. Inherent in the idea of adequacy is that there should be a minimal standard against which all the members of a given group are measured. When a person (or a piece of equipment) falls below this standard, it is assumed that corrective action must be taken.

Need, of course, is itself determined on a variety of bases, and many of them are in constant conflict. How much food does an individual "need" to remain healthy? Of what type? Do rural people "need" less of an allowance from the government than urban people because rural people can grow their own food? Do welfare mothers "need" a remote-control television? Should the taxpayers pay for it? These are the problems that come up continually in determining need. They have very little to do with contribution. They represent, rather, problems in defining what the relevant minimal standards are; in what realms such standards are appropriately set; and about how much of the standard, once set, should be granted. Throughout this process, however, there are continual exceptions. I have mentioned the urban-rural difference as a common one. Old-young is another. What do elderly people really need? Material support? Friendly visiting? Health care? The list of questions is potentially a long one because needs are many and varied, relative and individual.

In the realm of social judgments, adequacy and equity standards conflict with each other. We make such judgments on a regular, daily basis, going through the balancing process suggested by the conflict theory of values. Alves and Rossi (1978), for example, surveyed a number of people with respect to their views and judgments on how income was evaluated, based upon providing the respondents with some information about the distribution of earnings in the United States. Their conclusion is worth mentioning in some detail: "Considerable agreement exists concerning what principles are relevant to earnings-fairness judgments, while disagreements concerning how to apply these standards in practice is admitted. Apparently the standards for earnings judgments derive both from conceptions of the empirical distribution of earnings and from underlying values concerning what is fair and just" (p. 541).

What are these conceptions and values? "In general, judgments concerning the extent to which a household is overpaid, fairly paid, or underpaid *involve balancing both merit or performance considerations and those of need*" (p. 563, emphasis added).

What Alves and Rossi call "merit" and "need" are, in my terms, "equity" and "adequacy," or "contribution" and "need": "Further, without nullifying findings describing central tendencies in earnings-fairness judgments, respondents' position in the American social structure systematically influence their balancing of merit or performance considerations against those of need" (p. 563).

Two types of considerations are important in determining what these positions were. Because Alves and Rossi gave respondents vignettes of families, both the characteristics of those in the vignette (or the "judged") and the characteristics of the respondents (or the "judges') are important. According to Alves and Rossi, "[H]igh status respondents place greater weight on merit considerations, while low status respondents give need considerations more weight" (p. 559). Other characteristics of those situations judged made a difference, however, especially whether merit was that of the husband or the wife: "[A]lthough respondents were sensitive to both husbands' and wives' characteristics, they were more sensitive to the former than the latter, indicating that husbands' 'meritorious' attainments justify a given level of household income more readily than those of wives" (p. 553).

This analysis reflects also that the race of respondents is an important factor in fairness judgments, a finding that foreshadows my own in a later chapter. The key conclusion here, in a fairly direct test, is that dualism does, indeed, exist; that these two dimensions conflict with each other; and that the balance depends upon both the situation judged and the characteristics of the judge.[2]

In the Social Security Act, of course, one would expect such fundamental issues as fairness and need to become manifest. Wilbur J. Cohen (1977), in looking at the Social Security Act in the current period, sees the conflict between equity and adequacy as perhaps the most central one:

The problem of determining benefit adequacy in relation to equity is possibly the most difficult issue on OASDI (Old Age, Survivors, and Disability Insurance]. Such a determination is hard because it involves integrating two different answers to the same basic question: Who should receive how much? The principles of social adequacy and individual equity represent two different concepts about how payments should be allocated. (P. 1360)

Ozawa (1974) makes a similar point. In doing so, she captures, as well, a difference between personal values (she calls them "individual") and social values:

Old age insurance is a social insurance, and thus has two objectives: "individual equity" and "social adequacy." Although these are broad philosophical concepts, an accepted way to define them is as follows: individual equity treats the retired workers' benefits as annuities bought by the contributions made by the insured; social adequacy purports to provide a "basic floor of protection" or a "minimum subsistence level of income" for the aged. (P. 24)

Cohen, in adding the modifiers of "social" to adequacy and "individual" to equity, captures the currently accepted balance: rates are set on the basis of *social* (not individual) adequacy and *individual* (not social) equity. This means that the individual benefit, above the minimum, is related to the individual contribution, not to the individual need.

This policy idea of making the minimum a social standard and the range above it an individual standard is a brilliant way to resolve conflicting values. It is, however, rapidly coming under challenge. One could as easily argue that individual adequacy and social equity are what is needed, and there is some evidence that social thought may be moving in that direction.

Adequacy and equity, then, represent competing commitments that will influence policy opinion. Attempts to provide answers to policy-opinion questions will most assuredly tap into these conflicting perspectives.

PRIVATE VS PUBLIC

Another of the great policy-value conflicts in the United States is that between private and public. It is a conflict that exists on several levels. Private implies "a normative element: the right to exclusive control of access to private realms" (Simmel, 1968, p. 480). It is consistent with our notions of liberty, freedom, and a minimum of outside control, especially by church and state. To a degree, private, in its most intimate sense, is analogous to internal matters. This differentiates it from public, which is analogous to external matters. American society is internally oriented; and, as Simmel points out: "The internalization of norms may be considered a functional alternative to external social control. . . . Hence, the greater the internalization of norms, the greater the privacy granted and, therefore, the greater the development of privacy norms" (p. 483).

In a society as sparsely populated as ours has been, it would have been impossible to have social control that was essentially external. (This same point might be made about other societies and regions.) Thus, there needed to be a mechanism that permitted social control to be carried on from within the individual. That mechanism had to rely more on self-scrutiny and less on scrutiny by others. As it is likely that situations where behavior is observed are also those situations where behavior is compliant, then it is also likely that situations where behavior is not observed are likely to be those situations where behavior is noncompliant. The stress on privacy and its accompanying internalization, therefore, was, and is, an extremely functional form of "social" control (Simmel, 1968, p. 483).

Further, privatism links to individualism and, by extension and implication, to individual responsibility and choice. In our particular society we place emphasis on the unique ability of the individual to make his private judgment, whether that judgment is about voting or hitting a child or spouse. We hesitate to interfere; at the same time we insist, under the rules of equity, that the individual take responsibility for his or her actions. It is also likely that the situations in which there are strong elements of external control are those situations that generate systematic lack of compliance.[3] In a sense, the competing values of private and public are accommodated and "balanced" within the society at least to some degree. Simmel makes this interesting observation, quite consistent with my dual approach to values: "*In collectivities with strong privacy boundaries, subcollectivities will tend to be relatively open; in open collectivities, subcollectivities will tend to be closed*" (p. 484, emphasis in original).

The legendary American friendliness and openness coexists, then, with a strong emphasis upon privacy and individualism rather than publicism and collectivism. I'll pick this theme up again in my discussion of the person and the family.

The policy arena is one where both public and private compete. The sense of tension between public and private has been manifest as one between government and non-government sectors. Historically, of course, private means of welfare were among the most predominant. Such organizations as the Association of Benevolent Societies in Boston and the New England Home for Little Wanderers were highly significant for their time. Nor has the involvement of private organizations and institutions abated. By 1982, there were just under 120,000 private human-service organizations (96 percent of all charitable non-profits), with a total budget of $40 billion (30 percent of the total non-profit sector) (Salamon, 1984, p. 17). In 1982, Americans reported charitable tax deductions of over $48.76 billion (Briar et al., 1983, p. 219). And the total non-profit sector contained 124,000 organizations with a total budget of $131 billion (Salamon, 1984)!

Cohen (1977) details the pattern of evolution of U.S. approaches to private and public funding of welfare:

If any generalization can be made about the evolution of this . . . [public/private mixed] . . . system it would be this: Americans seem to rely initially on private protection plans alone and demand basic public protection through federal programs only when it becomes apparent that protection under private plans is too limited in its coverage or is too costly. . . . When a federal program is established, the protection it provides is neither so comprehensive nor so complete that the need or demand for private supplemental plans wholly disappears. (Pp. 1363-1364)[4]

This mixture, with all its conflicts, is one that characterizes the U.S. system.[5] It represents the harmony—or at least the mutually supportive efforts—of public and private realms. It also underscores the fact that this value pair, like the others, does not necessarily represent either one or the other. As Cohen (1977) observes about the last forty years: "The entire public-private framework of programs and resources for the aged, sick, disabled, and unemployed have been strengthened. The tremendous growth of the social security program, in terms of both coverage and benefit levels, has been paralleled by increased enrollment in private pension, health insurance and life insurance programs" (p. 1364).

In recent years, then, public/private cooperation has been the norm. Clearly, however, the period from 1950 to 1975 represented an astounding growth in public services, especially for the elderly. The pendulum appeared to be swinging back in the middle 1970s, and that trend seems to be continuing.

In a sense, we have a mixed system or a non-system made of different public and private components. Gilbert (1983) makes a similar point; and the Reagan administration seems to propose a somewhat different mixture of public and private, diminishing the "social" part of "public" while increasing defense portions and claiming to rely on "private" realms to meet social needs. Sharon Jablonski (1986) has suggested that, in addition, the Reagan administration relies on "public" morality and "private" activity as a way of balancing these competing claims.

INDEPENDENCE VS INTERDEPENDENCE

Independence vs interdependence is a crucial policy-value conflict within U.S. society. It is particularly important to us because of our historical tradition. People fled to this country, at least in the popular view, to be independent. Indeed, Americans were not here for very long before they declared their independence. In fact, our Declaration of Independence might have had more far-reaching impact in social and cultural terms than we have ever imagined before. Fischer (1978), a historian of old age, makes this point specifically in arguing that the decline of respect for the elderly person was in some respects coterminous with the Declaration of Independence. Freedom from the "old country" generated permission to be free from the "old man" as well. It seems clear today that, with respect to the elderly adult, remaining independent and being able to be independent is a highly prized value. Many of our social programs are aimed at making this possible.

On the other hand, interdependence is surely the typical situation of the human condition. We depend upon others for the accomplishment and achievement of almost all our goals. The helpfulness of people and communities together has long been a hallmark of *gemeinschaft* ethos. The old cooperative barn raising and harvest gatherings have been emblematic of U.S. society almost as much as the self-reliant mountain man. These cooperative efforts have been detailed by Vidich and Bensman (1968) and Carol Stack (1974), among others. In recent years U.S. society has seen both extremes of independence and interdependence manifest themselves. On the one hand there is the rise of belief in individual values and narcissism, where people are self-concerned and trying to free themselves from commitments to and interrelationships with other people and institutions. On the other hand, there is the rise of communal efforts and some strengthening of group activities, therapies, and interactions. Naisbett (1982) comments on the rise of networking and self-help groups.

There still remains, however, a conflict to be resolved: How much interdependence and how much independence? When and under what conditions should these occur? Yankelovich (1982) sees a new ethic of interdependence arising. It remains to be seen whether his prognostications are correct.

STRUGGLE VS ENTITLEMENT

American society has been characterized by a tension between the values of struggle and the values of entitlement. The former emphasizes competition and contentions and tends to see the need for continual preparation and vigilance. "Rights" exist only as long as one suffers for them. At the individual level, the phrase "no pain, no gain" embodies the all-important struggle. Entitlements, on the other hand, capture the notions that people have rights in and of themselves and are—and should be— guaranteed those rights without continuous individual and collective struggle. Some rights, free speech, for example, are assured by the Constitution and/or the courts (Simmel, 1968). In still other instances there is a lack of this assurance. The Constitution itself permitted slavery to continue, and early laws did not give everyone the right to vote and to participate in the activities aimed at the commonweal. As time passed, tension between the promise and the practice became an especially American dilemma.

The tension, then, exists not only between the values—the ideology of struggle and entitlement—but between each ideology and its manifestations. Tenure and seniority, for example, become focal points for these controversies. On the one hand, people should be entitled to a job after certain requirements are met. On the other, people continually should be competitive within the workplace for their job. Americans try to resolve these conflicts by creating entitlements in such a way that there is some aspect of contest, some aspect of risk and contribution. One is entitled to a profit, but one must take risks. One is entitled to constitutional protections, but such liberties require eternal vigilance. One is entitled to the protection of the law, but must on occasion take the law into one's own hands.

To some extent, as well, the differences between the conflict theories of society and those of a more consensus-oriented approach represent some of the same inclination. Those of the conflict school emphasize the gaps between values and reality. Those who emphasize agreement and consensus point to the ways in which conflict is prevented.[6] Both perspectives are necessary, as Coser (1968) points out. Too much emphasis on the one leads to a distorted sense of social reality. Coser states: "We deal here not with distinct realities but only with differing aspects of the same reality, so that exclusive emphasis on one or the other is likely to lead the analyst astray'' (p. 236).

In an important sense, too, the major entitlements on which this country was founded were restrictions on governmental actions rather than proactive statements about what should be done. LaFrance (1979), in his volume on the structure and entitlements of welfare law, observes:

Until recently, courts were willing to protect rights such as speech and religion from arbitrary governmental infringement but were unwilling to extend similar protections to public benefits, no matter how essential to life. . . . The guarantees of the Constitution are, by and large, restrictions on the scope and activities of government. . . . All they require is judicial enforcement. In contrast, programs of public assistance are not restrictions upon government, but affirmative undertakings. (P. 82)

As LaFrance suggests, the basic affirmative structure of public assistance in the United States remained, essentially, one that followed the English Poor Law. In this it was consistent until the Social Security Act and Roosevelt's "Four Freedoms."

One of the reasons this increase in social (vs political) freedom was slow to develop was the intellectual celebration of the contest motif, especially in terms of Social Darwinism. Social Darwinism was the social application of the struggle of the population to let the fittest survive. It was argued that public assistance was not only costly and a problem, but it was positively harmful because it kept alive those who otherwise would not have survived (Tax and Krucoff, 1968). While this celebration might not have had much of a lasting scientific impact, it emphasized two qualities that remain with us today when we talk about people's rights and gaps between the promise and the performance. First, it transforms the social order into a moral order, suggesting that there is something "natural" about the fact that some people have more than others and that some are behind in rights and rewards. Tax and Krucoff quote William Graham Sumner on this point: "The men who have not done their duty in this world never can be equal to those who have done their duty. . . . They may, then, be classified in reference to these facts" (p. 404).

The authors do not stress the potential political significance of Sumner's use of the word "equal" in this context nor do they come to the obvious conclusion that this line of thinking can, however subtly, be used not only to sanctify the current social order but also can be used to provide a satisfying, scientific, natural explanation of the discrepancies that can everywhere be observed. Distinctions, then, based upon physical properties (youth and old age, gender, race, ethnic origin) that have always been made become somehow more appropriate, more natural. So one need not feel guilty.

The second residue left by Social Darwinism is a strengthening of the distinction between the poor and the pauper. This distinction, developed in the English Poor Law reform of 1834, altered to some degree the stigma of poverty. Poverty was bad; accepting charity was worse, especially if the charity was public. There was a fear that too much "entitlement" would blunt the contest and develop into some kind of societal sinecure (Himmelfarb, 1984).

The moral connotation and quasi-religious emphasis in Social Darwinism needed to be countered by another moral force, which came at the same turn-of-the-century period as Social Darwinism. That moral force came in a movement called the Social Gospel movement: "The rise of the social gospel precipitated renewal and reform on many fronts across America. A dominant evangelical tradition had long emphasized an individual salvation. Now the church was awakened to the possibilities of a social salvation as well" (White and Hopkins, 1976, p. 3). This movement preceded the Townsend movement, and that, in turn, set the stage for the Social Security Act.[7]

In terms of the Social Security Act, the need for compromise between struggle and entitlement was plain. First, struggle produced the income from which people paid the Social Security tax. By paying this tax, at some later point they would be entitled to the benefits of Social Security without any questions. Their entitlement had been assured by their contribution. In the Old Age Assistance program, however, need was a determining factor. There was no preexisting right to benefits independent of need except age. Nonetheless, as LaFrance (1979) suggests: "Since this (the Social Security Act) represented a legislative declaration of entitlement or protection for welfare beneficiaries, in contrast to the preexisting notion of welfare as a dole or charity, it inevitably influenced a similar shift in constitutional interpretation by the Supreme Court" (p. 83).

Entitlements to aid had developed. Such policies, though, did not come without transforming, through the concept of need, some of the character of those entitlements into a struggle motif. The Social Security Act is the clearest example. While it provided some assistance in income support, it was only minimal "social" security. More comprehensive benefits remained to be developed during the period of the 1960s, where we, as a society, finally had the chance—and may have missed it—to bring into the fold of society some of the people still excluded.

In a real sense, the welfare state can be seen as one that moves from struggle to entitlement and in which the harsh consequences and great benefits of struggle are tempered. According to LaFrance, one way to look at the development of entitlement is through the prism of society's relationship to education, at least in America. He cites several examples of ways in which the right to an education has been upheld. Similarly, in the provision of welfare and Social Security benefits, problems of equal access to public entitlements have been addressed:

By thus protecting education, the Supreme Court altered the constitutional status of public benefits generally. Privileges become akin to "rights" if they are protected. The same approach has been developed with respect to welfare. There the Supreme Court rejected the proposition that welfare is a property right, but has nevertheless held that—like education—it is protected by the Constitution. (P. 85)[8]

As I have suggested, with respect to the elderly the issue is not solely civil rights, but program rights as well. Criticisms of Social Security have contained articles like Longman's (1983) "Taking America to the Cleaners," and Fallows' (1982) "Entitlements." They argue that entitlements have become too widespread and too generous and have problematic, aggregate effects. The Gray Panthers represents a "struggle" group of elderly adults intent upon retaining entitlement rights and civil rights. The American Association of Retired Persons is similarly active though stylistically different. A group organized by Wilbur Cohen and others, called "Save Our Security," is battling for retention of benefits under Social Security.

WORK VS LEISURE

From the earliest days of this country the philosophy of work has been a central cultural feature. Max Weber (1956 [1904-5]) called attention to the importance of the "work ethic" or the "Protestant ethic." As a motivating concept, it has come to be a driving force that keeps Americans' noses to the grindstone and shoulders to the wheel. Yet leisure has also been an important part of U.S. life. Sunday has traditionally been a day of rest, and leisure has been enforced through Sunday Blue Laws and other regulations in which there are prohibitions against doing certain things on Sunday: "Time out is of course as venerable an institution as work itself" (Dumazedier, 1968, p. 248).

Marx, like Calvin, saw labor as central to personal meaning; and, to the extent that the capitalist class was also the leisure class, its crime was doubled. The leisure class was not only living off the work of others; they were not themselves working. Indeed, leisure implies not only freedom from work, but also something much more sinister from society's perspective. Dumazedier (1968) states: "Leisure also includes freedom from the fundamental obligations prescribed by other basic forms of social organization such as the family, the community, and the church" (p. 250).

And, while noting that work and leisure occur together, Dumazedier poses a question crucial to our interests: "Will commitment to leisure values be balanced by commitment to occupational, associational, political, and spiritual values, or will leisure threaten all these other values?" (p. 253).

An answer to this question has been provided, in part, by the work of Talcott Parsons. Parsons (1964) argues that the key element in the U.S. value system is something he calls 'instrumental activism.'' In a sense it means keeping busy while also feeling as if one is making a contribution. Parsons (1978) comments:

From one point of view, work is considered decidedly meritorious and leisure is the earned reward for meritorious work. However, . . . it is not possible to make things as simple as that. [We discussed] at some length the reservations that various "elderly" people, including myself, have about the life of leisure. In the history of thought, I would associate this very closely with the classical ideas about the "disutility of labor." It seems to me very largely fictional and ideological that labor in any sense is a source of disutility or [what] one might somewhat more strongly [feel] constitutes suffering on the part of those who work and therefore needs to be compensated by some nonwork we call leisure.[9]

Parsons' point is that work is the medium through which much meaning is found, both personal meaning, in the sense of contribution, and economic reward. Work is not to be viewed as a negative thing, something to be done and done with. Rather, work is positive and inspiriting. The satisfactions of work and leisure are bound together and cannot be easily separated. It is for this reason that he sees activism as the crucial element and something that contributes to both work and leisure.

These issues relate to social policy generally and involve the elderly specifically. Historically, work programs have been a hallmark of social policy. In 1576, for example, the first detailing of a work program contained, according to De Schweinitz (1943; reprint, 1961),

the same mixture of purpose that has characterized the use of work relief ever since. The Elizabethan lawmaker proposes work as training for the youth, as prevention of roguery, as a test of good intent, and a means of providing employment for the needy. In the background is the House of Correction with its threat of punishment. How ancient is the confusion about work, and how deep-rooted is our conflict of feeling concerning it! (Pp. 26-27)

Work is not only the means to one's own resources, it is also the vehicle through which one contributes to the community. Leisure is somehow thought of as non-productive. If, however, leisure is considered an opportunity for "recreation" or "re-creation," it has a somewhat different history from that of leisure itself, with its "leisure-class" connotations.

While the fact of work has changed little over the years, the setting of work has changed dramatically. The setting of work at the time of Calvin and Luther, for example, was much different from the setting of work observed and criticized by Marx. And the setting today is different still. It is out of these differences that a concept of recreation grew. Before industrialization and urbanization, work, home, and family were concentric activities. The individual had some control over the totality of the tasks he or she undertook. Industrialization and urbanization brought the separation of home and work. Inherent in that separation is the idea that work is not woven into the warp and woof of life itself, but is something one does for certain periods of time, after which one does not work. This process also developed specialized work tasks so that one's contribution to the whole was increasingly minimal. It was specialization that Marx saw, and specialization moved apace in the United States up through the turn of this century. By thus changing the setting and nature of work, urbanization and industrialization changed both the meaning one derived from work and the time one had to spend at it.

It was in this context that recreation became a definition of leisure. The definition became a problematic one because it raised the possibility that recreation, rather than work, might become dominant. Dubin and Champoux (1975) argue that leisure activities are becoming a central interest of the U.S. worker. Sessoms (1977) contends: "The need for recreational experience stands on its own merit; recreation is simply the voluntary pursuit of any activity in which one derives satisfaction from the act of doing. The job is a means of financing those interests" (p. 1171). Underneath, however, is the notion that work productivity will be enhanced and strengthened if one rests and is therefore more productive.

Still, several attitudes complicate even the tension between work and leisure, work and "re-creation." One is that recreation is time-filling, a sort of bread-and-circuses approach that keeps people out of trouble. A second is that it is the locus of meaning. A third is that it is a vehicle where proper values can be taught. In this last connection, it has been thought to be most appropriate for childhood. Activities such as Boy Scouts and Girl Scouts are representative of this orientation. Leisure without work, however, becomes a central problem in the retirement of older workers. In this case, leisure becomes purposeless. As Maddox (1968) suggests: "Departure from the world of work, with the implication that the separation is intended to be permanent, is an event of considerable social and personal significance in our society. . . . Retirement is a rite of passage, usually an informal one, between productive maturity and nonproductive old age" (p. 357).

It is clear, then, that while the event is important, less attention than is appropriate has been given to the differential meanings of retirement, to men as opposed to women, to groups across the society, and to the different values that retiring workers have. Those workers, for example, who viewed employment as merely a job to provide money to do what they wanted may find retirement something to look forward to. Workaholics may experience the reverse. For others, perhaps, the truth will lie somewhere in between.

Vaillant (1977), in his study of best and worst outcomes among Harvard graduates, found that one characteristic of the best outcomes was a vigorous use of leisure.

The orientation toward work and leisure/recreation is a central dilemma in American society. The elderly have often been compared to children, and the attention to leisure within both groups is as misleading as it is informing. It may be one reason, in fact, why leisure is rejected and work championed, as in the extension of the maximum age of mandatory retirement. The proportion of work to leisure represents a crucial policy question for the elderly. What kind of work and what kind of leisure is another such question.

Does the purpose of work remain always and everywhere the same? Probably not, as De Schweinitz suggests. But neither does recreation. In the final analysis, some balance between the two is the most likely path. Combinations of leisure on the job and ways to make leisure productive beyond recreation are possible. The argument that leisure activities at one stage in life may evolve into a second career at some later stage represents another line of thinking that is now gaining in prominence.

SECULAR VS RELIGIOUS

The tension between secular orientations and religious ones is another policy dilemma with strong historical roots. The terms *secular* and *religious* are often hard to define. Indeed, in this analysis, I will suggest several meanings. At one level the distinction refers to the differences in a scientific-rational (secular) view of the world as opposed to a spiritual understanding of the world (religious). On another level, secular-religious distinctions refer to the moral imperatives that empower social action. Religious motivation has almost always suggested that there is a need to help those less advantaged and has stressed the communal aspect of care: "The obligation to be charitable is a fundamental tenet of all Judeo-Christian religions. . . . This framework of values provided a way for Western man to justify and organize his humane impulses, even to generate them. If there is one source of American social work, it perhaps lies here. . . . More specifically, modern forms of social work have essentially religious origins" (Reid, 1977, p. 1244).

At the social-policy level, religious orientations provide, as Reid suggests, the impetus for many of the social movements and social pressures that have moved us toward equality, toward righting the wrongs of society itself. The Social Gospel movement, noted earlier, is an example of this point (White and Hopkins, 1976). Another is the activity of church groups during the 1960s in civil rights and anti-war protests and in sheltering those who were seeking to flee from arrest and imprisonment because of their political activism.

In spite of this emphasis, it is hard to draw a clear distinction between religious and secular orientation because America has, for many reasons, emphasized both. The dominance of Protestant society until the middle of the nineteenth century led to a kind of secularization of religions. Public rituals, which one would think to be secular, have always had religious aspects and overtones to them. The historic doctrine of religious freedom in this country meant that religions had a secular blessing. They also provided one vehicle through which the pluralism of the society could be legitimately expressed. Thus, sectarian social agencies became popular both because charity expressed religious intentions, as Reid suggests, and because they represented an acceptable arena in which differences could be expressed.

Lenski (1963) purports that religions are not just groups of beliefs, they are communities. He believes we need to think of "American religious groups not only as associations, but as subcommunities as well; not merely as the carriers of religious norms in any narrow sense, but as the carriers of complex subcultures relevant to almost all phases of human existence" (p. 344).[10]

Recognizing that religions are communities and not simply abstract doctrines holds tremendous implications for coming social policy. This impact will be felt as the nation shifts from one dominated by a Protestant orientation to one in which Catholics exert ever-increasing force and power. If, as Shrag (1971) suggests, we are in a period of the "decline of the wasp" (white Anglo-Saxon Protestant), then we may fully expect certain changes in orientations toward social policy to become evident.

The extent to which society is becoming more "Catholic" and less "Protestant" can have implications of fundamental importance relative to social policy, generally, and to the care of the elderly, specifically. In a sense it relates to the relative position of the Protestant ethic both in terms of work-leisure and of a whole attitude toward what is valued, what is important, what is desirable in life. An emphasis on external control, as opposed to internal control, characterizes this changing attitude.[11]

Lenski (1963) offers his conclusions as revealed in his research and that of others on the difference between a Protestant orientation and a Catholic one:

We have repeatedly observed important differences on a wide range of matters. *Our overall impression is that Catholics and Protestants alike have assimilated the materialistic values of contemporary society to the point where they equally value a good job with high income, and are equally likely to aspire to such a position. However, Catholics seem to be at a disadvantage in the competition because of a series of values to which they apparently become committed as a result of their involvement in the Catholic church and subcommunity.* (P. 345, emphasis in original)

What are some of these orientations? Lenski suggests:

For example, they [Catholics] seem to become more strongly attached to the kin group than Protestants, and therefore less able to make the break with home and family that is required in many of the more demanding, and hence better paid, positions in contemporary American society. Also, involvement in the Catholic group apparently fosters a de-emphasis of intellectual independence which is ill adapted to the more creative and responsible positions in our rapidly changing social order. In addition, involvement in the Catholic group leads to higher than average fertility, which certainly creates difficulties in securing higher education, and which may have some effect on I.Q. (p. 345)[12]

Given these differences as Lenski sees them, what might be some of the implications for social policy and social orientation? To his great credit, Lenski does not finesse this crucial question in the least. He does indicate that his suggestions are not predictions but, rather, "patterns linked with the Catholic group" and are likely to develop if the population composition changes to include more Catholics. He suggests changes such as the following:

1) Rising rates of church attendance . . . ;
2) Strengthening of religious group communalism;
3) Strengthening of both the nuclear and extended family . . . ;
4) Declining emphasis on educational independence;
5) Increasing support for the Democratic Party;
7) Shifting focus of interest from work group to kin group;
8) Slowing rate of material progress, and perhaps also of scientific advance;
9) Rising birth rates;
10) Narrowing latitude for exercise of the right of free speech;
11) Increasing restraints on Sunday business and divorce, and possibly birth control;
12) Declining restraints on gambling and drinking. (P. 361)

Of course, Lenski left himself open by putting such "probabilities" down on paper. We will have the opportunity later to look specifically at religion as a variable in a regression analysis to assess its predictive power.

Should the orientation suggested by Lenski be accurate, the application to policy of some of the ideas is obvious, including support for welfare state policies. The emphasis on the family and the increased interest in the kin group suggest that the family would take care of the elderly person. Any increase in the vitality of the extended family must, perforce, include elderly parents. On the other hand, welfare state policies imply an increase in the institutional location of certain services, perhaps services for the elderly. Both can occur, of course, and this pattern has been the one characterizing Catholic orientation here and abroad: larger, family-oriented systems coexisting and interlaced with a large system of bureaucratic religion. Still, a recent study by Alwin (1984) argues that American Catholics are becoming more like Protestants, and, especially, are favoring autonomy and disfavoring obedience.

In a recent study, Alwin (1984; 1986) makes the following conclusions, comparing changes in Catholic and Protestant orientations toward child rearing: "these changes have resulted in a general convergence of parental values among major religioethnic catagories" (Alwin, 1986, p. 436). While childrearing is only one possible dimension of values assessment, the idea of convergence there suggests that there may be convergence along other dimensions as well, a point Alwin recognizes. However, it is not necessary that there be "all" convergence or "all" divergence. The concepts of dimensions of values, like the one offered here, suggests that there could be convergence along some vectors while substantial divergence could exist along others. Indeed, to the extent that this study provides empirical support, I would certainly agree with Alwin. Religious identification (Catholic and Jewish were used here) do not predict well to value orientations. But that analysis was global (see tables 3 and 4). More refined analysis might suggest areas where power still exists.

PERSONAL VS FAMILY

Debates about the decline of the family, though no doubt as old as the family itself, have taken particularly vigorous form during this century as the trend toward urbanization and industrialization accelerated. Christensen (1964) quotes Hobart as calling in 1963 for a "value revolution": "in which the family would play a key role—a revolution that would displace 'the now pre-eminent success, efficiency, productivity, prosperity values by the more human oriented being, knowing, caring, loving values'" (p. 986).

Conflict between the family and the world was mirrored within the family, too. Hobart took a standard view that:

the priority of these love and concern values is directly challenged by success and achievement values which may imply that status symbols are more important than babies; that what a child *achieves* is more important than what he *is*; that what we *own* is more important than what we *are*. Thus the stage is set for conflict between a success-oriented husband and a child-people welfare oriented wife, or for a rather inhuman family which values things over people, and which may raise children who have difficulty living down this experience of worthlessness. (P. 986)[13]

These forecasters thought they were Cassandras. They appear, indeed, to have been more like gloom-and-doom sayers without her prescience. Family observers, such as Lasch (1977) and others, have indicated that the demise of the family, however probable it appeared at the turn of the century, has not yet arrived. The extended family has been pared down a bit. But it has not quite descended to the nuclear family, living in splendid isolation from kin and neighbors (as many predicted). Instead, what we see is the modified extended family in which modern technology has brought people together as much as it has torn them apart. Family and community appear to be here to stay.

Nonetheless, the stresses of personalistic values, as implied by Hobart, cannot be set aside completely by any means. There is real stress. Kirkpatrick details it in much the same terms—dual conflicting orientation—that I have used here. Among a series of conflicts he identifies are the following: "Work achievement versus the love-reproduction function; personal self-expression versus devoted child rearing." (Quoted in Christensen, 1964, p. 989. See also Kirkpatrick, 1963.) There are conflicts between the personalistic orientation that would advance the fortunes and prospects of the person and those that would advance the fortunes and prospects of the family collectively (whether extended, modified-extended, or nuclear). Simmel (1968) states that "in some societies—for example, contemporary Japan and Greece, as well as in most of the developing societies—the claims of the family or larger group far outbalance the rights of the individual. One may expect to find this the case wherever family or group honor is the ultimate criterion by which the individual is judged" (pp. 483-484).

Today may be the age of the New Narcissism. Certainly, books and popular magazines point to such a trend. If it is movement bursting on our scene, it represents less of a radical shift in values than a shift in emphasis, stressing more personalistic values that have always been present in our culture and subordinating more collectively familial values.

I believe that these former values have always been more prominent. In this judgment I agree with J. R. Pole (1978), who has the virtue of being both an understanding outsider to our country and a noted historian. His conclusion to his history of *The Pursuit of Equality in American History* bears directly on this point: "It is the individual whose rights are the object of the special solicitude of the Constitution and for whose protection the Republic had originally justified its claim to independent existence" (p. 358).

It is no accident that we have no "family policy" in the United States, no specific set of laws designed to promote and enhance family living. In fact, it is sometimes not possible even to define what the "family" is. Such inability has led to the regular confusions in the White House Conference on the Family. Concern over the neglect of the family in policy matters has led to the formation of the Family Impact Seminar under the auspices of George Washington University's Institute for Educational Leadership. The basic value assumptions of the Family Impact Seminar are useful to consider:

We have a mutual interest in the well-being of families and their ability to care for their members.

We believe that public policies affecting families should seek to support and supplement families in the exercise of their basic functions.

As a general rule and consistent with the protection of constitutional rights, we believe government policies should provide families with broadened options and choices. (Johnson, 1981, pp. 11-12)

One might think this is a far cry from Pole's statement. There is, however, one last goal: "We believe public policies designed to support families should give priority to those families *and family members* who have least access to the needed resources of society" (p. 12, emphasis added).

It appears that the individual, as a family member, may have crept in after all. The fact that the individual in this case is a disadvantaged one is of less importance than the fact that, even within the promoting of the family, personalism appears. The Family Impact Seminar feels that families are threatened by the progress of society. It seeks, if possible, to identify the impacts that legislative activity will have upon them: "[When] assessing a particular policy, the Family Impact Seminar will seek to state the values and value trade-offs involved in options" (p. 12). One of the trade-offs, quite clearly, will be that between the family as a unit and the individual.

Wilbur J. Cohen notes, for example, that the Social Security Act as a program centered upon the family in terms of benefits and benefit packages.[14] Certainly, there is some argument for this position, and Cohen notes that, when the family orientation was introduced in 1939, no one anticipated that as many women would be working as are currently. Neither, too, did anyone anticipate that the private system would develop as it has. For this reason, providing additional benefits to the family on a family basis seemed, at the time, sound policy. Now, however, in the period of rising personalism, such a benefit structure may have to be changed.

Policy conflicts between familial and personal orientation have direct effects upon the elderly. As individuals become older, should they live with their children? Who is to take care of them? Should they have a place of their own? If they do, how are they to get some of the small yet needed social services that are routinely provided within a family setting? Ladd (1978) reports a decline in public opinion regarding the sense of filial responsibility. Lois Glasser and Paul Glasser (1977) attribute the decline in family values to hedonism. The plethora of nursing homes, absorbing the responsibilities of family members, and whole areas of cities filled with elderly people living alone suggest that a personalistic orientation has captured a dominant place in the minds of many, old and young.

As always, several caveats are in order. This personalistic approach does not represent the abandonment of the elderly population by the younger. It is, rather, a choice of the elderly population to be alone (privatism) and independent for as long as possible. There may also be important differences in the provision of care when it is needed. Recent figures in the

Wall Street Journal (June 4, 1986) suggest that gender may be significant in this regard: "Almost 40% of disabled men (aged 65 and older) are cared for by their wives; only 10% of disabled women are cared for by their husbands" (p. 29).

CONCLUSION

The perspective offered here on policy opinion seeks to put it into a context of competing commitments and oppositional orientations. These are within all of us, and the pattern I see in policy opinion at any moment is the outgrowth of this competition. It helps us to understand where we are coming from and where we might be going. It puts policy opinion in perspective.

One might ask at this point, what causes policy opinion to change, to move from one particular balance point to the other? There are at least three possible answers to this question, and they will be discussed in more detail in the last chapter. Suffice it for now to say that a dualistic framework, such as I've suggested, aids materially in understanding both change and stability. For one thing, the tension between juxtaposed values is itself generative of the need for balance. Too much emphasis on the personal or the family, too much emphasis on equity or adequacy, indeed, too much emphasis on any one of the paired values we carry with us generates a rebalancing dynamic. The tension and pull between any two values is part of the generative force here, but disappointment, as Hirschman (1982) suggests, with the current emphasis is also part of the generative force. It is also important to keep in mind that there are not only tensions and disappointments *within* each value dimension (in Hirschman's case it is public and private), but also *among* the various dimensions.

With these perspectives in mind, then, let's look at the distribution of policy opinion itself. The next three chapters—"The Eclipse of Public Function," "Righting Civil Wrongs," and "The Wavering of Traditional Commitments"—discuss the policy-opinion pattern in each of the three areas of interest here. Chapter 7, "The Mosaic of Culture," seeks to answer questions about the kinds of characteristics that are most likely to be associated with particular kinds of policy opinion. Chapter 8, "The Personal Roots of Commitment," uses a factor analytic approach to look at the clustering of policy opinion in the volatile vortex of social space. The concluding chapter, "American Values and the Elderly," looks at cultural change and its dynamics. A constant theme in each of these chapters, the leitmotif of discussion, is the role and perspective of the elderly respondent.

In short, the researcher and scholar is always interested not only in what is seen but in what is not seen, in what is said and unsaid, in the figure and the field. Without both parts of that analysis, only the most partial and skewed picture is available.

NOTES

1. Merit alone, however, without the evidence of "work," is often resented. To some it seems unfair that a particular student receives an A + for sitting down and writing an excellent essay with no apparent trouble or effort. Even though an essay thus produced would be recognized by all as the very best on merit, it is likely that students and teachers would be unhappy with it because merit is somehow connected, at least in part, with effort.

2. Interestingly, age itself was not a strong predictor, something we also found using different types of dependent variables. What is common is the fact that both the vignettes contributed by Alves and Rossi and our public-opinion-type questions involved judgments.

3. Historically, too, the major elements of external control, the church and the state, were both repugnant to Americans. It was freedom from both that brought the Pilgrims to these shores.

4. There is a question about when to begin counting here. In a sense, Cohen is correct. Americans did try to rely on private welfare, as we suggested, until the Depression made it impossible. On the other hand, the initiative represented by the New Deal and the Social Security Act did generate, along with supporting federal tax law and union pressure, substantial private activity.

5. *Private* has many meanings. What we call private now (meaning a "private" enterprise) in some instances was, years ago, public (in the sense of "open"). Life insurance is a good example. Before life insurance, death and its implications were met in the private circle of family and friends. The idea of going "public" through insurance, of somehow placing a dollar value on life itself, was initially rejected. Only later did it come to have acceptance and, later still, appropriateness. See V. A. Zelizer (1978), "Human Values and the Market: The Case of Life Insurance and Death in 19th Century America."

6. For a summary, see Lewis Coser, "Conflict," (1968), vol. 3, pp. 232-236.

7. See both Achenbaum (1978) and Fischer (1978) for discussions of the social activities of special relevance to the elderly prior to the passage of the Social Security Act.

8. This quote is from LaFrance's extensive discussion (Section 8) on the "Right/Privilege Distinction," which is much the same as entitlement vs struggle.

9. Personal correspondence, September 25, 1978.

10. There is the question, of course, of which came first, the religious orientation or the community? For our purposes, it does not matter. It is important to note, however, that groups of beliefs might have produced communities. The distinction Lenski makes, therefore, needs to be tempered.

11. A generalization is useful here in gaining perspective: Catholics are oriented to external control; Protestants to internal control. Catholicism is a religion that sustains itself through a highly structured bureaucracy that is everywhere operative, everywhere the "same." (One caveat: "Same" is inadequate because of differences in national churches.) It is the church bureaucracy that sets the rules and makes judgments. An elite priesthood maintains the dogma and the standards of the faith. There is little in the system that encourages the parishioner to undertake the role of thinker or judger. Instead the parishioner is a reporter, reporting his sins and seeking forgiveness for them. To the extent he has control, it is only relative to compliance,

never relative to the criteria themselves. The Protestant is encouraged to read and think for himself. While he may not, ultimately, control his salvation, he must decide, wonder, and worry always about being saved, think about it, assess the criteria that might indicate it, and so on. Individualism and intellectuality are encouraged. While they are not discouraged in Catholiscism, neither are they fostered.

12. Lenski's comments give credibility to Glazer and Moynihan's point about the legitimacy of religious distinctions. (Tropman, 1976). No one would think of making a similar point using race as the chief variable. Yet, today, similar comments are frequently made. Andrew Greeley, in commenting about the case of a professor suing a college over his firing because of alcoholism and the problems of alcoholism as a policy that have developed since the Rehabilitation Act of 1973, defines alcoholism as a handicap and remarks, "One of my social science colleagues remarked that it might be a secret conspiracy to provide more college professorships for the Irish. I doubt it because everyone knows that Irish Catholics can't be good scholars." From "Next: It's Quotas for Hiring Alcoholics," *Detroit Free Press* (February 20, 1979), p. 9a.

13. I've quoted from a much longer quote. The full text is in W. C. Hobart (1963), "Commitment, Value Conflict and the Future of the American Family."

14. Personal communication, 1978. Achenbaum (1978) points out that the program changed from an individual to a family orientation before benefits were ever paid. Perhaps the emphasis "shifted from the worker as an individual to the worker as a breadwinner for a family group" (p. 136). He quotes Frank Bane (1939), "The Social Security Act Expands," pp. 608-609.

PART *II*
POLICY OPINION AND THE ELDERLY: 1952–1978

4
THE ECLIPSE
OF PUBLIC FUNCTION

INTRODUCTION

There is great controversy in the United States concerning how the public sector should function. Should it, for example, move more toward a welfare state position, with private systems receding in importance? Alternatively, should public agencies act only in cases of need, leaving all else to the private sector? In looking at the role of government in welfare activity, the distinction Helen Witmer made years ago between institutional and residual social welfare orientation is still serviceable (Wilensky and Lebeaux, 1956; Gilbert, 1983). Institutional functions develop pervasively and as an ongoing part of public activity; residual ones come in only after all else has ceased to work, representing a sort of fail-safe approach to social welfare activity.

How these functions are played out is of considerable importance to elderly citizens. They well understand that, while private companies may pass away, the public bureaucracy is likely to keep going—and the government-assured benefits with it. This possibility is bound to be appealing to many elderly citizens, fearful that a bankruptcy, a takeover, or some other factor could deprive them of earned benefits. Experience of the Depression is likely to have reinforced this worry. Private coverage, moreover, does not include everyone. Some may have substantial pensions. Others may have little or none, depending on where one worked, one's position in the organization, seniority, and so on. While a large corporation may provide excellent benefits, a small one may not.

Whether financial security for one's old age is being provided for is of interest to old and young alike. It is the one benefit that can be shared by all because it is gradually accrued by all. Medical insurance bears something of this character; but, given the greater likelihood that the elderly person will have medical problems, a medical program developed by the government is likely to be aimed more at elderly people, as in the case of Medicare. Younger people may support the program because they fear the devastating financial effect that a parent's incurring a major illness could have on them directly.

The government is not simply the source of social programs, however. It provides a social model, a standard by which we can all live—a moral model. In this sense, governmental programs must be both just *and* compassionate, egalitarian *and* equitable. Government must also establish and maintain some standards below which its activities will not fall. Then it must act to insure that such principles and such minimum standards are established throughout the society itself. The protection of equity and adequacy in welfare activity has become a crucial function of government in the American polity.

The state can become more than an enabling center. It can also come to have an all-encompassing effect on an individual's life, as the church has in some societies. Church and state battle because they carry similar roles. It could be argued that the welfare state is a secular version of the sacred state, placing its emphasis on current benefits rather than on preparations for the life to come.

In this sense, limited government is similar to limited religion in that both can become alternative influences upon one's life. Accordingly, the fear may arise that too great a dependency on such external forces will develop "other-reliance," rather than a fundamental self-reliance. Interdependency can be seen as a lack of willingness to make one's own way, to rely on the efforts of external institutions rather than on one's own efforts.

Within recent American history the development of a more liberal governmental orientation has been associated in the minds of some with a greater orientation toward interdependency, with diminishing emphasis on self-reliance. In some areas of public policy more conservative orientations have tended to highlight self-reliance and to support limited roles of government, which tends to mean less governmental expenditures and activity. The ideological picture has rarely been so clear-cut as this liberal-conservative distinction suggests, however. The value conflict can be seen in the various directions taken by both sides.

Public function is, therefore, depicted in this study as encompassing three areas of values where crucial issues are seen regularly to arise: public vs private issues, equity vs adequacy issues, and independence vs interdependence issues. These issues touch both on the intensity (depth of feeling) of public activity and on its nature and extent. The nine figures to be presented below depict some changes that seem to have occurred in societal views on these issues over recent decades.

TRUST IN GOVERNMENT

No democratic government can operate without consent of the governed. How that consent is developed—and, in particular, how the government and others go about the engineering of consent—is a major constituent element in the political system. As a result of this process, trust is an essential part of the political capital with which democratic governments operate. Figure 1 demonstrates that in the United States there has been a substantial loss in trust in government over the decades.[1]

Between 1958 and 1978, the confidence that Americans had in the idea that "you can trust the government in Washington to do what is right" fell from a total of 73 percent of those interviewed who expressed views of "always" or "most of the time" to 30 percent holding those views twenty years later. (In order to avoid too much "chart junk" in the figures, the actual proportions are not present here. They are listed in the tables in appendix A.) The decline appears to have come in three stages. Between 1958 and 1964, around 60 percent of the respondents said "most of the time." At that point there was a downturn. Between 1966 and 1972, only about 50 percent of the respondents took that view. In 1974 and 1978, this limited approval dropped considerably, with 34 percent and 27 percent, respectively, trusting government officials "most of the time."

The elderly's view was similar to that of the youngest, though somewhat more pronounced. In each measuring period from 1958 to 1978, those over sixty-five were the least trusting among the various age groups. In 1958, 63 percent said they trusted the government in Washington "always" or "most of the time." In 1978, only 24 percent said this. The percentage of those with high trust, those who think the government always does what is right, slipped from 15 percent in 1958 to 5 percent in 1978. The spread between the oldest and youngest groups remained about the same over the period. The middle-age group, however, was a little closer to the younger group than their older compeers.

For all age groups there has been a substantial shift in the degree to which the public trusts the government over the past twenty years. This is expressed in a steady downward pattern.

Both aging and period effects seem to be evidenced here. A life-cycle effect is suggested since, for every year for which there is a measure, the young are the most trusting, the elderly the least trusting, with the middle-aged group generally in between. A period effect is suggested as trust seems to decline in a similar fashion in all three age groups.

Figure 1
TRUST IN GOVERNMENT, 1958-1978

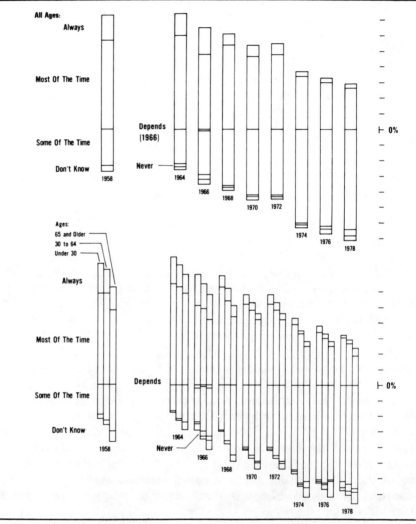

Year(s)	Question
58, 64, 68, 70, 72, 74, 76, 78	How much of the time do you think you can trust the government in Washington to do what is right -- just about always, most of the time, or some of the time?
66	How much do you think we can trust the government in Washington to do what is right: just about always, most of the time, some of the time, or almost never?

It is fascinating to consider why this eclipse of trust has occurred at the very time when governmental activity has shown unusually rapid growth, especially in areas concerning the elderly. Rising taxes may represent one possible explanation. Services have increased, however, and some of them have been especially aimed at the elderly—Social Security, the Older American's Act, and Medicare. Despite this fact, the response of the elderly has definitely not been one of approving gratitude. Rather, it has been one of increasing criticism.

The ambiguity of the phrase, "the government in Washington," may be another contributing factor, including as it does both elected and civil officials, ranging across the board from Congress to president to Supreme Court to clerks to cabinet members. Someone in this group is bound to offend—but someone in this group has *always* been bound to offend.

It may be that the rapid growth of government is associated with the critical attitudes expressed. As government does more, it must both please and offend more. Policy alienation could develop with increasing numbers of those on the left, who think that government is not doing enough, and increasing numbers of those on the right, who think government is doing too much. Janowitz (1978) makes an excellent case that as government does more, it tends to please less. To some extent the large shift away from the "most of the time" category for all age groups may indicate this trend.

An unpopular war in Vietnam may have been another contributor, but the decline had begun before U.S. entanglements in that war reached crisis proportions. Furthermore, it is important to remember that the Vietnam War was not widely unpopular in the beginning.

An obvious possibility for the decline might have been Watergate. Indeed, although it has become academically chic to blame the loss of confidence in government on the events generated during the Watergate period (Lipset and Schneider, 1983), it is quite clear that the decline began before and continues well after Watergate. Viewed in terms of public sentiment, Watergate may have been as much a product of a loss of confidence in government as it was the cause of such a loss. Prior incidents—including the Bay of Pigs, clouds surrounding the investigation of the Kennedy assassination, to mention only a few of the events that raised questions about the extent to which government could be trusted—may have made the public more interested and suspicious than it might otherwise have been. That interest and suspicion may thereby have created the "climate of concern" into which Watergate plunged the nation.

The elderly respondents to this question present a consistent pattern of less trust from the very first (1958) through the most recent period covered in this analysis (1978). Elderly respondents are, thus, more hesitant to trust than younger ones. Does this result mean that they are more "conservative"? I think not. Other evidence does not support such a conclusion, as will be seen here and in subsequent chapters. Rather, elderly respondents here, as in some other questions ("stop crime," "family size," "rights of women") exhibit specifically focused and targeted (rather than global) responses. In this particular case, a "lived life" perspective may suggest that a tempered trust of government is a prudent course.

GOVERNMENTAL BENEFIT

One specific reason for low trust reflected in the polls may be that people feel that government is not working for them, helping them, or being responsive to them. Instead, it may seem that the government is primarily working for the benefit of itself or for others. Figure 2 presents data on the responses to a question relevant to this point: "Would you say the government is pretty much run by a few big interests looking out for themselves or that it is run for the benefit of all the people?"

Here, too, the data are quite revealing. Since 1964, the idea that the government is "run for the benefit of all" has been receiving less and less support, dropping from 64 percent in 1964 to 24 percent in 1978. Here, as in figure 1, the proportion of "don't knows" has remained fairly steady. So, too, has the proportion of "other, depends" responses. Increasingly, people have chosen the alternative response available, that government is run for the benefit of a few big interests.

The 1958 version of this question is arresting because the question-response categories were different than later years and were not repeated. (A space or a dotted vertical line indicates a substantial difference in the question or the response categories.) While half the question is the same as at other times—namely, the "big interests" portion—the more "democratic" alternative was "give everyone a fair break" rather than "for the benefit of all." There were other differences in wording that suggest, as does the response pattern, that the question was quite a different one and should not be included in our considerations here.[2]

All three age groups showed increased feeling that the government is run by a few big interests for their own benefit. The elderly were slightly more likely, by a percentage point or two, to have no opinion. Their opinions, however, presage those of younger age groups in later years. In 1964, 57 percent of the elderly felt that government was run for the benefit of all, while 70 percent of those under thirty felt that way. In 1968, four years later, only 56 percent of the under-thirty age group felt that government was run for the benefit of all. By 1976, the under-thirty group had dropped to 25 percent. This compares with 23 percent of the group over sixty-five for that year.

The pattern by age group is one of greater doubt on the part of the elderly, relative to those of younger years, at every measurement period except 1958. This pattern suggests an aging effect. Both groups show

Figure 2
WHO IS THE GOVERNMENT RUN FOR THE BENEFIT OF? 1958-1978

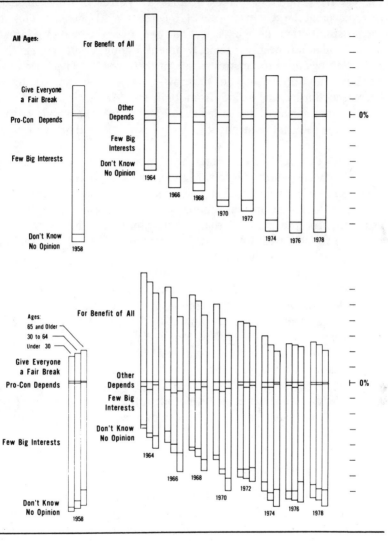

Year(s)	Question
58	Do you think that the high-up people in government give everyone a fair break whether they are big shots or just ordinary people, or do you think some of them pay more attention to what the big interests want? (1= give everyone a fair break; 3= pro-con, it depends; 5= few big interests)
64, 66, 68, 70, 72, 74, 76, 78	Would you say the government is pretty much run by a few big interests looking out for themselves or that it is run for the benefit of all the people? (1= for benefit of all; 3 or 7= other, depends, both boxes checked; 5= few big interests)

increasing doubt as time passes, with the gap between age groups gradually narrowing. In 1964, the youngest group was 13 percent more positive than the elderly group (70 percent versus 57 percent), while in 1978, the difference had largely evaporated (26 percent vs 21 percent). This suggests the possibility that the aging effect has been overwhelmed by a large period effect, which has been particularly potent among recent cohorts.

Two things need to be stressed about these results. The elderly are both similar to and different from those who are younger, and the differences decreased during the period from 1958 to 1978. In a sense, the elderly respondents appeared to be leaders, holding in advance views that they themselves took more strongly in later years, views that younger cohorts came to share.

As with the previous question, this response pattern reveals a consistent decline in positive attitudes toward the fairness of government. This decline occurred at the very point that government was moving—during the 1960s and early 1970s—to increase the range of its action to promote fairness, especially for the poor. Perhaps that is precisely the point. If so, the response in 1958 was not so offbeat after all, differences in the question notwithstanding. Surely, the vision set forth in the Kennedy inauguration and the early programs in school-community relationships and delinquency prevention took those 1958 perceptions as a point of departure.[3] It may have been exactly the 1958 perception that the government favored a "few big interests" that the Kennedy administration was seeking to rectify. Then, as we progress toward the 1980 period, we find movement toward the higher level of scepticism than was present in 1958.

The questions in figure 1 and figure 2 will be discussed further in chapter 7. When they were included in a factor analysis, they appeared together in the factor pattern, thus constituting one important dimension of political reality that may cut across both the idea of adequacy-equity and the idea of public-private.

SAY IN GOVERNMENT

Political cynicism and a feeling that the government is run for the benefit of a few may stem from (or be related to) a sense that the respondent has little influence on the processes of government. Data on this point are displayed in figure 3, which reports the distribution of responses to the statement, "People like me don't have any say about what the government does."

These data run the full span of years from 1952 to 1978 and reveal only moderate fluctuations and changes over that span. In 1952, 31 percent of the respondents agreed with that statement, suggesting a sense of political impotence and alienation from the processes of government. That response decreased to a low of 27 percent in 1960. It then began to creep up, reaching

Figure 3
PEOPLE LIKE ME DON'T HAVE ANY SAY ABOUT WHAT THE GOVERNMENT DOES, 1952-1978

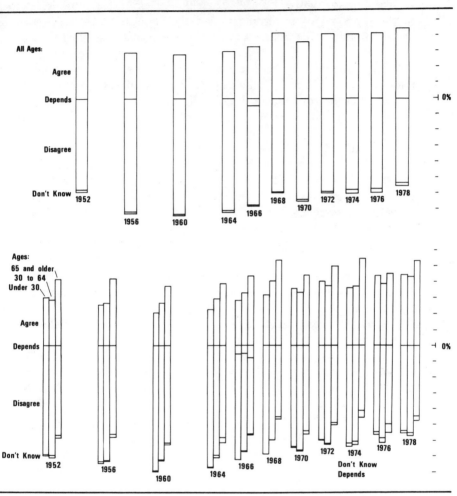

Year(s)	Question
52,56,60, 64,68 70,72,74, 76,78	People like me don't have any say about what the government does. (1= agree; 5= disagree)
66	People like me don't have any say about what the government does. (1= strongly agree; 2= agree; 3= not sure, it depends; 4= disagree; 5= strongly disagree)

a high plateau of around 40 percent in 1968, then rising once again to 45 percent in 1978.

The patterning by age group is also displayed in figure 3, revealing results much like those of figures 1 and 2. The elderly seem to feel more isolated from the processes of government than the younger and, here, by an important amount. The figures show that agreement of the elderly spikes markedly above that of the other age groups in every year except 1976. Elderly groups apparently feel decidedly more alienated than their younger counterparts, as the 52 percent agreeing that "people like me don't have any say about what the government does" indicates (in 1978).

Here, the pattern of cultural change revealed in the previous data is seen only among the youngest cohorts. About 30 percent of the under-thirty group felt alienated in 1952. That proportion dropped to 20 percent in 1960. It then crept upward to 45 percent in 1978. That year, the position of the youngest finally arrived at the near 40 percent level consistently held by the elderly population since 1952. (The elderly population, however, by 1978, had risen to 52 percent.)

These responses have some interesting characteristics. First, relative stability rather than change seems to be a central characteristic of the period. Unlike trust in government, which declined, and a sense that the government is run for the benefit of a few, which increased, the proportion of people who believe that they don't have a say in government remains about the same.

This is not to suggest that there is no shift in opinion. Generally, the change proceeds to increasing feelings of powerlessness over the years, from a ratio of about 30/70 in 1952 to about 40/60 in 1978. That represents a considerable fraction of people who do not agree that they don't have any influence. There is a double negative here, and it is not altogether clear that those who disagree with the statement are, in fact, agreeing with an affirmative version of it; i.e., that people like them do have an influence. Still, one can take it as a positive sign that, through this period at any rate, substantial proportions of Americans did not feel a lack of distance from governmental processes in spite of all the difficulties and problems that occurred during the era.

Some of the change that did occur reflects a patterning by age, however. First, elderly respondents felt more powerless than the youngest respondents. That fraction increased from 42 percent in 1952 to 52 percent in 1978. Second, alienation of the under-thirty respondents rose, too, but slightly more: from 30 percent in 1952 to 45 percent in 1978. This movement is curious, given the flow of events. During this period, young people over eighteen were granted the right to vote, and the "youth culture" was having a far-reaching impact on the political system through both non-governmental and governmental channels. One might have thought that a sense of power and influence would have been at its height.[4]

The period, then, was characterized by an increasing sense of powerlessness in all groups, somewhat more among the elderly. Young people were less negative in 1952, but moved to be more like their older cohorts by the end of the period. All groups felt an increasing sense of disengagement or distance from the governmental process, with elderly respondents being opinion leaders throughout. This result, too, is surprising, because it was the heyday of governmental action for elderly Americans.

VOTER'S INFLUENCE

The voting question gives rise to ambiguous, contradictory interpretations. People were presented with the following statement: "Voting is the only way that people like me can have any say about how the government runs things." The responses were: "agree," "depends," "disagree," "don't know." One interpretation is that an "agree" response is a measure of a positive political attitude: "The vote is a good thing, and I'm glad I can exercise it, and there could be other ways, too, for me to influence the government, although I don't necessarily use them." On this interpretation, voting becomes a floor of participation that other modes of influence could be built upon. Other positive interpretations are also possible; for example, "For people like me, voting really is the only way, and I accept that." A contrary interpretation is that an "agree" response reflects a negative view: "Voting is the only way for me to have influence, and I feel bad about it." Even in this direction, the person might feel cheated and resentful or simply resigned or possibly even cynical. The point is that very different meanings are possible, reflecting very different values and assessments of reality.

Likewise, a "disagree" response could mean, among other things: "For people like me, even voting is not good," or "there are other ways" (whether or not the individual thinks them possible or feasible or desirable or even cares to try them).

In essence, interpretation of the answers to this statement hinge upon where one wants to take the phrases "only way" and "people like me." Does that way open the door for other ways to them, or does it suggest that the voter is alienated from the political system and has limited alternative ways? The answer seems to be, at the very least, both. The overall distribution is displayed in figure 4.

The distribution of data indicates that the proportion of the "agree" response has fallen over the years, from 81 percent in 1952 to 58 percent in 1978. Here, as in the other figures, there are no substantial proportions of people in the "don't know" column. Overall, the change in opinion occurred in essentially three segments: the period from 1952 to 1964, when the "agrees" ranged in the 70 percent area (except for 1952); the period

Figure 4
VOTING IS THE ONLY WAY THAT PEOPLE LIKE ME CAN HAVE ANY
SAY ABOUT HOW THE GOVERNMENT RUNS THINGS, 1952-1978

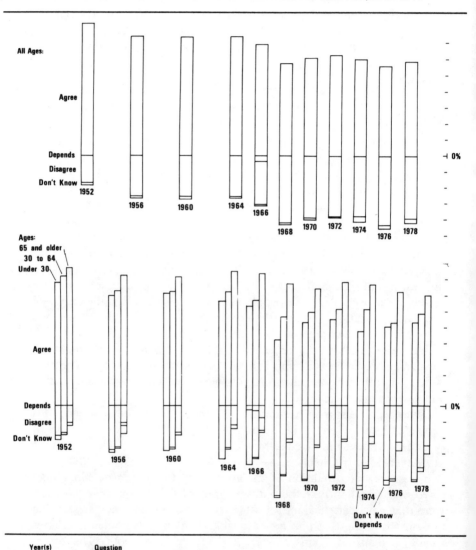

Year(s)	Question
52,56,60 64,68, 70,72,74, 76,78	Voting is the only way that people like me can have any say about how the government runs things. (]= agree; 5= disagree)
66	Voting is the only way that people like me can have any say about how the government runs things. (1= strongly agree; 2= agree; 3= not sure, it depends; 4= disagree; 5= strongly disagree)

from 1966 to 1974, in which the "agrees" were in the 60 percent range (except for 1968); and the period from 1976 to 1978, when the "agrees" were in the 55 percent to 58 percent range.

These overall figures conceal important age group differences. It is the younger age groups who have shifted, not the older. The elderly continue to agree with the statement, and strongly, registering an 85 percent agreement in 1952, which fell to a 70 percent agreement in 1978. The younger respondents, very close to older respondents in 1952 with a 78 percent "agree," fell to around 51 percent in 1978.

It is this pattern that suggests an interpretation of the statement. Older respondents think about this statement as they did the previous one (reported in figure 3), perhaps sensing themselves to be so alienated from control within the political system that they feel their voting does not do much good. Younger respondents, however, show a different value pattern or assessment of reality, one that reflects a contrary view of *voting*. While they may feel increasingly that they have no say, they may also see that there are ways other than voting that they could use, a conclusion that would have basis in the events of the past twenty years, extending from the civil rights marches to the Eugene McCarthy candidacy for president to the Vietnam War protests (to mention just three prominent non-voting examples of public influence).

In short, it seems that one plausible approach to this question, despite the possible ambiguity, is to view it as measuring a sense of overall loss of influence for most respondents, especially among elderly people, while younger people may see other possible avenues (such as activism) as means of influence. Voting is not the only way for the young; there are *other ways*. For the old, voting may actually be the *only* way—and even that may not be going too well in the eyes of some.

This line of argument raises a question of the meaning of voting itself, and, as a corollary, the public understanding of the idea of influence. People may think that while they do, in fact, vote, it does not have much influence, or that voting is really the only way, effective or not. Without belaboring all possible interpretations, it is useful to show how important varied public understandings and discriminations can be in interpreting the social meaning of a question.[5]

People in general, then—and especially the elderly—may be feeling increasingly estranged from government at the same time that government is moving more and more to help them—less able to influence government and more dependent upon it. Further, the old may sense that their vote is not very influential just at the time when their numbers are increasing. We must bear in mind the possibility that, for the elderly especially, questions about political influence that tap into a sense of personal control may well refer to much broader phenomena than a narrowly political kind. They may, for example, be triggering a feeling that the government treats them as mere policy objects rather than as citizens with political rights.

It also may reflect some of the ambivalence in the dual-value approach to policy opinion. On the one hand, the elderly may feel positive that governmental programs are improving their lot and that of others. On the other, they may retain notions of privatism, that the government should not be doing this or should be doing less. The results may be the amalgam of conflicting orientations. Indeed, this point is a central focus of the argument I am advancing, that "behavior" (in this case, expressing the choice of answers) may well be stimulated by more than one attitude or value. Schuman and Johnson (1976) raise this issue when they ask "How do we know when a particular attitude and a particular behavior should be related?" (p. 201). This question is a good one, but they do not stand aside from the one-to-one relationship. I suggest that two attitudes or values may be related to a given behavioral opportunity. Indeed, if this contention can be shown to be true, then a whole new perspective on the relationship between thought and action might be possible. In this particular case, it is helpful to assume that conflicting commitments may inform the elderly respondents' (and, perhaps, the younger ones, too) final answer.

I would add to this line of thinking that the conflict between independence and interdependence must surely arise. More programmatic activity on the part of government (and big business, too, to follow Lipset and Schneider, 1983) might generate threats to, or concerns about, independence. Big Brother may be helpful, but on his terms, not the elderly's, and they may find it hard to control him.

SHOULD THE GOVERNMENT ASSURE A JOB AND A GOOD STANDARD OF LIVING?

A "mindless public" hypothesis would presuppose that mass publics would be relatively insensitive to subtle changes in wording, to shifts in the meaning of questions, or to a range of possible interpretations. The figures so far suggest that such is not the case, that the responding public *has* opinions, expresses them consistently over the years, and appears to discriminate when differing interpretations are possible. This certainly appeared to be the case among different age groups in response to the voting question. The question about government assuring a job and a good standard of living provides another excellent illustration of this tendency.

Between 1956 and 1978, a series of questions were asked about the extent to which the government should assure a job or work to everyone who wanted it. These data are displayed in figure 5.

In this question the public places itself between a rock and a hard place. On the one hand, it favors people working and even feels that some government benefits are all right if the recipient is working (Tropman, 1978). On the other, there is some reluctance to use the public coffers for support, the feeling being that people should fend for themselves. The results are suggestive of such split orientations, with proportions of "not sure; it depends," and "don't know; no opinion" ranking among the highest in the data set. In this data series, these proportions increase to the point that, in 1978, such answers together represent a full 20 percent of the respondents. Although there are surely other reasons for this result, such high levels of indeterminacy on questions about which people are highly opinionated in daily life would seem to reflect the presence of cross-pressures and of conflicts in value orientation.

There may be some situations where the individual cannot come to a decision that accommodates well to conflicting policy-value pressures. A question such as this one—stimulating as it does conflicts between what is needed and what is fair, conflicts between what the government should do and what the private citizen should do, and, especially, conflicts between the independence of the citizen and his or her interdependency—is a most difficult one to answer. People may simply conclude by saying "I don't know" not because they have no opinion, but because they have sets of opinions in which portions of one come into conflict with portions of the other and because they are forced to choose between competing commitments.

This series is a fine test of extent to which people respond to question wording because such wording was changed, once substantially and once in a minor way. The substance of the question remained much the same from 1956 to 1960, given the references to public assurance on the one hand, and to job on the other. People were asked, at bottom, whether the government should "see to it" that everyone who wants a job should get one. The results, as presented in the left-hand panel of figure 5 were quite consistent: about 57 percent of the respondents approved of this orientation. There were, however, high levels of "not sure; it depends," and "don't know; no opinion" responses relative to those of the other questions used in this study.

In 1964, the wording (and I think the essential sense) of the question was changed in two ways. First, the government job assurance portion was modified to government assurance of a job *and* "a good standard of living." That addition permits many interesting interpretations. No longer was the respondent simply agreeing/disagreeing with the initial, single orientation. Another option was also presented: that the government "should let each person get ahead on his own." In essence, the choice was between government taking charge of everyone's having a job and a good standard of living private mobility. This was a tough choice and one likely to be titled in favor of personalistic, private values, and it was. In 1964, 43 percent of the respondents believed that the government "should let each person get ahead on his own." The number rose slightly to 47 percent in 1968, the heyday of governmental help (vs self-help) programs. Between 1972 and 1978 the numbers dropped somewhat into the high-30 percent and low-40 percent ranges. The interpretation of this change is uncertain because the coding underwent a slight change. Essentially, though, the addition of "and a good standard of living" to the question appears to have changed the response pattern of the U.S. public from a positive orientation toward governmental responsibility to one of uncertainty and negativism.

In the rough coding of value conflicts and questions, I linked concerns of struggle vs entitlement to the questions on rights (civil, women's, and criminals). That dimension, however, affects other realms as well. For example, here, struggle (using a job and, if necessary, governmental help to get a job) conflicts with entitlements ("and a good standard of living"). Too much entitlement is not good. Thus, each person "should get ahead on his own."

In this question the elderly respondents do not differ much from younger citizens. Over the twenty-year period of this question, their proportions are similar to other age groups. They changed their response as the question changes, just as the others did. They also show just as much uncertainty. This uncertainty increased somewhat as the question itself forced choices between and among competing commitments. By 1978, 46 percent (28 percent plus 18 percent) of the elderly respondents, 38 percent of the middle-aged respondents, and 39 percent of the under-thirty respondents were in the "not sure; it depends" and "don't know; no opinion" categories. On this question, then, the middle-aged and the youngest respondents were very much alike, with a slight tendency in the later years (especially in 1976 and 1978) for the elderly respondent to be more unsure of how to respond to the question.

This question also reveals a substantial difference between what people think and what is actually happening. The period of 1964 through 1978 was one of high governmental activity in the social-policy area. If there was any time in U.S. history when the federal government was trying to "see to it that every person has a job and a good standard of living," it was then. Yet, less than a third of the people supported this approach. A substantial number took the opposite view: "let each person get ahead on his own." It reflects what Michael Schiltz (1970) said: "In the practical order, this means that a proposal attracting support of a relatively small proportion of the electorate—perhaps 25 percent—during the discussion stage, may well enjoy a majority or even massive public support after enactment, not because it is everyone's preference, but because it is acceptable to most people" (p. 183).

Thus, is this the difference between policy opinion and policy action? Part of the answer lies in the uncertainty of many Americans (as expressed in the "don't know; no opinion" response). Part of the answer, too, may come from the idea that we all carry sets of dual and conflicting commitments. While we may support one side or another at a particular moment, residual support remains for the opposed course of action.

Figure 5
PUBLIC ATTITUDES TOWARDS GOVERNMENT ACTION TO INSURE EVERYONE A JOB (AND A GOOD STANDARD OF LIVING), 1956-1978

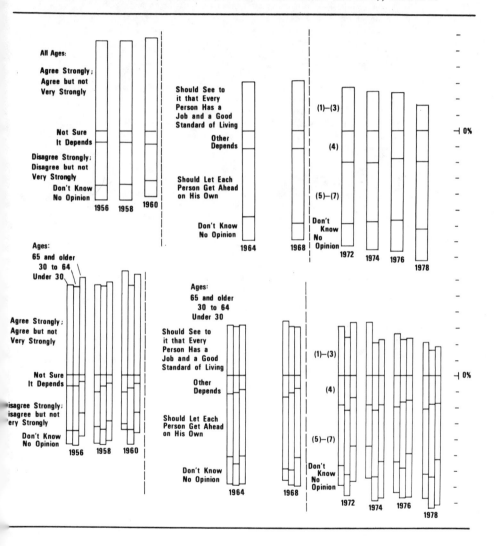

*See next page for text of Questions

Figure 5
(CONTINUED)

Year(s)	Question
56	The government in Washington ought to see to it that everybody who wants to work can find a job. (1= agree strongly; 2= agree but not very strongly; 3= not sure, it depends; 4= disagree but not very strongly; 5= disagree strongly)
58	The government in Washington ought to see to it that everybody who wants to work can find a job. Now would you have an opinion on this or not? (if yes) Do you think the government should do this? (same as above, except that 7= no opinion)
60	Around election time people talk about different things that our government in Washington is doing or should be doing. Now I would like to talk to you about some of the things that our government might do. Of course, different things are important to different people, so we don't expect everyone to have an opinion about all of these. ...The government in Washington ought to see to it that everybody who wants to work can find a job. (codes are same as above)
60	Over the years most Democrats have said that the government in Washington ought to see to it that everybody who wants to work can find a job. Many Republicans do not agree that the government should do this. How about you: would you agree with these Democrats that the government ought to see to it that everybody who wants work can find a job? Would you say you agree(disagree) strongly or not very strongly? (same codes as above)
64,68	"In general, some people feel that the government in Washington should see to it that every person has a job and a good standard of living. Others think the government should just let each person get ahead on his own." Have you been interested in this enough to favor one side over the other? (if yes) Do you think that the government: 1= (yes) should see to it that every person has a job and and a good standard of living 3= (yes) other, depends, both boxes checked 5= (yes) should let each person get ahead on his own
72	Some people feel that the government in Washington should see to it that every person has a job and a good standard of living. Others think the government should just let each person get ahead on his own. And, of course, other people have opinions somewhere in between. Suppose people who believe that the government should see to it that every person has a job and a good standard of living are at one end of the scale--at point number 1. And suppose that the people who believe that the government should let each person get ahead on his own are at the other end-- at point number 7.Where would you place yourself on this scale, or haven't you thought much about this?
74,76,78	Some people feel that the government in Washington should see to it that every person has a job and a good standard of living. Suppose that these people are at one end of this scale -- at point number 1. Others think the government should just let each person get ahead on his own. Suppose that these people are at the other end-- at point number 7. And of course, some other people have their opinions somewhere in between. Where would you place yourself on this scale, or haven't you thought much about this?

THE FEELING THERMOMETERS

Beginning in 1964, the Survey Research Center at the University of Michigan asked a question known as a "feeling thermometer." Groups were presented (Democrats, Republicans, liberals, conservatives), and the respondents were asked to indicate how "warmly" or "coldly" they felt toward each one. They were not asked at this point if they were a member of any of the groups nor how they felt in any other way. The warm/cold distinction elicits ambiguous responses. Generally, though, a positive/negative orientation can be assumed. Data are presented in figure 6.

The dots represent mean degrees of "warmth" that the respondents have felt over the years with respect to the groups in question. Citizens seem to feel most warmly toward the Democrats, though less so as the years go by. Their warm feeling was highest in 1964 and has been dropping ever since. In 1978 it resided just above 60 degrees. The Republicans have hovered around 60 degrees. In 1978 they had a place just below the 60-degree line, close to but lower than the Democrats' rating.

In terms of age differences, one can see divergence. With respect to Democrats, all ages clustered warmly (around 70 degrees) in 1964, with an increasing diversification of response by 1978 and a cooling of the orientations of younger respondents. Older adults always felt most warmly toward Democrats (with a slight exception in 1964, when middle-aged adults felt most warmly). In regard to Republicans, older respondents also always felt most warmly and younger respondents always least. The nature of these responses seems to indicate closeness to established institutions in general.

Looking at coolness and warmth toward conservatives and liberals expands our perspective on this complex picture. The respondents under thirty always feel most warmly toward liberals and least warmly toward conservatives. Warmth toward liberals and conservatives increased after 1970. (The liberal and conservative thermometers were not asked in 1978.) So, while the increasing conservative trend is spotted here, so, too, is increasing warmth toward liberals, although the rise in warmth is not as great.

Overall, younger people are warmer toward liberals and cooler toward established forms. Older respondents are warmer toward conservatives and established forms.

These links also have other associations. In particular, one can see tensions between interdependence (as represented by Democrats and liberals) and independence (Republicans and conservatives) represented in these findings. There are also tensions between public orientation (Democratic/liberal) and a more private one (Republican/conservative). But, again, one should take care not to assign all these "values" to a single person. Each of us is a "little liberal" and a "little conservative," and these preferences are at times at odds with each other.

Figure 6
FEELING THERMOMETERS, 1964-1978

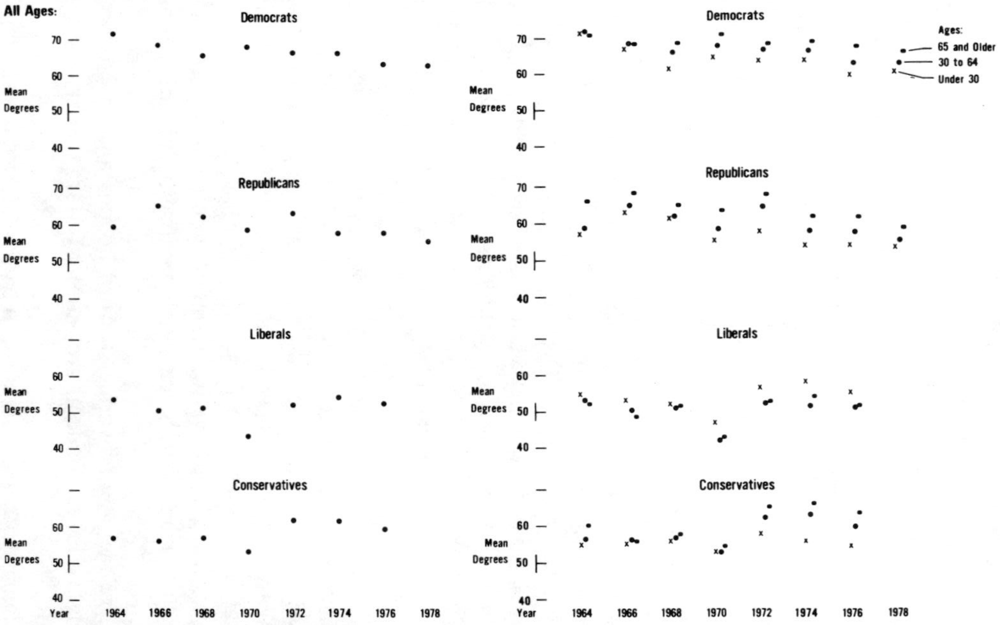

DESCRIPTION:

Respondents were asked how warmly or coldly they felt towards a particular group (very warmly = 97, 98, or 100 degrees; neutral = 50 degrees; very coldly = 0 degrees). Note - From 1964 through 1968, those respondents who replied "don't know," were coded by SRC as 50 degrees. Also, due to limitations of computer software, all responses of zero degrees were recoded as one degree.

YEAR(S)

64, 66, 68, 70, 72, 74, 76, 78

This series of questions, because it asked for orientations rather than either/or, mutually exclusive responses, tends to be among the most illustrative of the competing-orientations perspective. Differences and commonalities of values exist within us all. It is in the shape and pattern of these differences and similarities, existing simultaneously side by side, that a fuller understanding of policy opinion exists.

HEALTH CARE

Most of the questions discussed so far have suggested a particular change in American values, one generally directed toward greater privatism. However, since none was explicitly connected to a policy, policy implications of the values shift could not be clearly drawn. The question on health care (and the next on governmental involvement in electric power) touches directly on governmental action.

Few issues of domestic policy have been more tenacious or controversial than that of governmental medical care. As conflicting views on this subject have continued to be deeply entrenched for many years, the issue must have close links to deep undercurrents within the U.S. value system. As might be expected with such an issue, figure 7 reveals a high proportion of "not sure"/"don't know" responses.

The wording of this question, too, shifted somewhat from year to year. The most significant shift, and accompanying shifts in proportions of favorable responses, occurred in the period after 1970.

The overall proportions suggest that support for governmental action in the health care area stood at about 54 percent in 1956, rose to a high of 61 percent in 1962, and has been dropping in recent years. It stood at a low of 35 percent in 1976 and rose to 37 percent in 1978. "Not sure/don't know" responses have been rising, standing at a combined total of 28 percent in 1978.

The public is responding to something; exactly what is not clear. The proportions that support health care in the early years are substantial, but not overwhelming. Nothing like a clear-cut mandate emerges from the overall proportions. Furthermore, the age-group data in figure 7 do not tell us much in this regard. In the earlier years, elderly people were decidedly in favor of governmental action. The highest level of support, 74 percent, was reached in 1960. This support has subsequently declined. In 1976 it stood at 35 percent in favor, rising to 45 percent in 1978.

It could be argued that the elderly group is either cynically or protectively voting the politics of self-interest. Those over sixty-five now have governmental medical care. Supporting it for others could mean a possible loss to themselves. Medicare was passed in 1965. The earliest point after 1965 for which we have data on this question is 1968. At that time support was still high, 60 percent. The elderly did not change with their victory.

Figure 7
PUBLIC SUPPORT FOR GOVERNMENT INVOLVEMENT
IN HEALTH CARE, 1956-1978

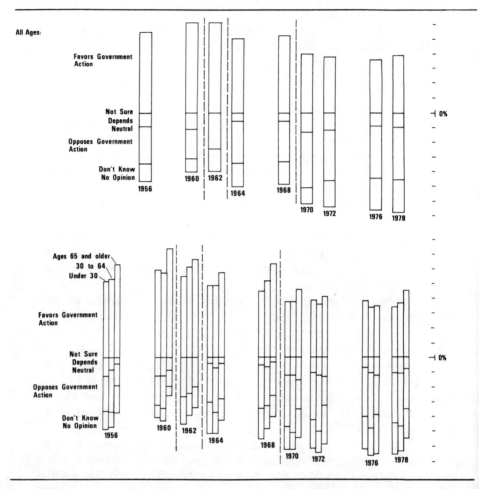

Year(s)   Question

56,60   The government ought to help people get doctors and hospital care at
        low cost. ()= agree strongly; 2= agree but not very strongly;
        3= not sure, it depends; 4= disagree but not very strongly; 5=
        disagree strongly)

62   Now on a different problem. The government ought to help people
        get doctors and hospital care at low cost, Do you have an opinion
        on·this or not?   ()= yes, 5= no) if yes:
        Do you agree that the government should do this or do you think
        the government should not do this? (1= yes; 2= yes, qualified;
        3= yes, for the aged or 'Medicare'; 4= no, qualified; 5= no,
        except for the aged or 'Medicare'; 7= yes, for those who need
        it, for those financially unable)

64,68   Some say the government in Washington ought to help people get
        doctors and hospital care at low cost, others say the government
        should not get into this. Have you been interested in this enough
        to favor one side over the other? (if yes) What is your position?
        Should the government in Washington:
            1= (yes) help people get doctors and hospital care at low cost
            3= (yes) other, depends, both boxes checked·
            5= (yes) stay out of this

70,72,76, There is much concern about the rise in medical and hospital costs.
78   Some feel there should be a government health (health omitted in
         1972) insurance plan which would cover all medical and hospital
         expenses. Others feel that medical expenses should be paid by
         individuals and through private insurance like Blue Cross.
         (show card to R) Where would you place yourself on this scale,
         or haven't you thought much about this? (1= Government health
         insurance plan; 4= midpoint; 7= private insurance plan
         (individual should pay))

Neither did others change who, based upon this line of thinking, should have changed. A good hypothesis cuts both ways. The self-interest hypothesis, therefore, should produce higher levels of approval among those who did not have this benefit. It did not. Even in the 1970 period, the elderly remained "high," relatively speaking, although it is true that their approval rate has dropped more than others.

Still, it is also true that the elderly respondents were most supportive of governmental action, though at differing levels, in eight of the nine questions asked during the period. Thus, while the support of both the elderly respondents and other respondents is shrinking, that of the elderly respondents remain at the top of the pile.

It may be that the change in question wording is as reflective of societal change in concern and focus as the change in answers. In 1970, for the first time, the question *began* with this statement: "There is much concern about the rise in medical and hospital costs." Introducing the notion of cost raised a sensitive issue and brought to the fore one particular aspect of the health care problem. It also raised, implicitly, the specter of governmental control of costs, thus changing the question appreciably. One cannot now be sure whether the change in the pattern of responses was due to changes in opinion or wording. The answer is most likely both. A decline in support of governmental involvement in medical care is consistent with the pattern of decreasing support for public functions seen in previous tables and to be seen in the next two. Some of the drop is doubtless due to this embracing cultural shift, one that affects all age groups. Some of the shift must also be due to changes in question wording, a change that highlights the possibility of governmental control of costs rather than that of its helping people with their health needs. Some aspects of the cost picture, moreover, have recently raised the issue of the extent to which people contribute to their own ill health and, therefore, to the costs of health care through smoking, excess weight, and so on, another aspect not reflected here (Brown, 1978).

Once more it is necessary to emphasize the politics of polls; i.e., some element of self-fulfilling prophecy is likely to be involved in presentation of results, whatever their cause initially. Most reporters and policymakers are not likely to be as sensitive to question wording as we have been in these discussions—and the wordings are certainly open to still further analyses. Moreover, public policy analysts are not likely to have the historical perspective made available in this presentation of the data. Thus, the conclusion that support for medical care is falling is a conclusion likely to be bandied about without careful reflection. To the extent that a bandwagon effect develops, the conclusion may gain additional adherents among politicians, policymakers, and journalists, who, in turn, affect the views of opinion leaders who have direct contact with the public and affect subsequent registrations of public opinion. Thus, the conclusion turns out to be correct, even though public opinion has in part been shaped by the inaccuracies of the earliest readings. This central fact gives the data a political character above and beyond its "scientific" reality. Even if wording made an important difference, as I think it did, there is no way of preventing a snowballing effect as people begin to hear what others think is happening.

Overall, though, we see the results, even considering the issue of cost, as another manifestation of the shrinking of public values (in the sense of support for public functions) and a resurgence of private values (in the sense of support for people doing it themselves). Public cost may be one important feature of this trend and may continually act as a prod for it.

The medical area has another interesting element: the wish that people would assume responsibility for keeping themselves healthy. Government cannot make people do that. It can only pick up the pieces (and the tab) later, after ill health has occurred. It can move, as well, to prevent some unhealthy situations through control of drug abuse and environmental regulation. These actions, however, do not come under the rubric of health insurance in the common usage. The meaning of *health* that focuses on control of one's own body, on modifying behavior such that health is enhanced through health foods, jogging, or whatever, seems to be gaining ground. To a degree the trend is reflected in these data.[6]

POWER AND HOUSING

Two public issues of national import and scope are electric power and housing. How these two important goods are to be handled within society is a matter of constant concern to policymakers. To ordinary citizens, however, these issues may seem remote from everyday affairs (Converse, 1964). A question is available on whether the public thinks that "things like electric power and housing" should be left to private business. An "agree" response is a vote for the private sector's responsibility. A "disagree" response is support for the public sector. A "don't know" is, as always, a refuge for many who are uncertain or have no opinion. Unfortunately, the data on this question go only to 1964. Some trends can be discerned, however. These are displayed in figure 8.

In the eight years between 1956 and 1964, support for the public sector, having begun at 23 percent, dropped to 19 percent. Support for the private sector was higher, rising from 42 percent to 48 percent, then dropping back to 39 percent. We mention both proportions because they are not simply mirrors of each other. In this case, as in some others, the categories of "don't know" and "it depends" also stand out. The "not sure; it depends" group remains about the same throughout. The difference comes in the "don't know; no opinion" categories, whose combined percentage drops from 29 percent to 23 percent, then rises to 37 percent in 1964. The jump in "don't know; no opinion" after 1956 is largely due to the pressures

Figure 8
OPINION ON GOVERNMENT INVOLVEMENT IN ELECTRIC
POWER AND HOUSING, 1956-1964

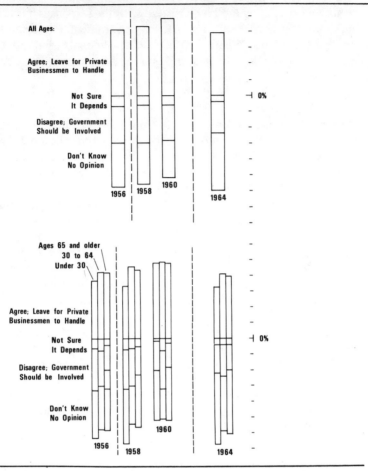

Year(s)   Question

56   The government should leave things like electric power and
           housing for private businessmen to handle. (1= agree strongly;
           2= agree but not very strongly; 3= not sure, it depends;
           4= disagree but not very strongly; 5= disagree strongly)

58,60   The government should leave things like electric power and
           housing for private businessmen to handle. Do you have an
           opinion on this or not? (if yes) Do you think the government should
           leave things like this to private business? (same codes as
           above, except for 9= no opinion)

64   Some people think it's all right for the government to own some
           power plants while others think the production of electricity
           should be left to private business. Have you been interested
           enough in this to favor one side over the other? (if yes)
           Which position is more like yours, having the:
                 1= (yes) government own power plants
                 3= (yes) other, depends, both boxes checked
                 5= (yes) leaving this to private business

of an added question that asked respondents whether they *had* an opinion or not. Most striking (and inconsistent with the responses in the health care question) is the lack of support for governmental intervention among elderly respondents. Where did the older respondents wind up? They placed themselves in the "don't know; no opinion" categories, larger for their age group in all four sampling years.

Several observations might be made here. First, to be sure, the support for privatism needs to be noted, but so, too, does the issue of "salience." Medical care is highly salient to the older (65 +) adult and may appear less so to younger (under 30) persons. Electric power may be a bit removed from the day-to-day concerns of respondents (that is, the question of production of power). Housing, however, is certainly close to "home," especially one would think for younger respondents. The older (65 +) respondent may, for good or ill, have taken care of her or his own housing situation. The younger (under 30) respondent may be seeking help in starting out and, hence, may favor governmental action, at least in this area. But, whatever one might say about age *differences,* the strongest message in these data is one of age *similarity.*

The mixture of responses is striking. No direction is overwhelming. While significant fractions favor action, significant fractions do not. Still other significant fractions respond with a "don't know" or a "no opinion." Without much stress one could find support for almost any orientation here. As in so many other areas, policy opinion is not clear cut and crystallized. Rather, it is highly ambiguous. This uncertainty is especially true if one looks at only a single administration of a question at one time. The results of a patterned process, captured as it were stroboscopically, become trendless because one does not know where things have been or where they might be going.

IS THE GOVERNMENT TOO POWERFUL?

The best way to sum up the entire series of indicators used here may be to focus on the significance in U.S. political history of controversy over governmental power that underlies much of our political system, from the Pilgrims right through present-day protesters. A rushing stream of privatism was diverted by the Depression and by World War II. The period of the 1930s made massive governmental action legitimate. World War II showed that such action could be effective and vital. It may be no coincidence that governmental leaders of the 1960s were veterans of World War II, were impressed by the awesome display of public power during that period, and were themselves beneficiaries of public services (such as those distributed by the Veterans Administration after the war). Now that they had a chance to run the show, wouldn't a "War on Poverty" be an appropriate campaign slogan?

The next query begins in 1964, where the questions on governmental activity in electric power and housing left off. Data are displayed in figure 9.

In 1964, 30 percent of the populace thought the government in Washington was getting too powerful "for the good of the country and the individual person." This proportion rose to 41 percent in 1968, dropped to 31 percent in 1970, rose to 49 percent in 1976, and dropped again to 43 percent in 1978. The "don't know" answers increased. The counterview, that "the government has not gotten too powerful," ran about one-third until 1972. In 1976 and 1978 it dropped to 20 percent and 14 percent, respectively.

Once again, the overall responses register a mix of support, with respondents split close to one-third each for too much governmental power, not too much power, and don't know/no opinion. Again, I want to mention how important the "don't know/no opinion" categories are. In an "Opinion Roundup" in *Public Opinion,* in the September-October 1978 issue (p. 34), this same question was reported. The data given there is reproduced here, with proportions from this analysis available for comparison:

PERCENTAGE WHO AGREE THAT GOVERNMENT IS TOO POWERFUL

	1964	1968	1972	1976	1978
Public Opinion, 1978	44%	55%	57%	69%	—
Tropman	30%	41%	41%	49%	42%

The *Public Opinion* figures were apparently arrived at by dropping the "don't know/no opinion" categories. While the procedure is an acceptable one, it certainly changes the conclusions analysts are likely to draw, making the country look more conservative and possibly less uncertain that it actually is.

The age-group distribution in figure 9 is interesting. The year 1968 was a transitional one for the policy opinions of elderly Americans. In 1964 and 1966, larger proportions of elderly than of the younger age groups thought the government in Washington was too powerful. In 1968, however, these proportions dropped below comparable ones for the younger age groups. They have remained below ever since. Several factors might have been operating to account for this cross-over.

The beginnings of political action on behalf of the elderly may have placed the government in a new light. Once viewed as a benevolent or paternalistic provider of social services, the government may now be coming to be seen by this group as the benevolent controller of important resources who, like the person guiding one's trust fund at the bank, will not agree to let one have what one wants in all instances.

Figure 9
IS THE GOVERNMENT IN WASHINGTON GETTING
TOO POWERFUL? 1964-1978

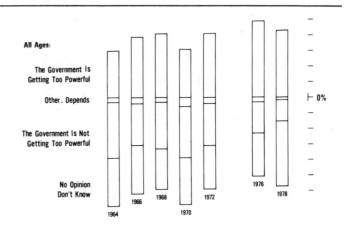

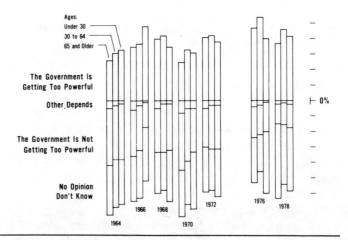

Year(s)	Question
64,66,68	Some people are afraid the government in Washington is getting too powerful for the good of the country and the individual person. Others feel that the government (add "in Washington" for 66,68) has not gotten too strong for the good of the country. Have you been interested enough in this to favor one side over the other? (if yes) What is your feeling, do you think: 1= (yes) the government is getting too powerful 3= (yes) other, depends; both boxes checked 5= (yes) the government has not gotten too strong
70,72,76,78	Some people are afraid the government in Washington is getting too powerful for the good of the country and the individual person. Others feel that the government in Washington has not gotten (substitute "is not getting" for 72,76) too strong for the good of the country. (omit "for the good of the country" in 1972) Have you been interested enough in this to favor one side over the other? (substitute "Do you have an opinion on this" in 1976) (if yes) What is your feeling, do you think the government is getting too powerful or do you think the government has not gotten (substitute "is not getting" in 72,76) too strong? 1= the government is getting too powerful 5= the government has not gotten (substitute "is not getting" in 72,76) too strong 7= other, depends; both boxes checked

Perhaps the actual change was not a cross-over of the elderly, but the younger groups catching up with their elders. Over the period since 1964, the elderly have shown modest increases in the proportion of their numbers who think that the government is getting too powerful—from 33 percent to 42 percent. The greatest increases have come from the younger groups, groups that overtook and then surpassed the elderly in this dimension. The under-thirty group almost doubled at one point within the period, from 26 percent to 47 percent in 1976, before falling back to 37 percent in 1978. The middle-aged group shot from 31 percent to 46 percent. These are substantial shifts that make the 9 percent shift of the elderly population look quite modest. It is my view that the elderly remained consistent, if consistency is seen as slow movement with the general tide, and that younger age groups, not the elderly, were the heavy movers. Rather than seeing the politics of protection, in which the elderly, having achieved substantial benefits through governmental action in medical care, are now closing the door to others, I see the politics of disenchantment, with citizens of all ages becoming annoyed at the government's actions and hence withdrawing their approval. (Hirschman, 1982, calls this "disappointment.")

Partly, too, the overall trend, leaving aside for a moment the spikes within the younger age groups, may be reflective of an overall wish to limit public functions. This conclusion, however, must be viewed in the light of substantial support for the contrary though slightly diminishing position that the government has not gotten too strong. Over the years, from one-fourth to one-third have felt positively about governmental power. It would seem relatively easy for a respondent to affirm, in response to the question wording for most years, either that "the government is getting too powerful" or that "the government has not gotten too strong." This possibility raises still another: that some respondents, seeking to register a denial of one statement, chose the other instead, even though it is not a direct contrary and did not express what they meant.

In 1964, leaving aside responses that affirmed neither of the alternatives, the balance was pro-government. Greater proportions said that the government was not getting too strong. In 1966, which could be a year of transition overall, the balance shifted from pro-government to anti-government. The magnitude of the shift was not overwhelming; but then, and up to the present day, more people thought the government in Washington was getting too powerful than people who thought it had not gotten too strong. In this connection, one cannot ignore subsequent events, such as the Vietnam War and Watergate and the effect of the polls themselves. Indeed, even taking the measures exactly as they were presumably intended, one may wonder why the level of approval of governmental action dropped only 22 percent, from a position of around 36 percent in 1964 to one around 14 percent in 1978 in view of the many problems that have become exacerbated since the mid-1960s.

CONCLUSIONS

Several conclusions emerge from this review of the trends over recent years. Although they are necessarily provisional, it seems useful to lay them out for consideration.

Limitation of Public Function

There seems to be an unquestionable trend in favor of limiting public functions. Trust in government is down, as is the sense of government being run for the benefit of all. It is seen, rather, as serving a few big interests. There is an increased sense of alienation from the public weal. And there appears to be an increased sense of powerlessness among the electorate. Older respondents are among the least trusting, the most suspicious, and the most alienated. Substantial proportions of the electorate feel that the government in Washington is getting too powerful. It is unclear, however, how many of these believe it has already gotten too strong.

While the elderly share fully in this trend, there is an important—and very likely substantial—counterorientation in which they also share. I shall comment on this point shortly.

Public vs Private Orientation

This crisis of confidence in the government could have several possible outcomes. One that can be expected (and one that is suggested by the figures in this chapter) is an eclipse of support for governmental action. In this I refer to the kind of New Deal–World War II orientation that the government can solve problems. In the two questions that deal with this issue, health care and governmental involvement in electric power and housing, it appears that there is a waning, not waxing, of support for governmental intervention. The most clear-cut case is in health care. Here, respondents, after a surge of support, show declining support. This drop may be due to an emphasis upon cost in the question itself. Such an emphasis was not present in previous questions. Even so, that addition, which is surely on the minds of respondents in any event, is a significant new wrinkle and need not invalidate the trend. It may simply suggest different components. This decline is evident across all sectors and can be related only tangentially to more specific questions of medical interest.

The power and housing questions, where public and private were counterposed directly, show a similar resurgence of emphasis on the private sector. This trend is consistent with the one manifest in health care.

Be aware, however, that it is not completely clear what "public" and "private" may mean to respondents to this question. The housing industry, for example, has existed with substantial public support, from the governmental permission to take income tax deductions on mortgage interest and real estate taxes to more specific (and sometimes exotic) tax incentives for investing in housing. New tax rules in 1987 will alter these benefits fundamentally. Whether the respondents, in affirming private orientations, were taking these types of benefits for granted (which does not seem an unreasonable assumption) cannot be specifically determined. Thus, a mixed system with a current tilt toward the private may be a more accurate rendering of the data.

Indeed, this interpretation is supported by the close balance of proportions of respondents preferring one alternative over another as we get to more specific policy questions. While there is always a mix of some sort, it seems to appear closer where more refined discriminations are possible. In exploring both the public and private areas, there are substantial proportions of respondents who do not choose to affirm either of the options when given alone. This may result from ignorance of policy issues, from ambivalence, or as a result of making discriminating responses to question wordings.

The responses of the elderly specifically are mixed. They show support for governmental involvement in health care (though sharing in the overall decline in support for governmental involvement) and yet are not so positive with respect to governmental involvement in electric power and housing.

Equity vs Adequacy

The best question for assessing orientations toward equity-vs-adequacy issues is the question on government providing jobs (and a good standard of living). Early versions of the question asked simply whether people felt that the government should assure a job for those who want one. These versions did not tap the adequacy issue to the extent the later one did, and the early responses were definitely affirmative—in the upper 50 percent range, with 10 percent "don't know" and another 7 percent "not sure".

With the addition of overt adequacy assessment language in later election studies (1964, 1968), and especially the most recent when the words "and a good standard of living" were added, affirmation slipped noticeably. About 31 percent of the respondents agreed with that proposition, and 22 to 26 percent were in one of the categories of uncertainty. In these years, over 40 percent of the respondents took the view that we should "let each person get ahead on his own." (It is not clear whether they believed each should be allowed to fall behind on his own, as well.) The answer to this question suggests a movement away from adequacy (a good standard of living) toward equity (let each get ahead on his own). Simultaneously, it also appears to be a movement that embraces privatism. The government was supported earlier when it provided the individual with the *means* to get ahead (i.e., a job and, hence, income) rather than income itself.

Elderly respondents joined with others in manifesting a decline in support for this governmental action. This was especially true given the more recent wordings. They did not flip to the other side, however. More of them seemed to wind up in the uncertain categories, possibly reflecting a conclusion from their life experiences, which suggested that clear-cut answers are never easy nor permanent.

Independence vs Interdependence

To the extent that interdependence is assessed through governmental efforts, the data suggest a rising support for independence during the analysis period. This seems to be true whether one is talking about people getting ahead on their own, of leaving electric power and housing to private interests, or of feeling warmly about conservatives. Interdependence makes demands. The question on governmental power may be reflecting a recognition of and a questioning of such demand. Certainly, both old and young alike share these tendencies.

Dualism

In chapters 2 and 3, a perspective on the U.S. value structure was set out that outlined dual, opposed value orientations within the electorate and within each person. We cannot here assess whether such orientations are present within the person except by implication. While it may be reasonable to assume that in a populace with such a balanced pattern of responses some of these juxtaposed orientations would be present, that conclusion would have to be tested by studying individuals.

What can be said from the data analyzed here is that U.S. feeling on these issues is not clear cut and that many issues are rather close in terms of the proportions of respondents expressing an opinion one way or the other. It is important to emphasize that the proportions are never overwhelming. These tend to waver from three-fourths to one-fourth to one-third to two-thirds. It would be difficult, therefore, to argue that policy was "caused" by the reflection of values discernible from public opinion responses. The proportions are too uncertain, even in the medical care case. Rather, the values so reflected might be said to anchor policy or give it roots and sustenance. They provide a base of support that is substantial (though not always representing a majority view) and permit policy to go forward. They further provide a base of opposition that tempers and trims the same forward effort. In this respect, the politician is a craftsman, fashioning pieces out of a multi-colored political fabric. While values may energize policy initiatives, politicians and policymakers crystallize it. It is precisely because the masses *are* discerning that attempts to combine and recombine pieces of policy package can be successful.

A dualistic approach sees answers emerging as a result of competing commitments, with some respondents weighing things in one way, some respondents weighing them in another way, and some unable to resolve their orientations one way or the other. A dualistic approach, then, helps to focus and interpret their responses. What is important about aging respondents is not that they may differ in policy opinion-policy value, but that they may combine orientations in somewhat different ways.

The Elderly

With respect to the analysis by age, I believe the overall similarity of the elderly and younger respondents is striking. If one thinks in terms of theme and variations, the central theme is one of similarity, commonness, oneness across the age span. The data, supported by factor and regression analyses, simply do not support the commonly held view that there are clear-cut generational splits and differences across age groups.

There are some important variations, but these should be seen as variations only. The elderly are somewhat more distant (i.e., they see themselves as distant) from the processes of influence though this, too, may be changing). The elderly appear to be slightly more suspicious and less trusting of government. These findings are consistent with the conclusion of Campbell and Strate (1981) that the elderly are not essentially more conservative.

SUMMARY

Overall, we see an eclipse of the movement toward support of public function and a strengthening of tendencies toward equity, privatism, and, by implication, self-reliance (rather than "other reliance" or governmental reliance). It may be that a period of our history, beginning in the Depression and strengthened by the success of World War II, is now coming to a close. Government lost both the war in Vietnam and the War on Poverty during the 1960 to 1970 period, completing the circle begun years ago. It may be time for something new—or something older than the Depression.

NOTES

1. Figures do not contain the proportions.
2. Respondents are, apparently, quite sensitive to the details of question wording. This is a point well worth remembering when thinking about the "fickle electorate" hypothesis or the idea that attitudes swing wildly. My experience in looking at public opinion questions suggests that, if anything, a "fickle scientist" hypothesis would be nearer the truth. Very few questions are repeated year after year; when they are, there is often a consistent pattern of response. When they are varied, response patterns also vary.

3. It is an important point in the politics of polls to recognize that the administration was doubtless aware of these results, as other elected officials have been at other times.

4. This discussion raises very concretely the whole attitude-behavior problem. For extensive and excellent discussions, see Schuman and Johnson, 1976; Dawes and Smith, 1985; and the "attitudes and actions" section of McGuire's "Attitudes and Attitude Change" (1985, pp. 251-253). It is possible that attitudes (values) support or reflect actions. In that case consistency would be the expected result. Alternatively, attitudes and values may counterbalance actions or, conversely, actions may counterbalance attitudes and values. In such a case, we would not expect consistency but, instead, patterned inconsistency. A competing-value perspective allows both these hypotheses to be simultaneously true, if only partially.

5. As it turns out, this question is closely related to the previous one in the factor analytic study reported in chapter 7. Thus there is additional reason for considering it, overall, as of the same character as the influence question.

6. It is important to consider that to some, then, the health issue may only be a manifestation of the more important variable of personal control. In this instance, people may be reasserting the wish for personal control over their own bodies, directly and indirectly. Other issues may arouse other manifestations of this kind.

5
RIGHTING CIVIL WRONGS

INTRODUCTION

U.S. society is built on the proposition of liberty and justice for all. Equality, fair play, and so on, have been our expressed national philosophy. Nevertheless, as Myrdal (1944; reprint, 1962) has observed, we have an "American dilemma": in spite of our having carved out numerous institutions to serve these ideals, blacks, women, the handicapped, and the elderly do not do as well as their counterparts. Slavery was a mark against American culture, but its demise did not end poor treatment of people of color. Rather, as slavery came to a close, a less extreme but similarly problematic social form, racial discrimination, began. It was made legitimate by the Supreme Court's separate-but-equal decision (*Plessy* v. *Ferguson*, 1890). It was not until the middle of this century, with the outlawing of restrictive covenants in property deeds (*Shelley* v. *Kraemer*, 1948), that some progress began to be made. Harry Truman desegregated the armed forces (at least in theory), and in 1954 *Brown* v. *Topeka Board of Education* continued the struggle to achieve full equality.

Then, in the 1960s, U.S. society experienced the full force of the civil rights movement, with those whose rights had been denied, abrogated, or curtailed coming forward. Along with their supporters, they used other options (class action suits, for example) legally granted by our political system to make their plight known and to demand redress.

U.S. society is riddled with "isms"—ageism, classism, racism, sexism—in which people are judged not by their capabilities but by some other, ascriptive feature of their person. Only through the constant vigilance by those who suffer discrimination and others who are committed to civil rights is progress made. Even then, advance is slow.

Juxtaposed with the strong value of entitlement in this country is the equally strong value of struggle. Struggle insists that, if one wants advancement, one must "fight" for it, earn it by one's own efforts. Some help may be acceptable, but help from governmental sources is legitimate only if it is matched with some effort by the ambitious. The popular phrase, "No pain, no gain," exemplifies this value orientation. It implies that the struggle element must always be present if one is to take meaning and fulfillment from the efforts of daily life. Under such a perspective, entitlements are devoid of meaning and purpose because they do not require—or have—the personal struggle and investment that make the achievements sources of personal satisfaction.

GOVERNMENT ACTION TO ENSURE FAIR TREATMENT

How far should government go to ensure fair treatment of those whose rights have previously been denied—blacks, for example? Generally consistent data on this point are displayed in figure 10.

I use the term *generally* advisedly because the wording of the question has changed substantially over the years.[1] In 1952, a very long question, containing several probes, centered on the issue of whether "the government ought to take an interest in whether Negroes have trouble getting jobs . . . or should government stay out of this problem?" While housing was added to jobs as an item in later years, it was not included in 1952. The responses ranged from statements that the national government should "handle this," that "it should be left for each state to handle in its own way," that the state governments should "do something" or "stay out of it also," and that there should be some type of legislation, to "don't know," and more.

In 1952, 68 percent of the respondents thought some level of government should take action on the problem of racial discrimination in jobs. This proportion—68 percent—is surprising because in 1952 the "Red Scare" of the 1950s might lead us to expect the populace to be suspicious of collective solutions to national problems. Apparently, equal access to employment opportunity was not strongly associated in peoples' minds with fear of communism. Only 20 percent of the respondents said that the government should stay out of the matter entirely. A small proportion (6 percent) responded "don't know."

In the 1956, 1958, and 1960 periods, the question was greatly changed and simplified, as were the response categories. Respondents were asked if

Figure 10
SHOULD GOVERNMENT SEE TO IT THAT BLACKS GET FAIR TREATMENT IN JOBS AND HOUSING? 1952-1972

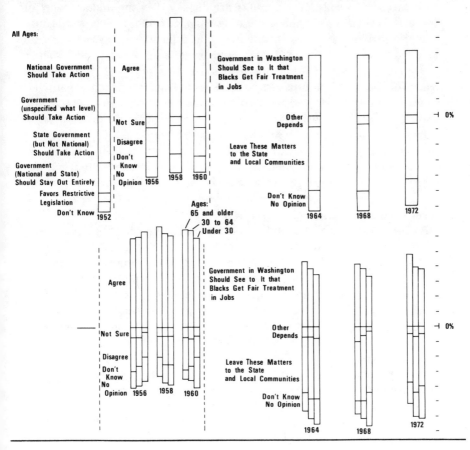

ar(s)   Question

(*47) There is a lot of talk these days about discrimination, that is,
people having trouble getting jobs because of their race. Do you
think the government ought to take an interest in whether Negroes
have trouble getting jobs or do you think the government should
stay out of this problem? (if the government should take an interest)
Do you think we need laws to deal with this problem or are there
other ways that will handle it better?(if 'other ways' to 22A)
What do you have in mind?(if laws to 22A) Do you think the national
government should handle this or do you think it should be left for
each state to handle in its own way? (if the government should stay
out) Do you think the state governments should do something about
this problem or should they stay out of it also? (00: national
government should pass laws and do other things too; 10: national
government should pass laws or NA national or state; 20: state
government should pass laws and do other things too; 30: state
government should pass laws; 40: government should do other things
only; 50: government should take an interest, NA how; 60 national
government should stay out but state government should take action;
70: government (national and state) should stay out entirely;
80: R favors restrictive legislation (include here clear anti-negro
statements)

56,60   If Negroes are not getting fair treatment in jobs and housing,
the government should see to it that they do. (1= agree strongly;
2= agree but not very strongly; 3= not sure; 4= disagree but not very
strongly; 5= disagree strongly)

58   If Negroes are not getting fair treatment in jobs and housing, the
government should see to it that they do. Do you have an opinion
on this or not? (if yes) Do you think the government should do this?
(same codes as above)

64,68,72 Some people feel that if Negroes (colored people) (omit "'colored
people)" in 1968) (substitute "black people" for Negroes in 1972)
are not getting fair treatment in jobs, the government in Washington
should see to it that they do. Others feel that this is not the
federal government's business. Have you had enough interest in
this question to favor one side over the other?
(if yes) How do you feel? Should the government in Washington:
1= (yes) see to it that Negroes (colored people) (omit "'colored
people)" in 1968) (substitute "black people" for Negroes in 1972)
get fair treatment in jobs.
3= yes; other, depends, both boxes checked.
5= (yes) leave these matters to the states and local communities.

the government should "see to it" that Negroes get "fair treatment" in jobs *and housing*. The "and housing" added a stimulus not present in 1952. People were asked to "agree" or "disagree," and there was a category of "not sure; it depends." The results are displayed in the middle panel of figure 10. (There was a minor wording change in 1958). The proportions who agreed with this statement favoring governmental action range around 60 percent—61 percent in 1956; 64 percent in 1958 and 1960. These proportions are similar to the pro-government proportion of 1952. In these years, too, about 18 percent disagreed. The "not sure; it depends" answers doubled, to around 12 percent. This may have been because of the addition of the phrase "and housing" to the question series. The conclusion must be drawn that, at a general level, there was substantial public support for governmental action in the direction of assuring fair treatment for blacks. It was, without question, that climate of opinion that surrounded the Supreme Court when it made the *Brown* v. *Topeka Board of Education* decision in 1954; and, in 1960, the U.S. public had not, as yet, much experience with governmental action in this area.

By 1964, however, the public did have some experience. The last panel of figure 10 demonstrates that the proportions supporting governmental action dropped sharply from the 60 percent range in the previous decade to around 40 percent. As has been the case so often, question wording confounds clear interpretation of this result. Housing was dropped from the series wording beginning in 1964, so we are back to "jobs." The negative response became "leave these matters to the state and local communities." It is unclear whether that "leaving" meant governmental action or not, and the issue was made to focus on the autonomy of state and local "communities" versus federal intervention. Given the wording of the state-ment, we must assume that respondents were free to interpret "leaving" as meaning "no governmental action." (There was no specific "government out" answer as there was in 1952.) If this assumption is correct, support for governmental programs dropped sharply in 1964. Negative views increased, and the proportion of noncommittal answers went up, though not sharply.

Was the experience of the 1960 period one factor in this drop of support? Certainly it had given respondents a point of reference about what might comprise a governmental action in this area.

The drop in support from previous highs should not obscure the fact that a truly substantial proportion of the respondents held firm in their beliefs throughout a period of great conflict and turmoil. In spite of the many problems and conflicts they saw, 40 percent of these citizens felt that national governmental action was still the way to go.

Figure 10 provides relatively clear data on the position of the various age groupings during this time of turmoil. In every measure, except 1956, the older respondents were no more negative than younger ones with respect to governmental action in the area of civil rights. (Data by age for 1952 were not available.) As governmental action and civil rights are two different topics, a confounding of response is surely possible. This is especially likely here because the oldest group has the highest "don't know' response, with one exception. (It tied with the youngest respondent group in 1958.) Elderly respondents did not exhibit negative responses much more than other age groups, so ambivalence is the most accurate way to characterize them.

On the whole, the over 65 adult looks very much like the under 65 respondents, with levels of support for governmental action close to, though somewhat lower than, others. The sharpest difference (about ten points) between the oldest and youngest respondent groups occurs in the last three administrations of the question (1969, 1968, 1972). The youngest groups appear more supportive of governmental action than the oldest. Given that the young respondent trusts the government more and is generally more accepting of liberal groups, this result should not be too surprising. The lessened trust of government by elderly (figure 1) may be manifest here as well.

THE SPEED OF CIVIL RIGHTS

Taking action is one thing; how fast is something else again. In 1964, a series of questions began on this very point: how fast did the respondent think the civil rights movement was going? The question remained the same over the twelve-year administration of the item. There are, therefore, few problems of comparability. Problems do appear, however, in trying to interpret the meaning of the response categories. The data are displayed in figure 11.

Between 1964 and 1976, the proportion of people who responded that the "civil rights people have been trying to push too fast" dropped from 63 percent to 39 percent. Correspondingly, the proportion of those who thought that the progress was "about the right speed" increased from 25 percent to 47 percent. The proportion of "don't knows" remained essentially stable.

Several considerations are necessary in the understanding of these findings. On the face of it, at least, the public's point of comparison is a factor. In the 1960s a large proportion of the public saw the pace as "too fast" or "somewhat too fast." From the perspective of this country's history since the Civil War, the speed of change must have seemed amazing—frightening, even—to the majority of Americans. One might think that for the majority any change is too fast in the area of civil rights, but minorities might not think so. (The average beta weight between race [0 = white and other minorities; 1 = black] and progress [1 = too fast; 5 = too slow] was .39 [table 4], a very high relationship for the data here.) And, of course, the focus of the question seems to center on the progress of civil rights with respect to blacks as that was the group most identified with

Figure 11
PUBLIC ATTITUDES TOWARDS THE SPEED OF THE
CIVIL RIGHTS MOVEMENT, 1964-1976

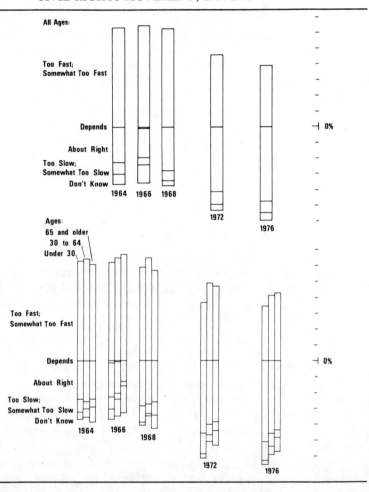

Year(s)   Question

64,66,68, Some say that the civil rights people have been trying to push
72,76   too fast. Others feel they haven't pushed fast enough. How
           about you: Do you think that civil rights leaders are trying to
           push too fast, are going too slowly, or are they (omit "they"
           in 1972,76) moving about the right speed? (1= too fast; 3= about
           right; 5= too slowly)

the movement we call "civil rights." The civil rights of other minorities, however—handicapped, women, gays, and so on—might well have been called to mind in the response to this question.

In any event, as the years progressed toward 1976, the proportion who thought that things were moving too fast declined. Perhaps the pace was slowing, and that was thought to be appropriate. Perhaps only the perception of what "too fast" was changed. After all, as just noted, the points of reference between respondents in 1964 and in 1976 in terms of what happened in society during that period were strikingly different.

In general, the public is not necessarily supportive of change. It is likely that some regard any change, even in a direction they approve, as "going too fast." Therefore, the decline in the proportion of people who think things are going too fast seems to reflect an overall satisfaction with the slower pace of change. Figure 12, below, supports such a conclusion.

The range of age-group differences is also displayed in figure 11. The elderly show no consistent pattern of response. Sometimes they are slightly *less* likely than their younger compeers to think that the pace of change is too fast (1964, 1968). At other times, they are slightly *more* likely to think this (1966, 1976). In 1972, the elderly scored lower than those aged thirty to sixty-five, but higher than those under thirty years. The proportion of "don't know" responses remains much the same across all age groups.

Age appears to function chiefly as a marginal modifier, not as a vigorous or consistent one. It may be significant, nonetheless, that the elderly consistently represent the smallest proportions of those who think that the progress is "about right." They may be expressing a twinge of dissatisfaction with civil rights relative to their own position. The proportion of the elderly who thought that progress was "about right" rose from 24 percent to 44 percent between 1964 and 1976. This was an increase of 83 percent. During this period the youngest group went from 24 percent to 51 percent, an increase of 112 percent. (The proportion of "too slow" responses among the elderly remained constant at 5 percent. The elderly do not appear to link themselves to the black civil rights movement. If the elderly thought they themselves might benefit from a civil rights revolution and if that perception was an element in their response, then the faster the pace the better it would be for them.)

HAVE BLACKS MADE PROGRESS?

Much opinion concerning whether civil rights people are pushing things too fast may be linked to the sense that progress is actually being made. For this reason, looking at a question on black progress may be helpful. The data are displayed in figure 12.

Although this question, too, changed slightly between 1972 and 1976, the effect does not seem to have been particularly great. Or, to play devil's

Figure 12
PUBLIC ATTITUDES TOWARDS CHANGE IN THE
POSITION OF NEGROES (BLACKS), 1964-1976

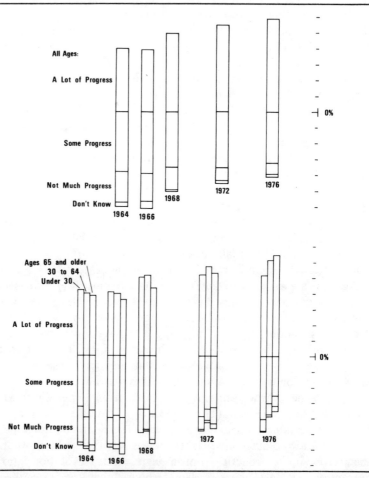

Year(s)   Question

64,66,68,   In the past few years we have heard a lot about civil rights
72   groups working to improve the position of the Negro (colored
            people)("black" was substituted for Negro in 1972). How much
            real change do you think there has been in the position of the
            Negro (colored people)("black" was substituted for Negro in 1972)
            in the past few years: a lot, some, or not much at all?

76   In the past few years we have heard a lot about improving
            the position of black people in this country. How much real change
            do you think there has been in the position of black people in the
            past few years: a lot, some, or not much at all?

advocate with ourselves, perhaps it is the change that is keeping the numbers similar; i.e., had there not been substantial change, the numbers would have looked quite different. In this interpretation, what appears to be stability is actually movement, given what the figures might have looked like had there been social sameness. (It is for this reason that "control groups" are used in experimental design; i.e., groups that receive no treatment. In any experiment there is always the nagging question of what the results would have been if nothing happened. Consider the comparison of laundry detergents. One should always wash one load of clothes in plain water only. This procedure allows one to compare not only the values of different detergents, but the value of all of them against nothing.)

Overall, the population felt that blacks had made progress. In 1964, 41 percent of the respondents thought the blacks had made a lot of progress. That response increased to 59 percent in 1976. The "not much progress" group declined from 19 percent in 1964 to 7 percent in 1976. In all administrations of the question, the phrase, "real change," was used. The respondent was to have the idea of actual progress in mind, not just paper progress. This pattern of response seems to suggest satisfaction with the pace of change for the public as a whole, measured in terms of "real change" in the civil rights realm. This point is suggested in figure 11, as well.

The age-group picture is not clear. Before 1972, the elderly showed the lowest proportion of the three groups who thought a lot of progress had been made. In 1972, that proportion was almost equal to that of the under-thirty group. Then, in 1976, their proportion became the highest, spiking at 64 percent.

One way of interpreting this shift is to assume that the elderly were using their entire life course as a frame of reference in answering this question. From that point of view, people over sixty-five would have had the entire span of this century as a referent for the purposes of comparison. Some even would have been born before the *Plessy* v. *Ferguson* decision.

From that long historical perspective, things may have looked much different in the 1970s relative to the 1960s and earlier. We will need to await further information from later years to see if this tendency among older respondents holds. The turmoil of the 1960 period may well have represented an unclear picture of progress to respondents who had seen the turmoil of two world wars, the Depression, and wars in Korea and Vietnam. In that light, they may have withheld judgment on how real the apparent progress was. By 1976, the smoke had cleared somewhat. This group of elderly, born around or before the turn of the century, had seen much progress in both technological and social areas. Their childhoods were spent in the horse-and-buggy days. Their late adulthoods saw men walking on the moon. In many ways they had a more extensive base upon which to judge the reality of progress.

RIGHTS OF THE ACCUSED

The struggle/entitlement dimension includes important elements other than race. Among these, the rights of persons accused of a crime and the rights of women are further indicators of the entitlement picture. Information on public perceptions of these rights provides a more well-rounded picture of the extent of support for correction of civil wrongs.

The data here, unfortunately, cover only a short period. The question on protecting the rights of the accused began only in 1970. Thus, only an eight-year span of information is available so far.

The question presented sharply poses the issue at hand: should we do "everything possible" to protect the rights of the accused, or "is it more important to stop criminal activity even at the risk of reducing the rights of the accused?" The overall proportions are displayed in figure 13.

The results have an arresting configuration. Twenty-nine percent of respondents felt that the rights of the accused should be protected. A higher proportion, in the vicinity of 40 percent (except for 1974), felt that crime should be stopped, even at the expense of reducing those rights. In this matter at least, the elderly are less likely to be fence sitters; fewer of them were neutral than their younger compeers. The largest proportions of elderly respondents distributed themselves, instead, into the "stop crime" group and the "don't know; no opinion" group.

This question is one of those where the age breaks are most dramatic. Older respondents at four time periods are substantially less likely to "protect the rights of the accused"; and, as just noted, they locate themselves clearly in the "stop crime" group. This answer is all the more striking because of its repetition over the years and because the over 65 respondents are clearly focusing on the question at hand. One could not attribute this response to any "general tendency" to be "conservative." There is no such tendency. But the respondents are not without some turmoil in their answer. The proportions of opinions in the "don't know; no opinion" category tell us so.

It is important to emphasize the high proportion of "don't know; no opinion" responses. Whether these responses are another way of remaining neutral or whether they represent something else is hard to tell. It is not clear what someone means when they say "don't know" or "have no opinion." I am inclined to think that it represents a values refuge. It is to this refuge that people repair when they are pressed too hard to take a position on values over which they feel conflict or when the choice and its implications are very specific and clear. The elderly have the highest proportion of "don't know" and "no opinion" answers. I believe this response pattern indicates tension.

There may be many reasons why the elderly group, above others, appear to be ambivalent or hesitant on this specific issue. Doubtless, the fear of

Figure 13
PUBLIC ATTITUDES TOWARDS PROTECTING THE RIGHTS
OF THE ACCUSED, 1970-1978

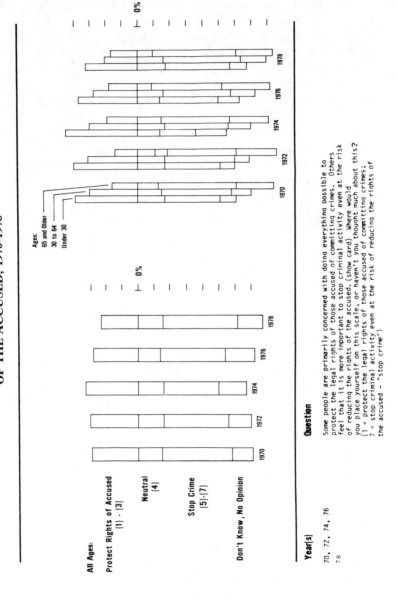

All Ages:

Protect Rights of Accused
(1) - (3)

Neutral
(4)

Stop Crime
(5)-(7)

Don't Know, No Opinion

Ages:
65 and Older
30 to 64
Under 30

Year(s)

70, 72, 74, 76

78

Question

Some people are primarily concerned with doing everything possible to protect the legal rights of those accused of committing crimes. Others feel that it is more important to stop criminal activity even at the risk of reducing the rights of the accused. (Show card) Where would you place yourself on this scale, or haven't you thought much about this? (1 = protect the legal rights of those accused of committing crimes; 7 = stop criminal activity even at the risk of reducing the rights of the accused - "stop crime")

crime is a factor. This issue has achieved a high visibility among the elderly as a problem likely to affect them. In earlier chapters, I suggested that the data reflected a sense of powerlessness to influence the world by this particular group. Here, too, power may be an issue. If one is concerned about crime, even if one has never been a victim, the issue may be the feeling of powerlessness, the anxiety that a person might become a victim, and that an accused lawbreaker might seek retribution even while that lawbreaker's rights were being protected.

Indeed, it may be the vision of violence rather than its reality that is the chief motivating force here. The elderly feel powerless in many ways when faced with crime. They have less physical strength than their assailants. They could not hope to flee from or to overpower those bent upon victimizing them. The elderly are vulnerable. Often they cannot relocate. They do not have the resources to secure protection from private police. The picture from the bleak house in which many of them view the situation is not one that contains many options.

Still, a substantial proportion of the elderly were noncommittal, due, perhaps, to the values tension just noted. While large numbers were willing to curtail rights to control crime, a large number had no opinion. It is the balance between "don't know; no opinion" and the "stop crime" responses that present the fullest, truest picture of the elderly's response.[2]

WOMEN'S RIGHTS

In recent years, the roles of women have undergone the most expansive transformation since the suffrage movement. With some exceptions, progress achieved in the context of that movement was slowed or eroded by conditions arising from the Depression and World War II. After a fallow period during the 1950s, the activism of the 1960s, among other things, began to have its effect on women's awareness of their rights. Groups for "raising consciousness" began to develop, and the movement for women's equality was mobilized on all fronts.

Beginning in 1972, a question was asked by the National Election Study on attitudes toward women's rights. Respondents were asked to indicate whether they thought women should have equal roles with men or whether "women's place is in the home."

Within the recent past, the overall proportions have been quite consistent. These are displayed in figure 14.

About 50 percent of the respondents felt that women should have an equal role. The proportion of persons who thought women should remain in the home was lower, dropping from 29 percent in 1972, to 21 percent in 1978. A substantial proportion of respondents, about 18 percent, were neutral.

These proportions illustrate, perhaps as well as any other set, the

Figure 14
PUBLIC ATTITUDES TOWARDS WOMEN'S RIGHTS, 1972-1978

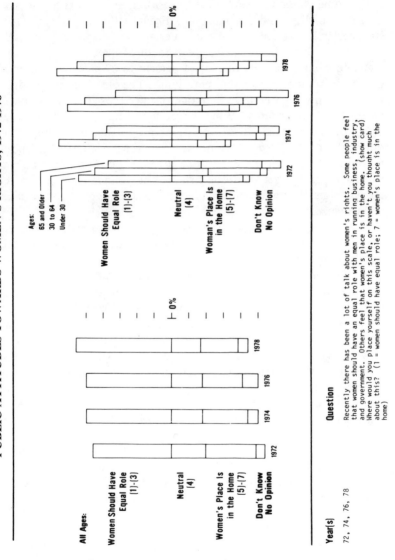

Year(s)

72, 74, 76, 78

Question

Recently there has been a lot of talk about women's rights. Some people feel that women should have an equal role with men in running business, industry and government. Others feel that women's place is in the home. (show card) Where would you place yourself on this scale, or haven't you thought much about this? (1 = women should have equal role; 7 = women's place is in the home) conflicting attitudes of the U.S. populace. In a land where "all men are created equal," and after more than a decade of vigorous effort to bring to the attention of the public the problems of women, only 50 percent of the population was willing to accord women an equal role with men.

We come closer to that "ideal," however, in looking at the age-group distribution displayed in figure 14. Because the age-group effect is so striking, it is essential to take a generational perspective here. Younger individuals, those under thirty, are in favor of the equality of roles among men and women on the order of 55 percent to 67 percent. The middle-age groups drop sharply from that percentage. The oldest age group drops even more so. Only slightly more than one-third of those over sixty-five support an equal role for women. What is seen here, though, as in the case of the rights of the accused, is an important proportion of "neutral" or "no opinion" or "don't know" responses. Between one-fourth and one-third of the respondents over sixty-five took a refuge position. That position was usually taken by less than one-fifth of the youngest age group. Clearly, there is a gender traditionalism among the elderly, one heavily mixed with ambivalence.

Lest we leap to a conclusion concerning the traditionalism of the elderly, a caveat is appropriate here that suggests an alternative interpretation. It may be that a question with gender roles reversed, in which respondents are asked whether men should have equality with women in home and family activities or whether their place was really "in the shop," would have elicited a similar response. The perspective of the years may have suggested to those respondents that a division of labor was appropriate. Many of them may have had rural backgrounds and may have grown up in a period in which home activities were respected and valued, perhaps more so than today. They simply might not want to discard the treasured habits, notions, and perspectives of a lifetime. The alternative form of the question might well indicate that the *status difference* between the two roles is as much a factor as the gender difference. It sometimes appears today that equality of roles is, as the original question implied, assumed to be equality of the workplace. That is not necessarily the case. In times past, certainly, it was not always the case.[3]

The distinction between gender-specific traditionalism and status difference may need some elaboration. Specialization and differentiation of tasks may not always lead to differences in prestige and rewards to those specialized units. An oboist is not more valuable than a bassoonist in an orchestra performance, for example. In the case of gender roles, a traditional division of labor has been established, which, for the older respondent, may have had a certain amount of mutual respect and meaning. And, certainly, when one thinks of the farm family, both male and female worked, and home and work were not separated.

CONCLUSION

The clearest conclusion to be drawn from this analysis may be that civil rights is, itself, a multi-faceted dimension, with responses varying in important ways depending on the sector and the level of specificity addressed by the question. Overall, there does seem to be both declining support for civil entitlements and less-than-enthusiastic support for them. Fewer people now than before think that government should assure that blacks get jobs. Respondents seem to think that the current pace of civil rights activity, with all its deficiencies, is "about right" (given that they were offered the option of saying it is going too slowly). Increasing proportions of people seem to think that blacks have made real progress. Citizens are divided on the issue of protecting the rights of the accused and of the equality of women's roles. While the picture is not dismal at all, it certainly is not overly enthusiastic to the provision of entitlements.

The elderly seemed to think much like everyone except for the issues of crime and women's equality. On those two specific issues, the elderly took a more conservative or traditional or hard-line position than those of the younger age groups. They were more willing to support "stop crime" activities and more likely to support more traditional roles for women. The potential vulnerabilities of the elderly group need to be taken into account. So, too, does that fact that a higher proportion of the elderly are women. A substantial number of them may have experienced equality of roles in a more traditional way, as, for example, in a farm family context. This may have provided a framework for their answers.

I suspect, based on the data, that the age of entitlements may have reached its current peak and may now be on the downswing. Among other pressures, cost looms large. Rights, whatever else they may involve, cost money. In a period of economic retrenchment people may begin to see a superfluity of rights. "Back to basics" may mean, in this context, back to a period when society did not have to pay fully for the fruits of all the labors it enjoyed.[4]

NOTES

1. The nature of this question spans three of our value realms: equity-adequacy, public-private, and struggle-entitlement. The "fair" treatment part suggests equity. The government part suggests public. The focus upon blacks suggests entitlement. As will be seen in a later chapter, the factor analytic approach links this question with some of those from the other dimensions. It was located here, however, because of the specific focus on blacks in the question wording.

2. Ignoring "don't know" answers can be the basis for major error. Assume we have one-hundred "no opinion" respondents, for example. They would be distributed as they are in figure 13. If we remove the "don't know" group from the

1976 wave, we have a new N of eighty-seven for the under-thirty group and seventy for the elderly group. Using those new Ns as the bases for computing percentages, then 41 percent of the younger group (vs the current 36 percent) and 62 percent of the elderly group (vs 44 percent) would be taking a "stop crime" stance. The difference between the current and recomputed figures is vast and would suggest that the elderly are far more negative toward criminals than they actually are.

3. A recent study by Gilbert (1983) begins to raise this perspective again. He has a section called, "An Alternative Perspective: In Support of domesticity" (pp. 108-114).

4. A thorough discussion of the whole notion of the "cost" of rights is beyond the scope of this study. Nevertheless, I do want to suggest some thoughts that have special relevance to the elderly. If one assumes that, in general, societal desires always and everywhere exceed the current societal resources, then all societies need to find ways to balance the social books. As this balance is not likely to be achieved through the lowering of expectations, there need to be ways to raise the resources. In a general sense, these resources are raised through free labor or contributions to society that are paid for at less-than-market rates. Historically, of course, slavery is a clear example of this mechanism. Other mechanisms have included the use of child and conscripted labor, the economic exploitation of women and blacks (whose wages currently run about 60 percent of the wages of white males in the United States). And, certainly, one must include the volunteer sector of activity, where people are persuaded (because "it is right to do so") to give of their time and energy for little or no monetary compensation. Current social trends are making whatever "surplus" may exist increasingly smaller, and a "deficit" looms ahead of us. The "Rights Revolutions" means that the exploitation of many groups is no longer the effective strategy it once was. While such exploitation still exists, its legitimacy has been undermined, and its occurrence has diminished. Equal pay for equal work is now the cry. Environmental forces have made exploitation of the environment far more difficult than previously, forcing us to pay the full cost (or more of the true cost) of goods made in this country. This is closing down the hidden subsidies inherent in products, the manufacture of which polluted the environment, the waste by-products of which were disposed of in less expensive but unsafe ways. Finally, the development of the welfare state, especially with the increase in benefits to the elderly, has reduced the need for volunteers (though in a climate of political conservatism, this trend may be arrested). The result of these changes is that our society currently needs more people to exploit, to give free service. The elderly would appear to be a prime target for any new wave of exploitation, both because they are the recipients of increased governmental attention and because they are less well equipped to defend themselves against exploitation. They are not yet well organized politically and are potentially subject to manipulation by guilt for receiving governmental benefits.

6
THE WAVERING OF
TRADITIONAL COMMITMENTS

INTRODUCTION

Work, family life, and religion are three of the United States' most traditional commitments. These are the values America celebrates as being at the foundation of its greatness. They are also values under stress.

I believe these values exist in juxtaposition with other values to which substantial commitment is also attached. While work-related values remained important during the period I examined in this study, leisure values gained significantly. During the third quarter of this century, productivity in the United States declined. At the same time there were many indicators of an increasing emphasis on leisure, e.g., higher sales of recreational vehicles, a rush to acquire vacation homes, and the growth of resorts and theme parks. Family orientation was also challenged, particularly in the 1960s and early 1970s, by narcissism and strong self-indulgence movements. Religion found itself in court almost as often as in church. Faced with a wide variety of cults and charismatic movements—some appearing to spring forth relatively spontaneously, others emerging from within existing religious bodies—organized religion began a period of self-examination and relevance testing that still continues.

There is not nearly so full a range of repeated measures available as one would like for assessing these areas. Such as I have found, however, can provide indicators of what is happening to various clusters within the culture. Reported church attendance will be used to assess religious orientation. Preference toward the hours of the work week will be used to assess work orientation. Attitudes toward the ideal number of children in the family will be used to assess famly orientation. Many other measures would, of course, be possible. Those that I have selected bear the important advantage of covering the entire period from 1952 on. Within such a time span, changes are a central feature of assessment.

As might be expected, these data show both support and lack of support for common wisdom. Slight shifts do occur, sometimes throughout the whole population, sometimes more prominently within one age group. Work and religion, at least as tested by these measures, do not seem in any imminent danger. Family orientation does seem to be undergoing some redefinition but may yet emerge, following Schumacher's dictum, as one of the institutions in which "small is beautiful."

FREQUENCY OF CHURCH ATTENDANCE

Good measures of religious attitudes are difficult to find. How, for example, does one distinguish between real commitment and surface compliance to religious forms? The measure I present here, frequency of church attendance, suffers because, as is immediately obvious, it tells us nothing about the extent of the personal religious commitment of the individual. It reports asserted behavior rather than attitude, and this represents a departure from other questions used in the study.

I do not believe these deficiencies to be fatal. There is, after all, no general agreement on what constitutes a true religious orientation. Regular participation in religious ritual may be, therefore, at least for the purposes of this study, a reasonable indicator of underlying attitudes toward religion within the general populace. To what extent, then, is it important to join in such public rituals? If, as Sennett (1978) feels, public man has "fallen," we would expect reported attendance at religious ceremony to decline. Figure 15 provides information of the extent to which this has occurred.

As to the behavioral aspect of this measure, note that it is *reported* church attendance being assessed here, not actual church attendance. Thus, it is less a measure of church attendance than a measure of the extent to which people feel it important to *indicate* church attendance (and, perhaps by extension, religious values). If people are on the side of overreporting, as I suspect, then that error reveals a sense that it is somehow better to over-report than to underreport. This is, itself, supportive of the value. Nevertheless, though it taps into the value, it in no way definitively describes religious orientation. None better is available, however.

Over the years since 1952, the National Election Study asked respondents to report their church attendance. Data for the general public are displayed

Figure 15
FREQUENCY OF CHURCH ATTENDANCE, 1952–1978

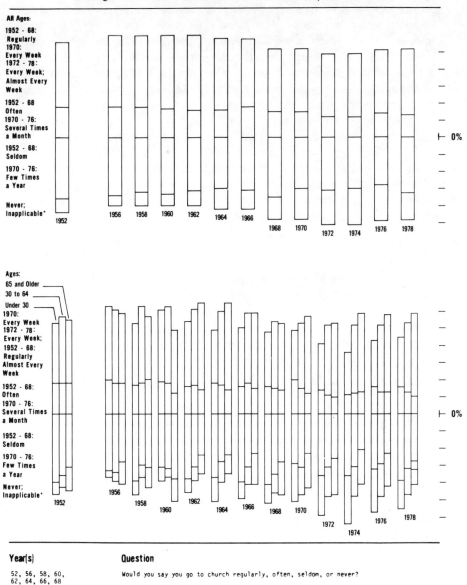

All Ages:

1952 - 68:
Regularly
1970:
Every Week
1972 - 78:
Every Week;
Almost Every
Week

1952 - 68
Often
1970 - 76:
Several Times
a Month

1952 - 68:
Seldom

1970 - 76:
Few Times
a Year

Never;
Inapplicable*

0%

Ages:
65 and Older
30 to 64
Under 30
1970:
Every Week
1972 - 78:
Every Week;
1952 - 68:
Regularly
Almost Every
Week

1952 - 68:
Often
1970 - 76:
Several Times
a Month

1952 - 68:
Seldom

1970 - 76:
Few Times
a Year

Never;
Inapplicable*

0%

Year(s)	Question
52, 56, 58, 60, 62, 64, 66, 68	Would you say you go to church regularly, often, seldom, or never?
70	Would you say you go to church-- every week, several times a month, a few times a year, or never?
72, 74, 76, 78	Would you say you go to (church/synagogue) every week, almost every week, several times a month, a few times a year, or never?

* includes agnostics, atheists, those who do not know
  their preference, those with no preference, and
  those giving uncodable responses

on the top panel of figure 15. There was some variation in the question-response categories. Between 1952 and 1968, "regularly" was the response category. In 1970 "every week" was used. Between 1972 and 1978, "every week/almost every week" were the categories. The degree to which these changes altered responses cannot be known. In 1952, 38 percent of the respondents said they attended regularly. In 1978, 39 percent reported attending every week or almost every week.

Change in proportions, thus, did not come from among those reporting regular attendance but, rather, from among those reporting "never/inapplicable." This category increased from 8 percent to 16 percent.

The elderly show a slight increase in reported church attendance. In 1952, 37 percent reported that they went to church regularly. In the most recent period, 48 percent so reported. The same is true for the other end of the scale, "never/inapplicable." In 1952, 14 percent reported this response. The fraction is the same for 1978.

The youngest group showed a slight drop in reported attendance. Since 1952, those under thirty reporting regular attendance declined from 35 percent to 29 percent. The trends are most sharply outlined if one looks at the differences between the oldest and the youngest respondents in 1952 and again in 1978. In 1952, the difference in reported regular church attendance was 2 percent (35 percent vs 37 percent). In 1978, that difference was 19 percent. Certainly, this difference is substantial; and it is caused by the two age groups moving in opposite directions—more elderly respondents and fewer youngest respondents reporting regular church attendance.

One's reaction to these results will depend, in part, on one's expectations. Those who would have expected a dramatic secularization of society, indicated by great drops in reported church attendance, are to be disappointed. Those who might have thought that older individuals would exhibit decline of church attendance must confront the opposite result. Younger people, to be sure, showed a drop, but at 6 percent, it is hardly a drop to be associated with the picture of "godless narcissism" so often associated with the young. With respect to religious values assessed by this question at least, traditional orientations appear to be alive and well, although there are some very modest shifts in the relative orientations of age groups.

REDUCING THE WORK WEEK

The United States has been characterized as a nation fueled by the Protestant ethic (Weber, 1958; Schrag, 1971). Work had had a near-religious importance in society and is frequently thought of as the universal nostrum for all ills. Women, unhappy at home, should work. The handicapped, without useful purpose, should work. Workfare is the answer to welfare, and so on. Work, today, most often means the concept of working for wages. Thus, the "work" the housewife does is not really thought of as work.

Again, many measures could be devised that would help assess Americans' attitudes toward work. Again, few were consistently available over the period under study. The Gallup Organization asked one question about the work week, which is available from 1953 through 1965. The question was, "Do you think the work week in most industries should or should not be reduced from forty hours to thirty-five hours?" Respondents could answer that it should or that it should not, or they could express no opinion.

It is not completely clear what a positive answer to this question might mean. It could reflect work dissatisfaction. It could represent a hope to retain salary while working less. It could reflect desire for the potential nine-hour day, four-day week plan, thus leaving a three-day weekend. It could, in fact, be indicative of any number of alternatives. Moreover, the question contained another important qualifier: "the work week in most industries." Thus, the respondents' overall assessment of what would be desirable is being sought, not his or her preference with respect to work hours. Some people may have expressed a preference anyway, even though it was not directly called for by the question. This orientation further complicates the interpretation of the question, in that a respondent might suppose, for example, that automation could take up at least five hours' worth of the work most people do. It seems reasonable to suppose, nevertheless, that those who answered "should" were expressing less commitment to work. The results are displayed in figure 16.

Overall, as measured by this question, there was a slight decline in work orientation during the period between 1953 and 1965. In 1953, 21 percent of the people thought that the work week should be reduced. The number increased to 28 percent in 1965. Large majorities on this question, from just under three-fourths in 1953 to just under two-thirds in 1965, felt that the work week should not be reduced. Uncharacteristic for a question of such specificity was the low proportion of those who had no opinion. The proportion ranged between 6 percent and 8 percent over the twelve-year period. While the change in support for work is not great in proportional terms, it is one that represents a substantial shift in the population and one that gives food for thought. Might it, for example, represent an increased commitment to leisure? While that question cannot be answered directly from these data, one would think that interest in leisure would be a part of what is involved in the decline of the commitment to the forty-hour work week.

The pattern by age groups shows some interesting shifts. Older respondents, consistent with a more traditional orientation, exhibit the lowest proportions of agreement with the question (the work week *should* be reduced). That is particularly true in the 1960s period. Younger respondents, on the other hand, do feel that the work week should be reduced. That may be what Yankelovich (1982) meant when he talked about redefining the giving/getting relationship. It may be that younger people (defined here as those below sixty-five) did not feel they were getting enough

Figure 16

**PUBLIC ATTITUDES TOWARDS THE ISSUE OF REDUCING
THE HOURS IN A WORK WEEK, 1953–1965**

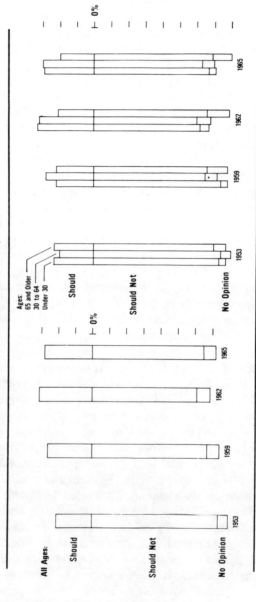

Year[s]

53, 59, 62, 65

Question

Do you think the work week in most industries should or should not be
reduced from 40 hours to 35 hours?

from work; i.e., that they were giving to work more than they were getting from it. As a result, they decided to reduce their commitments to work in favor of emphasis in some other area, very likely leisure.

Here, too, though, it should be noted that older adults have some ambivalence. Higher proportions of them report "no opinion" than other age groups, especially in 1959, 1962, and 1965. While traditional, they may be wavering relative to others.

THE IDEAL NUMBER OF CHILDREN

Family orientation is particularly hard to assess. U.S. society is complex and rife with multiple and conflicting values. Nowhere in recent years has there been more controversy and conflict than in the family area. What should the family be like? What are its legitimate demands on the individual's priorities? What weight should family responsibilities assume as opposed to individual ones throughout the life course? One widespread view is that older citizens are family oriented and expect their children, who are now in their middle years, to be "dutiful" to them. This is a view shared by the adult children themselves, perhaps even more than most parents expect. On the other hand, while the middle group is trying to be dutiful to *their* parents, they seem to feel that their children are not being dutiful to them.

In any event, the central issue here is children and the roles of children in family life. A question on the ideal number of children, therefore, is helpful in understanding shifts in family orientation among the public.

Children used to represent a valuable commodity, especially in rural areas. With urbanization, people have tended to prefer smaller families because costs rise dramatically relative to benefits. Children are simply more expensive in the city, and there is little they can contribute to the family's sustenance. Thus, we should expect to see a drop in the preferred family size over time. These data are displayed in the top half of figure 17, reflecting Gallup measures of the ideal family size, with only minor question-wording changes between 1941 and 1978.[1]

The data conform only partially to expectations. The distribution of preferred number of children was quite stable from 1941 to 1953. It rose somewhat in 1962 and 1967, then dropped again during the 1970s. The best way to consider these data may be to note that the proportion of people over this almost forty-year period who want three children has remained much the same: 30 percent in 1941, 24 percent in 1978. The proportion favoring large families (four or more) decreased, and the proportion favoring two children increased. Two-child preference increased from 27 percent in 1941 to 51 percent in 1978. Preference for four or more children decreased from 40 percent in 1941 to 23 percent in 1978. While 70 percent of the 1941 respondents felt that three or more was the ideal family size, 75 percent of

Figure 17
PUBLIC ATTITUDES ABOUT THE IDEAL NUMBER OF CHILDREN IN A FAMILY, 1941–1978

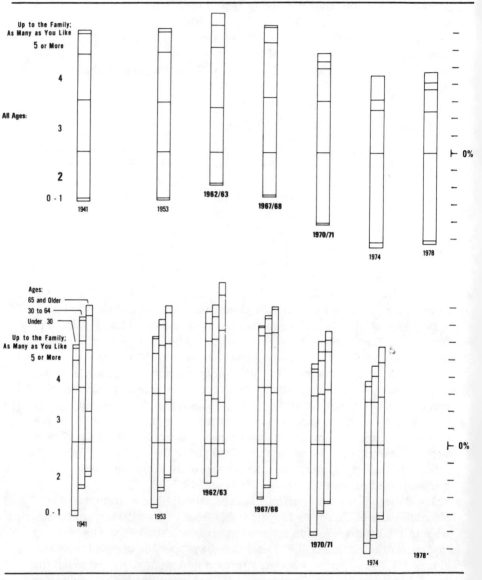

Year(s)	Question
41, 53	What do you consider is the ideal size of family – husband and wife and how many children?
62, 67, 70, 74, 78	What do you think is the ideal number of children for a family to have?

*data not available by age for 1978

those responding in 1978 felt that two or three was ideal. In the early period the median was three children. At the end of the period under study it was two children.

It is important to note, given all the current discussion about "modern" families who wish to have no children, that only a miniscule proportion has expressed this preference. And this group is so small that it is impossible to establish any trend in its size after taking sampling error into account. The proportion of people who express a view that zero-to-one child is ideal remain at 1 percent or 2 percent throughout the period. Preferred family size and actual family size are both shrinking; neither, however, is likely to go to zero.

Several things may have contributed to this decline. Consideration must certainly be given to the possibility that the change in the question wording, however mild, could be implicated. This seems unlikely because the question, whatever its exact wording, seemed to have the same meaning to respondents. Consideration should also be given to the fact that the 1960s was a period of rising prosperity. There were more dollars for children, and few cared about the "population explosion." Then, too, the interest in having more children may also express a tendency toward linking with others outside the self. This was clearly shown in the rising concern over the rights of others during that period.

What the social role of having children might mean is dramatically illustrated by the age-group breakdown, displayed in the lower panel of figure 17. Overall, the pattern of the elderly with respect to ideal family size follows the pattern of the society at large. It is high in the forties and fifties, rises slightly in the sixties, and then drops in the seventies. This parallel conceals, however, more than it reveals. In every period recorded here, the elderly age group has preferred more children than their younger counterparts.[2] In 1941, for example, 63 percent of those over sixty-five felt that four children or more was the ideal number. This contrasts with 27 percent of those under thirty. By 1974, 29 percent of the elderly saw four or more children as ideal, while only 12 percent of those under thirty shared that view. This figure represents an important relationship of the elderly to the rest of the population. While it is true that the elderly have followed the trend of the society as a whole, it is also true that they have had their own sharply different subpattern within that overall trend. Neither statement makes sense without the other.

To summarize the data, the overall trend is downward. The distribution of preferred number of children is anchored at two and three, and age-group differences are large. Preference for children is clearly patterned by age. Those under thirty want the fewest. These are followed by those of middle age who want more. Those over sixty-five want the most.

The linear nature of these findings immediately suggests one hypothesis that cannot be ignored: there are different feelings about taking responsibility for child care within the different age groups. Caring for children takes a lot of work. People in the childbearing years, primarily those under thirty, will bear the brunt of their work. Their perception of the actual work involved may temper to some degree any desire for larger families, especially if the corresponding benefits seem few. The memories of those hardworking days may fade a bit as age increases. To this group the pressures may seem less intense. These are the elderly who enjoy the grandchildren on an occasional Sunday, those who may have pushed thoughts of the actual work involved in the raising of these children into the dim recesses of their memories. Finally, both older groups may have actually had more children themselves, or may have wished to. (This point is not to disparage seniors who are raising children.)

This hypothesis may not be all of the picture, however. Indeed, there may be a certain poignancy to the desire of older people for the larger ideal family size that arises out of their need for companionship. One ambiguity in the question is relevant to this point. Typically, the question would seem to focus on one's own children as the central element. If one is an elderly respondent, however, *siblings* may become a significant point of reference. The elderly may, thus, be thinking that a larger family is better because of the potential companionship siblings can afford in older years. From another direction, the elderly may feel that at least one or two among a larger number of children could be friendly and caring toward their parents in later years.

The change in the family situation from extensive intergenerational contacts to sporadic contacts may also have some important implications. As time passes, the physical distance between grandparents and their adult children may mean that the grandparents are not able to provide as much help in caring for grandchildren, a historic function. This situation may, in turn, lead to decreased family-size preference on the part of the younger because of the work involved and the lessening of the family resources. Alternatively, as the grandparents get to the point of grandparenting, they may come to feel some regret that they did not have more children, believing that a greater earlier investment might be paying dividends in later years.

A related possibility may lie in a changing perspective on family as people get into their later years. The perspective of the seniors may be that, in spite of the knowledge of past tribulations, family relationships are much to be valued. As Talmon (1968) points out, they may cherish them more than their children do.[3]

CONCLUSION

In terms of traditional values, both change and stability characterize the respondents' attitudes. Change is evident because there is slightly less support for a full forty-hour work week than there was in the past; slightly fewer respondents reported regular church attendance; and there is a preference for a smaller "ideal number of children." Still, with the exception of the reduced family size, these changes are not dramatic ones. They represent, rather, the wavering of traditional values, with the changes occurring in an overall framework of constancy. Even within the ideal family-size shift, the largest in this group, there is an adjustment from several children into the two-child group. Among those who take one child or no children as ideal, there has been almost no observable change in nearly forty years.

A secondary conclusion emerges when the age breakdowns are examined. Younger groups are more likely to be less traditional than their elders. In each case it is the youngest age group who takes the less traditional position; opting for a shorter work week, reporting less frequent church attendance, and desiring a sharply reduced family size.

Although the data do not directly imply generational conflict, the potential for it is certainly there, with the more traditional—those over sixty-five—coming into conflict with those under thirty—the less traditional group. Except for the family-size question, however, the differences are not marked. Neither here nor in the other questions presented in previous chapters were there great cleavages between age groups. It is for this reason that I emphasize the similarities in value orientations as much as the differences. The basis for intergenerational conflict exists not simply because of the differences but because of the *way* the differences come about.

Not surprisingly, the young display greater divergence from earlier norms. The elderly have remained relatively constant. In many cases, however, it is also apparent that both groups have changed. It is popular to talk about the conservatism of people as they grow older, as if aging necessarily brings with it diminished willingness to consider new possibilities. The trends observed here suggest that fresh, entering groups of young people do, indeed, have new ideas that contrast with the ideas of their elders. As these groups age, their own views change slightly, moving in the direction of those held by their elders years ago. Work-week preference provides a good example. In the 1960s a higher percentage of younger people preferred a shorter work week. As that group aged, the strength of their views began to diminish. The trend, however, is hardly overwhelming.

Similarly, on the family-size question, the elders' larger-families ideal is retained, even though the proportion of people holding this ideal has diminished for all age groups. In church attendance, the elderly are actually reporting an increase in regular church attendance while the younger groups report a drop. Here, the two age groups do go in opposite directions.

There are several implications in these trends and patterns. One flows from making a distinction between individual-secular-leisure ("self") versus family-religious-work ("other") orientations of the age strata. In these terms, the younger appear to be less "other" oriented than are the elder. They are less connected to church, to work, and to children than are their older compeers. Contrary to theories that suggest that people become more self-centered as they grow older, these data hint the reverse; i.e., youth are more self-centered and become more other oriented as the process of aging progresses. This pattern is, with only a few exceptions, present in all the years covered by the surveys, regardless of whether there are overall shifts. Ideal family size represents such a pattern, even though every age group today has more of a preference for smaller families than they did in 1941.

The middle-age group is also intermediate on most questions. This suggests a life-cycle progression from a greater emphasis on self and self-reliance to a focus on interdependence, a posture that recognizes the importance of collectivity and interactivity. This tendency is not overwhelming by any means, but it is present.

Based upon a dual-values scheme, at least one important trend may be expected with respect to traditional commitments: a swing back to or a resurgence of previously high levels of commitment. To some extent that swing appears already to have begun. An emphasis upon the importance of work and productivity can be seen in new laws designed to prevent forced retirement of older workers. New emphasis on religion is also emerging, as evidenced by proposals for school prayers surfacing in Congress, increased reported church attendance among the elderly, etc. Finally, more emphasis on family also seems to be developing (Yankelovich, 1982).

Overall, then, traditional commitments are alive and well. The modifications in traditional value structures appear to be moderate. The public continues to be "sensible," resisting in their responses temptations to waft whichever way the winds of fashion may try to blow them. The distributional patterns and trends over the years show too much constant structure to suppose the contrary. Rather, there seems to be a clear cultural pattern, one slowly changing, slowly modifying its manifestations within the social fabric. It is to get a sense of the overall mosaic, the patterns of culture, as it were, that we now turn.

NOTES

1. Within certain limits the question changes may be regarded as minor. The questions do seem to presume, however, that the nuclear family is the norm. The idea that a one-parent family would be desirable or that a family might consist of two homosexual partners does not appear to have been considered in the surveys used here.

2. A sociobiological explanation might be that reproductive selfishness is a central human motive. People will have as many children as resources permit, subject to the proviso that, in modern cultures, if children are to be successful, the parents must spend more. So, one either raises a few and increases their likelihood of success, or

one raises many and hopes that at least some will succeed. For the most part, parents very likely do look ahead (more responsibly than they are often given credit for) both to their own resources and to the type of environment their children will face; and, in looking ahead, they gauge their strategy accordingly. The elderly want grandchldren. Costs do not greatly affect their judgment about this.

3. Talmon (1968) also points out that there is a bulge in the family life-cycle. The family is together while it is young and the children are growing up. There is then a spreading out, or widening, that involves separation. This is followed by a closing together again around aged parents.

PART III

PATTERNS IN THE STONES

7
THE MOSAIC OF CULTURE

INTRODUCTION

Of the several special issues that need to be considered, the first is the extent to which the seven pairs of values I identified earlier emerge as powerful factors.* Is there a structure to the indicators, seen in the responses to the questions this study reports upon, that looks something like the scheme I am suggesting? While the questions examined in this presentation were constructed for other purposes, it may be possible to organize them loosely within a pattern that would serve as a test of the framework itself and reduce the total number of variables to be considered.

Then, too, I combined the indicators into groups in the previous chapters. Do these groups, which seemed to be based upon the content of the questions, make sense? This relates to the general problem of whether the questions were grouped properly, *whatever* they were called.

A third issue relates to the grouping of questions over time. Typically, analysts interested in question grouping have only one time (e.g., one year) to consider. The problem of whether a particular set of attitudes or groupings endures over time is of special importance in this study. Assuming for a moment that the question wording remained identical from year to year, there could still be important shifts in the packaging of response clusters over time and thus fresh aggregations or disaggregations. Questions have

*I express special appreciation to Professor John Strate for doing the analyses for this chapter and the next.

shifted and, hence, indicate something new. And, if the wording of a question changed, as it sometimes did, these changes might contribute to or initiate such a shift.

FACTOR ANALYSIS

A factor analysis of the indicators by year was my choice of method for exploring patterns. Generally, a factor analysis is used in situations where one is not sure what to expect from the data and is seeking to explore the inherent structure in a set of responses. Kim and Mueller (1978) state: "Factor analysis refers to a variety of statistical techniques whose common objective is to represent sets of variables in terms of a smaller number of hypothetical variables. . . . [T]he distinguishing characteristic of the factor analytic approach is the assumption that observed covariation is due to some underlying common factors" (pp. 9, 22).

One might use factor analysis, for example, to measure the results from different tests to see whether there is an inherent factor that might be called "intelligence" or "math-music intelligence" as opposed to "verbal-aggressive intelligence" (Gardner, 1983). To be sure, I had some expectations of factors present in the data before undertaking this study, but the data did not fit my hopes perfectly, nor was the set of questions asked identical in each year.[1]

In thinking about the number of factors present in a set of data, one needs to consider the possibility that an opposite may not simply be a different end of the same factor—viewing "liberal," for example, as the other end of a continuum that moves from "conservative" to "liberal"— but may actually be located on a different dimension altogether. (Indeed, I found that liberalism/Democrat feelings *were* separate from conservative/Republican feelings, representing an independent dimension.) This point is a crucial one for the dual-value perspective; for, as I stressed in an earlier chapter, the dimensions of dualism are not simply the opposites of each other, i.e., equity is not the other end of an equity-adequacy continuum, nor is public the other end of a public-private continuum.

Factor analysis can be used for at least two purposes, which Kim and Mueller (1978) identify as "exploratory" and "confirmatory." One tests, minimally, the null hypothesis that there is no pattern among questions or, more substantively, that there is a particular, expected, or hoped-for pattern that will emerge. In the case where one has no idea of the nature of the structure, the analysis has exploratory—and descriptive—properties. It becomes one way in which Occam's razor can be applied, simplifying the conceptualization and presentation. If one has at least some idea of what the structure of dimensions should look like, then the analysis can serve to confirm or deny the idea. (Occam was a medieval bishop who argued that the simplest solution to any problem was the best one.)

Exploration-confirmation is not confined only to factors. It can also extend to the clustering of variables and the correlations of the variable with the factor ("loadings" on the factor). Both these approaches are important in this study. I was interested in seeing if the factors I thought would come out did, in fact, come out. I was also interested in considering the behavior of the variables that clustered to define the factor.

Factor analysis is an ideal approach to the kind of study being undertaken here. It would be good if only data from a single year were being considered. It is even more useful when working in time series. Further, one can look at breakdowns both for all groups and by age within years. A factor analytic approach is used to test the hypothesis that there are no significant differences among the patterns for any age groups. As we shall see, the analysis reveals that the factor structure by age group is, essentially, quite similar.[2]

It is important, of course, to understand that, as with any analysis, what comes out is entirely a function of what goes in. Chart 5 reveals the pattern of variables as they were entered into the series of factor analyses.

In 1956 and 1960, seven variables were used. This number was doubled from 1964 on, except for 1978, when the number was thirteen. There are slight differences in the number of variables in each of the later years either because of survey exclusion of specific variables or because of peculiarities of a particular survey and the subsamples used in administering a particular question.[3]

The factor analysis was done for each election year from 1956 to 1976 and for the year 1978. I believed this would give a sufficient picture of emerging patterns without overwhelming my readers with data.

OVERALL PERSPECTIVES

The Clustering of Value Indicators

The overall picture is presented in chart 6. For the early years, two factors emerge from these analyses. This may be due in part to a more limited number of variables than were available in later years. (See chart 5.) Later, two more factors emerge, giving a total of four. In the last year of analysis, one of the factors seems to have split itself, making a total of five.

The first factor I label "Questionable Public Entitlements." This factor appears to bring together elements of preference for trimming expanding governmental activity in the social-policy realms. I see this as a turn toward a more private orientation.

The second factor, which I call "Public Inadequacy," refers to problems of access to government, a distancing from it, and a repetition of the conflict between private and public orientations exhibited in the first factor. Two of the same variables load on both factors: Government Medical Care

Chart 5
THE DISTRIBUTION OF VARIABLES INCLUDED IN THE FACTOR ANALYSIS OF RESPONDENT OPINION

Variable[1]	1956	1960	1964	1968	1972	1976	1978	Figure
Say in Government	x	x	x	x	x	x	x	3
Voter Influence	x	x	x	x	x	x	x	4
Too Powerful	-	-	x	x	-	x	x[3]	9
Liberal Thermometer	-	-	x	x	x	x	-[3]	6
Democrat Thermometer	-	-	x	x	x	x	x	6
Republican Thermometer	-	-	x	x	x	x	x[3]	6
Conservative Thermometer	-	-	x	x	x	x	-[3]	6
Government Trust	-	-	x	x	x	x	x	1
Government Benefits	-	-	x	x	x	x	x	2
Civil Rights	-	-	x	x	x	x	-	11
Negro Position	-	-	x	x	x	x	-	12
Rights of Accused	-	-	-	-	x	x	x	13
Women's Rights	-	-	-	-	x	x	x	14
Church Attendance	x	x	x	x	x	x	x	15
Government Health	-	-	-	-	-[2]	x	x	7
Government Job	-	-	-	-	-[2]	x	x	5
Government Power	x	x	x	-	-[2]	-	-	8
Government Medical Care	x	x	x	x	-[2]	-	-	7
Negro Job	x	x	x	x	x	-	-	10
Government Work	x	x	x	x	-	-	-[4]	5
Help Minorities	-	-	-	-	-	-	x[4]	
# Variables =	7	7	16	15	14	16	13[3]	
# Factors =	2	2	4	4	4	4	4[3]	
N =	1046	1134	531	680	1351	3101	762	

1. The 21 variables key to the 17 questions and four thermometers surveyed in this study. The questions are listed in Chart 2. Help Minorities was added in 1978.

2. Government Job and Government Medical Care were deleted from the factor analysis in 1972 because only pre-election data were available. The sample chosen for analysis includes all those individuals interviewed in both pre- and post-interviews with complete data on all variables.

3. In 1978 Liberal and Conservative Thermometers were not asked.

4. Used in factor analysis only.

and Government Job. This suggests that the private orientation is tied both to a wish for government to do less and to a sense of removal from it.

These two factors, which emerge with reasonable clarity throughout the analysis period, buttress the notion of orientations that reflect increasing distance from government and a diminishing of support for the high level of social involvement that has come to characterize government.

Of the third and fourth factors that emerge in 1964, I call the third, "Privatism and Self-Reliance" and the fourth, "Public Inequity." Privatism and Self-Reliance reflect warm feelings toward Republican and conservative orientations and a sense that the government has become too powerful. Public Inequities describe a feeling of lack of trust in government and a belief that government is somehow unfair.

In 1978 Privatism and Self-Reliance appears to merge with Questionable Public Entitlements. Elements of that factor now also appear in the Public Inequity factor. At the same time, the Public Inadequacy factor appears to split. Women's Rights, which clustered with the Public Inadequacy variables in 1976, linked with Church Attendance in 1978 to form a new factor. I call this factor "Traditionalism."

The naming of variables should, of course, be viewed heuristically rather than definitively.[4] In the later years, especially, there is a confounding of variables and factors that makes clear-cut interpretation difficult. Nonetheless, one sees in the factors the same kinds of questioning of the public weal, of return to traditional orientations that were revealed in the individual questions.

Questionable Public Entitlements

This factor emerges in almost every year analyzed. In the later years the entitlement aspect of it becomes stressed, and it appears to merge with the Public Inadequacy factor. In the initial years, this factor contained three variables: Government Work, which deals with whether the government should provide a job (and a good standard of living) for people; Government Medical Care, which asks about governmental action in the health area; and Negro Job, which asks if the government should see to it that blacks get fair treatment in jobs (and housing).

This collection of questions suggests that conflict exists over public orientation or the extent and scope of public function. The race question, in particular, suggests conflict over entitlements. Two of the questions, Government Work and Negro Job, suggest that it is the adequacy of *opportunity* rather than the adequacy of *results* that is at issue.

In 1964, new questions became available: whether the government was getting too powerful, whether the speed of the civil rights movement was too fast, and four thermometers. The first two of these and the Democrat

Chart 6
THE CLUSTERING OF "POLICY" OPINION, 1956-1978: FACTOR ANALYSIS BY YEAR OF REPEATED QUESTIONS

Factor	Variable Clusters and Year*						
	1956	1960	1964	1968	1972	1976	1978
1. Questionable Public Entitlements	Gv Work Gv Med Ngr Job —— (1)	Gv Work Gv Med Ngr Job —— (1)	Ngr Job -Cv Rts -Too Pow Gv Med -Th Dem -Th Lib Gv Pow Gv Work —— (1)	Gv Work Ngr Job Gv Med -Cv Rts -Th Dem -Th Lib -Too Pow —— (1)	-Th Con -Th Rep Cv Rts -Ngr Job Th Lib —— (1)	Th Con Th Rep —— (1)(3)	Gv Job Help Min Gv Hlth -Th Dem Th Rep —— (1)
2. Public Inadequacy	Vote Inf Say Gv Gv Med Gv Work —— (2)	Say Gv Vote Inf —— (2)	Gv Ben Gv Trust -Too Pow —— (4)	-Gv Trust -Gv Ben —— (2)	Say Gv Vote Inf —— (2)	Rts Acc Women Rts -Say Gv -Vote Inf Gv Job —— (2)	Gv Ben Gv Trust -Too Pow -Th Dem —— (4)(3)

3. Privatism & Self-Reliance

		Th Con Th Rep -Th Dem Gv Med	Vote Inf Say Gv	Th Dem Th Lib
		(3)	(2)	(3)

Th Dem Th Lib	-Say Gv -Vote Inf
(3)	(2)

4. Public Inequity

Say Gv Vote Inf	-Th Con -Th Rep	Gv Trust Gv Ben	-Gv Trust -Gv Ben
(2)	(3)	(4)	(4)

5. Traditionalism

Women Rts -Ch Att
(5)

Cumulative Variance Explained

1. Factor 1	14.9%	13.1%	11.9%	12.8%	11.1%	8.3%	11.4%
2. Factor 2	22.2%	22.4%	19.3%	19.3%	17.2%	14.3%	19.6%
3. Factor 3			28.7%	28.3%	23.5%	20.8%	25.4%
4. Factor 4			32.4%	31.3%	30.1%	26.9%	29.9%

* The variable names used here are shortened forms of those appearing in Chart 5. The order of variables is the ordering of variable loadings. All variables with loadings of +.30 are included.

NOTE: This schematic portrays the flow of factors and their position over the years from 1956 to 1978. Factor 3, Privatism and Self-Reliance, appears to end in 1976. The survey did not ask two of the four thermometers in 1978, however, so it is difficult to tell whether there was an effect or not. A fifth factor, "Traditionalism," emerges in 1978, representing what appears to be a separation of two elements of the Public Inadequacy factor. It is made up of Women's Rights and Church Attendance.

and liberal thermometers linked with the question on governmental involvement in electric power and housing to emerge as part of the Questionable Public Entitlements factor cluster.[5] Taken together, the indicators continue to show conflict over public entitlements, with emphasis by some on the notion that government should leave these social-policy interventions to individuals.

Beyond 1964, noticeable change occurs as the questions included in this factor become fewer and the private or public dimensions, represented by the thermometers, become dominant in the sense that three of the five variables are thermometer variables (in 1972).

In 1976 only the conservative thermometers appear in this factor. I regard this result as a combining of the privatism dimension implicit in Questionable Public Entitlements with the private portion of the Privatism and Self-Reliance factor. In a sense, too, privatism also merges with the Public Inadequacy factor into a more negative picture of the public weal.

Questionable Public Entitlements re-expands in 1978. Government Job, Help Minorities (the 1978) version of Negro Jobs), and Government Health now cluster with the Democrat and Republican thermometers.

Public Inadequacy

Consistently, two questions have hung together. The first asks whether voting is the only way people "like me" have to influence the government. The second asks respondents whether people like them don't have much say about how the government in Washington runs things. These two questions emerge as important areas each year, and in most years make up the Public Inadequacy factor. In 1976 these two are joined by Rights of the Accused, Women's Rights, and Government Job in the Public Inadequacy cluster. This suggests that a sense of public inadequacy has combined with negative reactions to governmental activity and a traditional approach to gender roles and crime control.

This factor began as one that measured whether people felt able to influence or alienated from the public weal. In 1976, it involved traditionalism and ineffectuality; i.e., everything in the culture may be moving too fast. As a result, those individuals who were most sharply critical of the government may themselves have lacked a sense of efficacy. They may not have believed that they could influence things, even, perhaps, their own lives. Hence, the disenchantment with the perceived problems and levels of governmental activity may have been sharpened.

Generally, the Public Inadequacy factor may represent both a disenchantment with governmental programs and an enlarged sense that governmental action itself in the enhancement of rights violates the idea of struggle. Entitlements, after all, can and should go only so far—but the question of how far is open to discussion. The 1976 data may reflect the emergence of support for a more limited role of government. That role might be one that endorses both struggle (let each person get ahead on his own) and a more traditional role orientation, favoring "stop crime" over rights of criminals and favoring the place of women in the home.[6]

The 1970s have been characterized by some as a period during which the government developed many programs, yet during which many of those government programs seemed not to work. There may never have been a time in U.S. history when the government was so active, nor, at the same time, when there was a wider public perception of institutional failure. Schools didn't work and Johnny couldn't read. The prisons didn't work. Poverty was with us as much as ever. Medicare and Medicaid costs skyrocketed. The Social Security system was seen as doomed. What the data may reveal about this time is a mixed perception. On the one hand we have the image of government assisting or intruding (depending on one's point of view) into every nook and cranny of life. On the other hand we have the image of monumental governmental ineptitude. Such a mixed perception is a telling preface to the next two factors.

Privatism and Self-Reliance

Beginning in 1964, the thermometers emerged as powerful elements in the analysis. The historical image of the major parties suggests that the Republican-conservative orientation represents a more self-oriented, more self-reliant stance. Democrat-liberal orientation embodies a more other-oriented posture that recognizes (more fully) the interdependency of people.

Using this frame of reference, I identify a Self-Reliance factor. It emerges in 1964 and 1968. In 1972, the Democrat and Liberal thermometers emerged as a single factor. Privatism and Self-Reliance, which had been strong and had contained a variety of other variables in the two previous survey years, now begins to shift to the more entitlements-oriented factor that emerges in 1976.

By 1976, then, two thermometer groups emerged as separate factors. One stressed interdependency. The other stressed self-reliance.

In 1978, this factor does not appear among the initial four. A new factor does emerge, and I label it "Traditionalism." This might suggest that four factors of one kind or another remain. When I ran factors by age, however, five factors rather than four were requested as a check on the possibility that privatism might emerge as the fifth. It does for both the under-thirty group and the thirty-to-sixty-four group. It does not appear for the over-sixty-five group. Thus, it is safe to conclude that there continue to be the four factors that the analysis initially uncovered plus a new, fifth one that emerges from the 1978 data. (See chart 8.)

Public Inequity

The fourth factor emerges in the 1964 survey. It involves the issues of whom the government benefits and whether the government can be trusted to do what is right. Over the years there is a very discernible trend toward negativism on the part of respondents to both of these issues. The two remain together in each of the survey years in which they appear. This suggests a developing sense of public unfairness. The two variables represent a factor involving lack of trust of government and the view that government is run increasingly for the benefit of a few. Such perceptions, especially the latter, may appear incongruous when one realizes that the government's role is expanding and many groups are being helped. That point may be precisely the key one, i.e., that the many groups are really only a few special interests. The notion that government benefits a few special interests suggests, but does not require, that only a few interests among many benefit. Rather, one could hypothesize that in U.S. society it may be *many* fews, and part of the response package here may reflect the trivialization of government, a failure, as it were, of government to see the broad picture—in favor of an involvement with apparently every group that has (or that government thinks has) an issue.

It is paradoxical, nonetheless, that, at the very time the government is attempting to move to increase access to the system for the many to whom access has been denied, it is being perceived as moving unfairly. Part of the explanation for this may be related to the definition of "fair" as relating outcomes to inputs. It is not fair to get grades that were not earned. It is not fair to be punished for something one did not do. Fairness in the United States historically has been narrowly and individually defined rather than broadly and collectively defined. Governmental programs, especially in the last twenty years, that have tended toward collective equity and broadening the definition of fairness (equity) raise public questions about whether this new concept *is* fairness as we have known it. Pole (1978) thinks not, and at least some of the respondents agree.

Traditionalism

The last factor to emerge, that which I call, "Traditionalism," includes Women's Rights and Church Attendance. Rights of the Accused might have been included, but it missed the arbitrary cutoff point of .30 by two one-hundredths of a point. (It was .28. I chose .30 as a "reasonable" loading that a variable had to have to be considered part of the factor.) This factor suggests that the 1978 data revealed the emergence of a traditional dimension that emphasizes church attendance, traditional roles for women, and a hard-line emphasis with respect to those accused of a crime.

Before proceeding further, a caveat of sorts is necessary here, lest anyone take these factor names too seriously. Let me emphasize that the attempt at pulling patterns from the data is speculative and heuristic. The picture does not have the sharp focus I would have liked. Questions do not group cleanly and without ambiguity. Under these circumstances, the best one can do is strive to capture a sense of the data. While I hope that has been done here, I am keenly aware that other interpretations are also possible. I invite others to continue these multi-year analyses with more and different variables so that they may themselves look for patterns.

Overall Perspectives: Multiplicity and Dualism of Policy Values

Overall, then, did the factor analysis tell us about the patterning of the U.S. value system? Did it confirm anything? Was the exploration worthwhile? To all three questions I believe the answer is essentially affirmative.

The consistent patterning that emerged confirms the idea of multiple policy-value dimensions. To some extent, in addition, the data are at least consistent with a dual approach to policy-value dimensions. Certainly, the five factors seem to suggest competing orientations.

That there does appear to be some level of confirmation should not come as a surprise. Ours is a pluralistic society, which surely means a pluralism of policy values. But a new idea does present itself: what is present in the policy is also present within the personality, and change occurs along the lines dividing the various orientations. While considerably more investigation needs to be done, this study does provide some support for this idea.[7]

There are also some tentative links that can be made between policy-value sets represented by the five factors and the seven dual-value dimensions I defined earlier. Admittedly, the connections are very speculative at this juncture. The fit is imperfect and open to serious challenge. Still, as psychologist James V. McConnell (1985) has frequently observed all theory begins with a gut-level feeling that one has set a foot on a correct but fog-shrouded road. Each bit of confirming evidence dispels some of the fog until at last truth (or falsity) is revealed. This, then, is my sense about the connections:

1. Questionable Public Entitlement has aspects of the Struggle vs Entitlement dimension, with struggle seeming to dominate;
2. Public Inadequacy has elements of Equity vs Adequacy, with the implications of inadequacy and distance from government with respect to influence;
3. Public Inequity also links to Equity vs Adequacy, with the implications of lack of fairness, government representing only a few, and lack of trust in government;
4. Privatism and Self-Reliance, with private dominating and emerging alone in 1976, links with Private vs Public. From 1976 on, this factor divides into two factors, representing two different value dimensions.

VALUES OF THE AGES

The overall patterning of the responses to the available questions over time suggests four, and very likely five, factors around which opinion seemed to crystallize. The suggestion is not as crisp as I would have preferred, and the factors did not remain entirely stable over the years. An initially powerful one seems to deteriorate over time. That which I call Privatism and Self-Reliance seems to have strengthened, developing two facets. Both facets are apparently more conservative in orientation, but they apparently have different foci.

There is a popular belief to the effect that age makes a difference. For this reason, data from one year in each decade (1956, 1964, and 1972) was again factor analyzed to see if some sort of age-linked pattern emerged for the under-thirty, the thirty-to-sixty-five, and the over-sixty-five age groups. Relevant results are presented in chart 7.

Overall, there is a striking similarity between the breakdowns by age and the total set of responses. It is particularly clear in 1956 and 1972. In those years the pattern within each age group is almost identical to the total response pattern. In 1964, there is some mixing of questions loading highly on the overall factors. Privatism and Self-Reliance is not as distinctive by age as it is overall. Rather, the Privatism and Self-Reliance factor (as indicated by the thermometers) and the Questionable Public Entitlements factor (as indicated by Government Job, Negro Job, and Government Medical Care) intermingled.

This mixing is far more prevalent in the elderly and youngest groups (in particular, the youngest) than in the middle-aged group. In 1964, for those under thirty, there appears to be a greater emphasis on entitlements than is present in the other groups. I reach this conclusion after noting that an entitlement-type question emerges within every factor. In the initial overall analysis, the Questionable Public Entitlements factor had a decided entitlement cast to it (hence its name). In this age-group analysis, however, Public Inadequacy also contains the Civil Rights question and the Negro Job question. (Their coding goes in opposite directions.) The Privatism and Self-Reliance factor contains the Negro Position question. The Public Inequities factor also contains the Negro Job question. It is the pattern here that is strikingly different from the overall analysis and from the other two age groups.

Speculations about what this mixing might mean are at best hazardous. I note only that there were powerful conflicting streams within youth at that time, streams of conservatism that clashed with streams of radicalism. This clash might help account for why warmth toward conservative policy values appears in the Questionable Public Entitlements factor and a sense that progress toward civil rights is moving too slowly appears in the Public Inadequacy factor.

Other than this difference in emphasis in 1964, the factors appear to be quite similar.[8] Two other points of comparison are useful here. The first considers the relationship among age groups for a given year. In this respect the group over sixty-five is much like the younger groups. No unique factors emerge for the elderly group that are not present within the younger ones. In 1956 and 1972, even the order of emerging factors is similar. In 1964, the order of factors varies among the age groups somewhat. In the middle-aged group, the large Questionable Public Entitlements factor is followed by Public Inadequacy. The Privatism and Self-Reliance factor emerges as third. This is the order that appeared in the overall analysis.

For the youngest group, however, Public Inadequacy does not appear until the last factor. (Public Inequity appeared as the third factor for the elderly group.) Because of the overall similarity of the patterns by age to the overall patterns, there is similarity among the ages within each year as well.

There was an obvious problem of data comparability over the years. Furthermore, the year 1972 was relatively early in the 1970s while 1956 and 1964 were in the middle of their decades. For these reasons, and because an overall factor analysis had already been performed for 1978, one additional analysis by age was performed for that year. In this analysis an additional element was included that was not included in the previous analysis: five factors were requested instead of four. I wanted to be sure that I was not arbitrarily constraining the data to obscure factors that might otherwise be present. Relevant results are displayed in chart 8.

Overall, the pattern by age continues to look very much like the pattern for the society as a whole. The same factors emerge in 1978 for the age groups as emerge for the society as a whole. In each case the "new" factor, Traditionalism, emerges.[9] Church attendance, important as an indicator in the over 65 and under 30 groups, is not as important in the 30 to 64 group, failing to make the inclusion cutoff of .30. (We did include it, properly noted, because, at .28, it was close.)

The elderly look somewhat different in this analysis. Of the five factors, the elderly had four that were the same as the under 30 group, including Traditionalism. Privatism and Self-Reliance, however, does not appear for the elderly group. What does appear is a factor I have labeled "2/4" because I believe it to be a combination of Public Inadequacy (factor 2) and Public Inequities (factor 4). It seems to reflect alienation or a more explicit feeling of removal from the decision-making processes than would be true for the younger groups. The three variables that load on this factor (Too Powerful, Government Benefits, and Say in Government) all suggest that there is an element of distance, something that has not affected the elderly so explicitly before. Whether there will be a continuation of this trend remains to be seen.

It is not entirely clear whether the elderly have remained much the same over the years or whether there are differences within the group over time.

Chart 7

THE CLUSTERING OF "POLICY" OPINION, 1956, 1964, and 1972: FACTOR ANALYSIS BY YEAR OF REPEATED QUESTIONS BY AGE GROUPINGS OF UNDER 30, 30-65, AND OVER 65

	1956			1964			1972		
	< 30	30-65	> 65	< 30	30-65	> 65	< 30	30-65	> 65
	Gv Work Gv Med Ngr Job	Gv Work Gv Med Ngr Job	Gv Med Gv Work -Gv Pow	Th Rep Th Con -Th Lib -Th Dem Gv Pow Gv Med Cv Rts	-Th Dem Th Rep Gv Med -Too Pow Th Con Gv Pow -Th Lib Ngr Job Gv Work	Th Con Th Rep Gv Med -Th Dem -Too Pow Gv Pow -Cv Rts	-Th Rep -Th Con Cv Rts -Ngr Job Th Lib	Th Rep Th Con	-Th Con -Th Rep Cv Rts -Ngr Job Th Lib
	Say Gv Vote Inf	Vote Inf Say Gv	Ngr Job Gv Med Say Gv	-Cv Rts Ngr Job Gv Work -Too Pow	Gv Ben Gv Trust	-Th Lib Say Gv Too Pow	-Say Gv -Vot Inf	-Say Gv -Vote Inf	Say Gv Gv Ben Gv Trust Vote Inf
				Say Gv Vote Inf Ngr Pos Th Dem	Ngr Job -Th Con -Cv Rts	Gv Trust Th Dem Gv Ben	Th Lib Th Dem	Th Lib Th Dem	-Th Lib -Th Dem
				-Too Pow Gv Ben Ngr Job	Say Gv Vote Inf	Cv Rts Ngr Job Vote Inf		Gv Ben Gv Trust	-Ngr Pos Women Rts

% Variance Explained by Factors:

< 30	30-65	> 65	< 30	30-65	> 65	< 30	30-65	> 65
13.3%	14.9%	13.4%	15.5%	17.5%	16.6%	12.1%	9.7%	11.8%
18.2%	23.6%	25.1%	25.9%	24.7%	23.9%	18.3%	15.6%	20.3%
			32.8%	29.4%	32.8%	24.1%	23.5%	27.8%
			39.3%	33.1%	40.5%	31.3%	30.3%	32.1%

The variable names are shortened forms of those used in Chart 5. The order of the variables is the ordering of the variable's loadings. All variables with loadings of .30 or greater are included.

Chart 8
FACTOR CLUSTERING OF POLICY OPINIONS
BY AGE, 1978*

	1978	
< 30	30-65	> 65
Gv Job Help Min Gv Health	Gv Job Help Min Gv Health Rts Acc	Gv Job Gv Health -Th Dem Help Min Rts Acc Th Rep
Gv Ben Gv Trust -Too Pow -Th Dem -Say Gv	-Gv Ben -Gv Trust Too Pow	Say Gv Vote Inf Rts Acc Gv Ben
Vote Inf Say Gv	Say Gv Vote Inf	Women Rts -Ch Att
Women Rts Gv Health -Ch Att Rts Acc	Women Rts Rts Acc -Ch Att**	Gv Trust Gv Ben -Th Dem
Help Min -Th Dem	-Th Dem -Too Pow Th Rep Gv Health	Too Pow Gv Ben Say Gv

% Variance Explained:

	<30	30-65	>65
1.	8.5%	9.0%	14.6%
2.	16.8%	16.9%	22.4%
3.	21.4%	23.2%	28.5%
4.	28.5%	27.6%	37.5%
5.	32.5%	33.8%	43.7%

* Variable names are shortened forms of those used in Chart 5.
The order of factors reflected the computer-generated order.

** Although the Church Attendance variable at -.28 did not meet
the +.30 inclusion criterion, the newness of the factor that
emerged and the closeness to +.30 argued for its presentation.

This is because of some problems in comparability of data from survey to survey. The year 1956, for example, does not have all the variables that appear later. I will offer some tentative observations, however.

There seems to be a continuing emphasis across the years in Questionable Public Entitlements, although by 1972, the pattern is not as strong, with Privatism and Self-Reliance emerging even more powerfully. The elderly do not seem to change a great deal over time, given the variables available to assess such change. The general impression that can be derived from chart 8 is one of more stable orientation, an orientation with some consistency and integrity to it. It seems to be something like a common policy-value structure.

CONCLUSION

For people in general, five dimensions appear that have some consistency across the years: Questionable Public Entitlements, Public Inadequacy, Privatism and Self-Reliance, Public Inequity, and Traditionalism. The first factor disappears by 1976 but re-emerges in 1978. The last factor emerges only in 1978. All other factors continue over the years, demonstrating a vigorous staying power and creating confidence that these factors are, indeed, important. At the very least, these factors provide a framework into which the details of the specific questions can be fit and within which they take on an enhanced meaning.

It is important to understand that cultural structure does not mean cultural straitjacket. The proportions of variance explained by all the factors run in the range of 22 percent to 32 percent (43.7 percent in the case of the elderly in 1978). There is, therefore, ample room for divergence within the structure itself.

NOTES

1. The crucial aspect to understand is that this statistical technique looks for inter-relationships and, according to a set of criteria, determines the fewest number of dimensions, independent from one another, required to explain these inter-relationships.

2. This same technique could be used with any groups—men and women, blacks and whites, and so on—where one has a question about the extent to which the groups might cluster differently. It is especially appropriate where one has a prior suspicion from research or public belief or reading the entrails of a chicken or whatever that there is some important difference in the way in which people with a particular characteristic (or set of characteristics) combine to differentiate themselves from others.

3. Only National Election Study variables are used in this analysis.

4. To do this, I looked at the variables that loaded heavily on the factor. One

looks at the direction of the coding on the variables as an aid in understanding the substantive significance of the loadings. For example, the Women's Rights and the Church Attendance questions have positive and negative factor loadings respectively on the same factor, and large scores on both of these variables are associated with traditional orientations.

5. The factor solutions of particular years were rotated 180 degrees to insure that the signs on the factor loadings were the same over time because the signs of these factor loadings for the same variable would vary over time due entirely to the arbitrary nature of factor solutions.

6. Such an orientation, by the way, may be a help in the problem of lack of influence. If the government has gotten too big to influence and has too many programs and people to influence effectively, then a return to a more traditional orientation is also a return to a scale and a scope through which influence may be exercised once again. Some such combination of a return to a scale one can influence, a return to emphasis on a contest motif, and an equity or fairness-of-opportunity orientation may represent an emerging trend. I mention this point hypothetically and to indicate that those who are negative with respect to big government are often negative to big, national government. Those same individuals may, for example, support governmental initiatives on a local level in such areas as schools, libraries, and parks. In short, one is in error, I believe, to identify a value dimension here as pro- or anti-government solely. Rather, the scale issue needs to be taken into account. An "anti" on the local level may well be a "pro" on a national level, and vice versa.

7. See especially Erikson (1976) for a discussion of change in Appalachia using these terms.

8. Our criterion was that there needed to be substantial similarity between the factors. The year 1964 was the only one that might be thought different in this respect. In the other two years, the substantial similarity is visually obvious. In 1964, the under-thirty group had two factors different from the overall analysis; i.e., they had the Conservative and Republican thermometers while the overall analysis had Negro Job and Government Work instead. This difference appears to make it the Privatism and Self-Reliance factor because of the heavy and prominent loadings of the thermometers. The second factor of the under-thirty group contains the Civil Rights, Negro Job, Government Work, and Too Powerful variables that are, with the exception of Government Medical Care, consistent with Questionable Public Entitlement emphasis. The third factor for the under-thirty group is the Public Inadequacy factor involving Say in Government and Vote Influence. Here, however, Public Inadequacy has two more variables: Negro Position and the Democrat thermometer. The Public Inequity factor is fourth in the under-thirty group (second in the overall analysis), but contains one different variable from the overall; namely, Negro Job instead of Government Trust.

9. The regressions suggest, however, that, while the factors are more important for each of the age groups, the under 30 group and the over 65 group are at opposite ends. The elderly appear as traditional on Women's Rights and as not supportive of Rights of the Accused. The under 30 are reversed.

8
THE PERSONAL ROOTS
OF COMMITMENT

INTRODUCTION

Where do values come from? Some beg the question.[1] Weber (1956), as one example, observes merely that values shape the reality we see and in which we act. Important as that observation is, it sheds little light on the question. Those who do attempt to address the matter of value origins often speak in generalities that do not hold up well under careful scrutiny. Marx, an example from what is essentially the reverse perspective, argues that values come from the conditions of man's life. If, indeed, that were true, similar individuals in similar circumstances with similar characteristics ought to respond similarly; and, further, their reponses should remain relatively stable over time.

Where, then, do values come from? Are they a function of age or of income level or of race or of the geographical region where one lives or, indeed, of any of a myriad of characteristics one can identify? Are any of these characteristics alone powerful enough to influence the development of a value system? Or must they act in concert with some others or all others? Do some characteristics, while not important in and of themselves, significantly alter the influence of others that may be extremely important? And, finally, if one knows enough about the characteristics of respondents, should it not then be possible to predict with some degree of accuracy the values, the beliefs, the attitudes, the opinions a given respondent will hold or exhibit?

These are among some of the questions to which at least partial answers were sought through a multiple regression analysis of the respondents' answers in terms of their characteristics. As will be seen, the results of that analysis can be characterized as being of meager significance and of great interest.

A MULTIPLE REGRESSION APPROACH

The data set used in this study permits a look at various social identifications of the respondent in combination (e.g., age, gender, race, etc.). The method used was regression analysis in which a large equation with fourteen independent variables was used to predict individual responses in any year. Actually, two predictions were examined—the first, for a series of values questions; the second, and more powerful, for the factors developed in the previous chapter. The independent variables were selected on the basis of their historical importance in sociological research, not because I believed there was some specific theory that associated variables with values. (Rokeach, 1979, chapter 7, also sought to look at these relationships, but with different variables.) The variables selected were as follows:

1. age
2. level of education
3. race
4. region
5. income
6. marital status
7. party identification
8. subjective social class
9. blue collar
10. white collar
11. urban/rural
12. sex
13. religion-Catholic
14. religion-Jewish

In those cases where the variable was continuous (age, education, income, party identification, and subjective social class), an interval coding scheme was used for each respondent. Non-continuous variables were coded a "1 or 0." Chart 9 lists the independent variables and the approach to coding each.

Chart 9
CODING OF INDEPENDENT VARIABLES REGRESSION ANALYSIS OF REPEATED POLICY OPINION QUESTIONS: 1952–1978

Independent Variable	Code	Definition
Age	-	Coded in years
Education[1]	1	None
	2	1-7 grades
	3	8 grades
	4	9-11 grades
	5	9-11 grades, plus non-college training
	6	12 grades, high school graduate
	7	12 grades, plus non-college training
	8	Some college
	9	College graduate
Race	1	Black
	0	Non-black (white plus other minorities)
Region	1	South
	0	Other
Income[2]	-	Coded at midpoint of the income class interval
Marital Status	1	Married
	0	Other
Party I.D.	1	Strong Democrat
	2	Weak Democrat
	3	Democrat, leaning
	4	Independent
	5	Republican, leaning
	6	Weak Republican
	7	Strong Republican
Class[3]	1	Lower
	2	Working
	3	Middle
	4	Upper
Blue Collar	1	Working class occupation[4]
	0	Other
While Collar	1	Middle class occupation[5]
	0	Other
Urban/Rural	1	Farmers and farm managers[6]
	0	Other
Sex	1	Male
	0	Female
Catholic[7]	1	Catholic
	0	Other
Jew	1	Jewish
	0	Other

1. Coding through grade 8 included those with non-college training. Codes for education varied somewhat throughout the years.

2. For those with very high incomes (no upper bound to the interval), income was set at $25,000+(.2 * Lower Bound); i.e, for the class $25,000 and over, income is at $25,000 + (.2 * $25,000) = $30,000. All income figures = family income.

3. Recoded from subjective assessments. The exact question varied somewhat throughout the years.

4. 400-799 on the political behavior occupation code. Any other individual (e.g., those without an occupation or those in a middle class occupation) was coded as 0.

5. 100-399 on the political behavior occupation code.

6. 800-840 on the political behavior occupation code.

7. Protestant was also available, but in order to make the "dummy" variable for religion, Protestant was coded as 0.

The regression equations are calculated within a given year. Because the data permit a view over time, it is possible to look at several relationships of interest. To begin with, the analysis allows a consideration in a series of years of how well one does at explaining the social roots of the commitments people hold. Second, one can see whether or not these social bases of value orientation change any as the years go by. Does education, for example, increase or decrease in importance as a predictor in relation to the other predictors. Third, and of special interest for this study, chronological age and the role it plays in determining values and commitments can be examined.

RESULTS

As I have already indicated, overall the results of this analysis were not impressive. Given the wide collection of predictors assembled in the regression equations, I hoped that substantive results would be achieved in understanding the generally personal links to policy opinion. It is true that in every single year, given the large sample sizes, many of the variables in the regression analyses achieved statistical significance. Significant or not, however, the results were not terribly important in the larger scheme of things. Table 1 portrays the range of R^2 values for different years and different variables. The R^2 values represent the proportion of variance that can be accounted for by the predicting variable, holding other variables constant.

The results are disappointing. They are mainly under 10 percent. In a few cases, which I will discuss individually, the proportions are higher. These are mainly in the thermometer variables, Government Medical Care, Church Attendance, and Civil Rights.

This low level of explained variance may speak to the multiplicity of value elements represented in a single question. If so, I believed the predictive power of the independent variables ought to improve if one could obtain "cleaner" dependent variables, those with less "noise" in them. *Clean* and *noise* have specific meaning in this context. In the case of the independent variables, it is not clear what such social characteristics as age and gender really indicate. We presume, or assume, that we understand what kinds of social construction of reality they represent; but in my view there is quite an admixture of elements represented here, some of which may well work at cross-purposes, lowering the predictive value of the independent variable in that instance. With respect to "noise" in the dependent measures, it seems clear that each dependent measure ("trust in government," "reported church attendance," and so on) is, itself, an indicator of a larger construct. It is for that reason that the factor analysis is useful in combining related variables into a new variable that represents a more coherent package of attitudes. Those factors developed in the last chapter are examples of such variables. A regression analysis was used to predict the factor scores. Results of this analysis are displayed at the bottom of table 1.

Table 1

**R^2 VALUES FOR DEPENDENT VARIABLES,
MULTIPLE REGRESSION ANALYSIS WITH
14 INDEPENDENT VARIABLES**

Dependent Variable	1952	1956	1960	1964	1968	1972	1976	1978
(National Election Study)								
Government Trust				.03	.03	.04	.03	.03
Government Benefits				.05	.05	.05	.05	.02
Say in Government	.09	.15	.10	.08	.10	.09	.09	.06
Voter Influence	.05	.13	.10	.12	.19	.19	.14	.12
Government Job		.16	.15	.06	.13	.08	.06	.14
Democrat Thermometer				.42	.36	.24	.32	.43
Republican Thermometer				.36	.26	.17	.20	.25
Liberal Thermometer				.10	.06	.14	.13	
Conservative Thermometer				.12	.07	.13	.14	
Government Health		.19	.23	.23	.15	.06	.05	.12
Government Power		.08	.09	.14				
Too Powerful				.24	.15	.03	.11	.06
Negro Job		.08	.10	.15	.11	.10		
Civil Rights				.20	.20	.17	.15	
Negro Position				.04	.03	.02	.06	
Rights of the Accused						.12	.09	.08
Women's Role						.08	.16	.13
Church Attendance	.15	.17	.17	.16	.15	.10	.13	.11
Dependent Variable Factors[3]								
1. Quest. Public Entitlements		.23	.23	.39	.35	.26	.21	
2. Public Inadequacy		.22	.21	.18	.25	.21	.19	
3. Privatism				.45	.23	.19	.23	
4. Public Inequity				.11	.06	.06	.04	

Dependent Variable (Gallup Poll)	1953	1962	1974
Family Size (A)[1]	.03	.08	.12
Family Size (B)[2]	.03	.05	.11

1. Includes all available independent variables.
2. Includes only independent variables common to all years.
3. Factors not available for 1978.

My guess seems to be confirmed. The R^2 values rise. That rise is not as much as I would have hoped given the array of independent variables used, but it was substantial, nevertheless. In three of the four factors, the R^2 values are, with only a few exceptions, greater than 20 percent. This is a decided improvement over the individual variables. For the Public Inequity factor, however, the variance accounted for is low.

These results are highly suggestive. First, it appears that no single opinion-question-value-indicator is heavily determined by elements in the social structure. Some variables (see tables 3 and 4) are more powerful than others in the prediction of responses to individual questions and the question clusters (factors). Overall, however, it would be an error to conclude that these responses are simply the product of social conditions. Policy values and opinion may behave independently of social conditions, at least to some extent. While they may interrelate, much more work is needed to chart the links between the two.

Second, the substantially increased R^2 values for the factors suggest that the individual questions themselves are at best confounded indicators of the value structure.[2] Typically, the questions tapped several different dimensions. This tendency toward overlapping was picked up in the factor analysis. Still, when one reads the question in isolation or hears about some poll report, there is a tendency to think that one "knows" what the question says and means—and, therefore, what the response means. Perhaps an alternative model might be a good corrective—to regard the question as "poems" in which time is spent attempting to understand exactly what the asker meant and, equally or even more important, what the listener thinks about in responding to such a question.

I have emphasized a dual-value system. That dual system is one made up of a set of seven different policy-value dimensions, each set itself composed of contradictory indicators. While this analysis cannot prove the existence of such a system, the low R^2 values suggest a pattern quite consistent with the hypothesis. If the value system were straightforward, even transparent in its structure, without important contradictions, then there ought to be high R^2 values because it would be easy to predict.[3] It is not. Additionally, if one is willing to regard the factors as approximations of the policy values, then predictions improve as the measures improve.

I should stress that precisely the same independent variables were not available for the Gallup questions and family size. (Work week was not run. See table 3 for exact differences.) The results of those two regressions are presented here to show the differences involved in using different independent variables. Using a similar equation, R^2 values using the Gallup data are not much better than data from the National Election Study. This may, in fact, be a positive result. It suggests that the findings are not the result of one study's unique features.

DIFFERENTIAL IMPORTANCE

Questions resisted explanation to a greater or lesser extent, a variability that may be best illustrated in table 2. In this table the proportions of the fourteen independent variables that were statistically significant at the .05 level or beyond are recorded for each dependent variable.[4]

The range of the proportion of significant variables may be higher than one might expect, given the low R^2 values and low beta weights.[5] They range from a low where almost nothing is significant (14 percent—Voting is the only way that people like me can have any say about how the government runs things—1952) to a high where almost everything is (Church Attendance—79 percent in 1960 and 1968; 86 percent in 1976). Reported Church Attendance is affected by the most things (i.e., more variables are significant in predicting it than any other variable), followed closely by Government Medical/Health and Government Work/Job questions.

Although the selection of independent variables was not guided by specific theory, I did expect more independent variables to be significant than actually were. Too, table 2 suggests how much the beta weights change; i.e., an independent variable does well for Church Attendance in some years and not in others, a pattern repeated for other variables as well.[6]

The factors themselves are not accounted for much better. While the R^2 values go up (see table 1), the proportion of significant variables does not differ much and is less in some instances.

What I am suggesting, then, is the hypothesis that certain value conditions are responsive to *specific* social conditions, not to an entire range of them nor to the same ones uniformly, although I'll suggest a slight modification on this point shortly. It seems relatively clear in looking at the specific predictors that a subset of them are important for specific variables while others are not.

POWERFUL PREDICTORS

Which of the fourteen independent variables turns out to have the most predictive power? A summary matrix is presented in table 3, which shows the proportion of times specific predictors were significant.

The clearest indication comes from the two right-hand columns, where mean proportions of significance are displayed. Crude though this measure is, it does provide some overall sense of the ranking of the predictor variables. Only a few of the independent variables are important, and the range is considerable: from a low average of 19 percent to 20 percent (White, Farm, and Blue-Collar Occupations) to a high of 72 percent (Race).[7]

Confirming the political and policy nature of these data is the fact that a

Table 2
PERCENTAGE OF 14 INDEPENDENT VARIABLES SIGNIFICANT AT .05 LEVEL FOR DIFFERENT DEPENDENT VARIABLES

Dependent Variable	1952	1956	1960	1964	1968	1972	1976	1978
					YEAR			
Government Trust				14%	21%	21%	43%	21%
Government Benefits				21%	36%	29%	29%	21%
Say in Government	21%	43%	29%	14%	21%	43%	43%	29%
Voter Influence	14%	36%	64%	29%	43%	57%	64%	14%
Government Job		57%	50%	14%	50%	21%	43%	36%
Democrat Thermometer				29%	43%	43%	57%	43%
Republican Thermometer				14%	36%	43%	79%	29%
Liberal Thermometer				36%	43%	50%	59%	
Conservative Thermometer				36%	36%	50%	71%	
Government Health		50%	64%	57%	43%	43%	64%	57%
Government Power		29%	36%	36%				
Too Powerful				43%	43%	14%	64%	43%
Negro Job		21%	21%	36%	43%	50%		
Civil Rights				29%	36%	50%	36%	
Negro Position				21%	29%	36%	43%	
Rights of the Accused						71%	64%	43%
Women's Rights						29%	79%	50%
Church Attendance	43%	64%	79%	57%	79%	57%	86%	57%

Dependent Variable Factors

	1952	1956	1960	1964	1968	1972	1976	1978
1. Quest. Public Entitlements		57%	57%	29%	36%	64%[1]	50%[2,3]	
2. Public Inadequacy		36%	36%	29%	29%	29%	21%[2]	
3. Privatism				21%	50%	21%	50%[2]	
4. Public Inequity				14%	21%	36%	64%	

1. Percentages for this year may be slightly exaggerated due to artificial expansion of sample size as a result of case replication weighting.

2. 1976 -- A "private" and a "public" factor emerged, called 1976A and 1976B on Table 8. Each had 7/14 (50%) of its variables significant. 1976A, "Privatism," is a split off from one of the factors in Dimension 1., Questionable Public Entitlements.

3. Factors not available for 1978.

Table 3
PERCENTAGE OF TIMES A PARTICULAR VARIABLE IS SIGNIFICANT AT .05 LEVEL*

Dependent Variables[1]

Independent Variables	Gv. Trust 64-78 %	Gv. Benr. 64-78 %	Say Gv. 52-78 %	Vote Inf. 56-78 %	Gv. Job 56-78 %	Th. Dem. 64-78 %	Th. Rep. 64-78 %	Th. Lib. 64-78 %	Th. Cons. 64-78 %	Gv. Hlth. 56-78 %	Gv. Pow. 56-64 %	Too Pow. 64-78 %	Ngr. Job 56-72 %	Ngr. Rts. 64-76 %	Ngr. Pos. 72-76 %	Rts. Acc. 72-78 %	Women Rts. 72-78 %	Ch. Att. 52-78 %	Family Size(A)[2] 53,62/3,74 %	Family Size(B)[2] 53,62/3,74 %	x̄	n
Age	50	0	43	86	17	75	75	50	100	50	33	25	20	50	50	100	50	57	(100)	(100)	57	(20)
Education	50	25	100	100	67	25	0	100	75	83	0	25	20	100	75	100	100	86	(100)	(100)	64	(20)
Race	25	50	29	57	100	100	100	50	100	100	67	100	100	100	75	100	0	86	(33)	(33)	72	(20)
Region	25	25	29	43	0	50	50	75	25	33	100	50	100	100	50	50	50	86			57	(19)
Income	0	25	43	0	17	75	50	0	25	67	0	25	0	50	0	50	50	14	(50)		28	(19)
Marital Status	25	0	0	0	0	25	25	0	0	0	33	0	40	0	0	0	0	86			28	(18)
Party I.D.	100	100	43	29	100	100	100	100	100	100	100	50	70	50	50	100	50	43	(0)	(0)	69	(20)
Soc. Class	25	50	43	71	33	0	25	25	50	67	33	50	20	75	25	50	0	57			30	(18)
Bl-Clr.Occup.	0	0	0	14	17	0	25	25	25	0	33	25	40	0	25	50	100	57	(33)	(0)	21	(20)
Wht.Clr.Occup.	0	0	43	29	33	0	25	0	0	17	0	0	20	0	0	50	0	14			19	(18)
Farm Occup.	0	0	0	0	0	0	25	0	0	17	33	0	40	25	50	100	100	57	(33)	(33)	20	(20)
Sex	25	0	14	43	17	100	50	50	25	33	33	50	0	0	50	50	50	100	(67)	(67)	39	(20)
Cath. Rlgn.	25	75	14	43	67	25	50	50	25	83	0	100	0	0	25	50	50	100	(100)		44	(19)
Jewish Rlgn.	0	0	29	43	83	25	25	100	50	100	33	75	60	50	25	50	100	86	(0)		48	(19)

1. The dependent variable Family Size is included in this table. Since this question was not asked in 1953, 1962, and 1974, it was asked at the same interval as the other variables.

2. With respect to the Family Size variable, regression analysis was run in two separate ways. For Family Size (A), all the independent variables available in 1953, 1962, and 1974 were included. For Family Size (B), only those independent variables that were available in all 3 years were used.

* Data for years 1960 and 1976 were case replicated so that the number of independent variables that are statistically significant in these years may be slightly exaggerated.

powerful variable is Party Identification, which achieves significance about 69 percent of the time. Not all personal attributes share the same predictive power. Social Class, a self-designated measure, comes in at a much more modest 30 percent. Slightly higher than Party Identification is Race. Important in its own right, race attributes received heightened attention during this period.

The next echelon of important predictors lies in the 50 percent-to-60 percent significance range. Education, Southern Origin, and Age achieve significance as predictors 64 percent, 57 percent, and 57 percent of the time, respectively. Education and Age have a particularly distinctive influence in the formation of values. Education, by its very nature, is concerned with ideas and approaches to problems. Certainly, education in some form is inextricably intertwined with the development of opinions on important issues. But Race and Southern Origin have effects independent of Education. This suggests that ascribed statuses (rather than achieved) are important determinants of the value orientations people hold. It is probably no accident that the two predictors most highly significant are those that, whatever else their characteristics, have cultural and social focus. The South, blacks, the educated, and the political party—all have communities of their own however internally heterogeneous those communities may be.

Age ranked as only the fourth best predictor. This suggests that Age is a far less powerful predictor than is usually thought to be the case. Age is, nevertheless, powerful in the sense that it is in the top group, sharing with other variables in a pattern of influence upon values. The variables with which it shares influence are crucial ones: Race, Party Identification, Southern Origin, and Education. This sharing should temper any idea that Age is the automatic producer of certain values and beliefs.

The next echelon of variables is Jew and Catholic, at 48 percent and 44 percent of significance, respectively. With these variables we move into the larger remaining group that are significant less than half the time, a point that reinforces the thinness of the results.

Catholic identification, at 44 percent on average, is 13 percent behind Age in importance. Like Age groupings, Catholic groups may share only modest common culture. They may share common organizational and procedural commonalities (although increasingly that is not the case), and these may be crosscut to some degree by ethnic ties. In this respect Catholics may differ from Jews, who are moderately higher at 48 percent. Irving Howe's (1976) comments about Jewish immigrants are quite to the point: "Others came to their new country with one culture; the Jews came with two, and frequently more than two, cultures. One culture they carried deep *within* themselves, within their spiritual and psychic being. The other they bore *upon* themselves, like an outer garment" (p. 71, emphasis in original). But, whatever arguments one makes, in this case at least, these two identifications are quite close to each other in power, with only minimal differences.

A fourth echelon of importance is occupied by the variables Sex (39 percent), Subjective Social Class (30 percent), and Marital Status and Income (both at 28 percent). Intuitively, it seems that Sex ought to be higher than it is for reasons I shall discuss shortly. There are doubtless other elements of the cultural system where these variables would all be of great importance.

The low performance of Income is particularly surprising. Money may talk, but it is not talking much here. It appears to be more like Occupation than Education in level of strength. A given level of income may be produced through a variety of means—high salary for one family member, a combination of husband-and-wife income, and so on. What is being measured here is the *family* income of the household in which the respondent lives. It may not always be, therefore, a personal characteristic of the respondent.[8]

The least powerful of the predictor variables are those related to occupation: White Collar, Blue Collar, Farm. This is also a surprising finding. Typically thought to be powerful and a determining factor of life-style, in these analyses they do not appear to make much of a difference (although more refined measures of occupation might well be more potent).

The use of average proportions of significant variables may reveal less to some than an actual array of specific measures. Table 4 presents the median beta weights for each variable grouping and, in the two right-hand columns, an overall median (a median of medians).

The story these data tell is substantially the same as that seen in table 3. An explicit comparison between betas and the proportion of significant betas is presented in table 5, along with their rankings. While the ranks are extremely close (a rank correlation of .96), it is important to note that the beta weights are not at all large.

Using three different measures, then, R^2 values, proportion of significant betas, and median betas, the same conclusion emerges: personal characteristics are of limited use in explaining much about what people believe (at least in this aggregate way). There is, however, some observable patterning: those statuses that are ascribed, which are difficult to change, are more likely to influence beliefs than those that are more malleable. There are several reasons why this might be so. While the argument has been elaborated elsewhere (Tropman and Strate, 1983), let me mention here that statuses that cannot be changed may exert a greater "power of time" over the incumbents; i.e., the incumbents may spend more time in those statuses, which facilitates learning and identification. Individuals in these statuses may also be excluded from a broader range of interactions or, by choice, interact with others like themselves. Discrimination and/or selection might tend to reinforce in-group perspectives. In addition, such interaction with out-group members as does occur may be stereotypic and stylized, with ritualism in both exchange and response.

Table 4

MEDIAN BETA WEIGHTS OVER TIME AND SELECTED INDEPENDENT VARIABLES*

Dependent Variables[1]

Independent Variables	Gv. Trust 64-78	Gv. Bene. 64-78	Say 52-78	Say Inf. 56-78	Gv. Job 56-78	Th. Dem. 64-78	Th. Rep. 64-78	Th. Lib. 64-78	Th. Conn. 64-78	Gv. Hlth. 56-78	Gv. Pow. 56-64	Too Pow. 64-78	Ngr. Job 56-72	Cv. Rts. 64-76	Ngr. Pos. 72-76	Rts. Acc. 72-78	Women Rts. 72-78	Ch. Att. 52-78	Family Size(A)[2] 53,62/3,74	Family Size(B)[2] 53,62/3,74	x̄	n
Age	.03	-.03	-.03	-.08	.00	.11	.09	-.02	.14	-.06	-.01	.02	.04	-.03	-.04	.15	.10	-.13	(.12)	(.12)	.065	(20)
Education	-.03	-.03	.21	.19	-.17	-.04	.01	.06	.05	.13	-.01	-.02	-.02	.13	-.06	-.14	-.21	-.11	(-.09)	(-.11)	.080	(20)
Race	.00	-.02	.01	-.06	-.01	.12	-.07	.13	-.10	-.13	-.03	.10	-.26	.39	-.02	-.06	-.03	-.09	(-.02)	(.02)	.103	(20)
Region	-.03	-.01	-.02	-.04	.04	.01	-.04	-.07	.10	.05	-.09	-.01	.09	-.11	-.05	.07	-.04	-.08	(-.04)		.05	(19)
Income	-.01	-.04	-.06	.05	.04	-.06	-.02	-.00	.04	.07	-.01	-.05	.01	-.01	-.02	.03	-.03	.05	(-.03)		.035	(19)
Marital Stat.	-.01	-.01	-.01	-.01	.01	.03	.02	-.04	.04	.02	.06	.00	.03	-.04	-.02	.04	-.03	-.09			.03	(18)
Party I.D.	.10	.05	-.02	.02	.08	-.53	.46	-.21	.21	.16	-.23	-.11	.05	-.06	-.08	-.08	.03	-.04	(.00)	(-.02)	.108	(20)
Soc. Class	-.04	-.06	.02	-.07	-.03	.00	.02	-.00	.01	-.03	.00	-.05	.04	.02	-.04	-.04	-.01	-.05			.025	(18)
Bl.Clr.Occ.	-.01	.04	.02	-.02	-.01	.02	-.03	-.00	-.01	.03	.01	-.01	.04	.00	-.01	-.03	-.08	.07	(.00)	(.01)	.024	(20)
Wht.Clr.Occ.	-.01	.03	-.03	.01	-.02	-.01	-.03	-.01	-.01	.03	.00	-.01	.02	-.01	.00	-.04	-.15	.00	(-.03)	(-.02)	.024	(20)
Farm Occ.	.02	.01	.01	.01	-.01	-.01	.02	-.02	.00	.02	.04	-.02	-.01	.00	.04	.00	-.04	-.04	(-.05)	(-.05)	.021	(20)
Sex	-.04	-.01	.02	.04	.02	-.07	-.06	-.03	-.01	-.03	-.03	-.04	.04	.00	.00	-.06	.03	.13	(-.06)	(-.06)	.044	(20)
Cath. Rlgn.	-.05	-.04	-.01	-.03	-.05	.01	.03	-.02	.04	-.09	-.01	.07	-.03	.02	-.03	.01	-.02	.29	(.15)		.058	(20)
Jewish Rlgn.	.01	.02	-.04	.00	-.06	.01	-.03	.07	-.05	-.09	.01	.08	-.06	.03	.00	-.01	-.04	.08	(.01)		.038	(20)

1. The dependent variable Family Size is included in this table. Since this question was asked in 1953, 1962, and 1974, it was not asked at the same interval as the other variables.

2. With respect to the Family Size variable, regression analysis was run in two separate ways. For Family Size (A), all the independent variables available in 1953, 1962, and 1974 were included. For Family Size (B), only those independent variables that were available in all 3 years were used.

* Data for years 1960 and 1976 were case replicated due to weighting of sample cases.

Table 5

RANK ORDER COMPARISONS OF INDEPENDENT VARIABLES

Independent Variable	% Significant $\geq$ .05 Level	Rank	$\overline{\text{Med. Beta}}$	Rank
Age	57%	4	.065	4
Education	64%	3	.080	3
Race	72%	1	.103	2
Region	57%	4	.050	5
Income	28%	9	.035	9
Marital Status	28%	9	.030	10
Party Identification	69%	2	.108	1
Social Class	30%	8	.025	11
Blue Collar	21%	10	.024	12
White Collar	19%	12	.024	13
Farm Occupation	20%	11	.021	14
Sex	39%	7	.044	7
Catholic Religion	44%	6	.058	6
Jewish Religion	48%	5	.038	8

Spearman's r for ranks is .963 (accounting for ties)

Ascribed statuses, then, limit the amount of interaction status holders have with others in different statuses, simultaneously increasing the similar messages received from the in-group and limiting contradictory messages that might come from other out-groups. It may also ritualize occasions of in-group/out-group interaction, as in some black/white interaction or some male/female interaction, so that the person does not come through, only the status.

Race is one such powerful ascribed status. Party identification may be also, but we probably don't think of it in that way. But if Party Identification acts like Race or some other variables that limit interaction to an in-group and focus and stylize interaction with an out-group, then it qualifies. Physical characteristics—such as Race and Sex—are often thought of first as ascribed statuses; but belief systems—such as Party Identification and certain religious orientations (cults, for example)—may act in the same way.

Age and Education may be quasi-ascribed positions, having some features of ascribed status but also some of achieved status. Sex should be such a variable, but it does not behave like one. The plethora of "consciousness-raising" groups at that time (and to some extent today) might suggest that women did not have as sharp an awareness of their position then as they do now. (See Ehrenreich, 1983.)[9] But that observation is hypothetical and speculative; more investigation on this point is in order. At the moment, the behavior of the Sex variable counts against the line of thinking developed here, with ascribed statuses being those that affect attitudes and values more. Perhaps there are variables that mitigate the impact of ascribed status, "consciousness," for example. Perhaps the theory is wrong. For now, one will have to think of the hypothesis as a suggestion, with some variables that "behave" and some that do not.

To summarize, then, an open system can be seen here. Policy opinion has links to personal characteristics but without the degree of determinism flowing from personal characteristics that has been thought by some to be virtually axiomatic. Further, the fact that these results are consistent over the years gives additional strength to the notion of such an open system.

EXPLAINING THE DIMENSIONS

If one assumes that there are integral value dimensions, as the R^2 values reveal, then these should be easier to explain than responses to individual questions. This expectation is legitimate even if one assumes substantial looseness between the independent variables (broadly considered as structural ones) and the dependent variables (broadly considered as cultural ones). In general, the greater the measurement precision, the stronger the observed relationship among variables. In this case, by using a factor rather than individual indicators to specify the value dimension more accurately, the association should be stronger.

The factors represent, I believe, more accurate and more compelling groupings of values than do the individual questions. However imprecise those original questons were, the answers to them fall into a pattern that is consistent over the years and, for the most part, by age groups. Such consistencies define a "policy-values pattern." For three of the four factors, as is shown in table 1, the R^2 values are higher than for the individual variables.[10] As we did not change the independent portion of the equation (i.e., the same independent variables were used for the factors as for the individual variables), the improvement must lie in the improved specification of the dependent variables. Such improvement implies that the value packages may be more closely related to people's location in the social structure than individual value questions, but that values are only partially tapped; or, more accurately, a value is only partially indicated by individual questions of the sort used in this study. An individual's policy-value orientation may represent a sort of unwritten personal policy that crosses a range of items and from which, incidentally, there may be occasional variation. That personal policy may change slowly over time, if it changes at all. The similarity of the dimensions in the different age and time groups suggests that there is not as much adjustment within the life course as one might have thought.[11]

The first finding, then, is the substantially improved capacity for prediction on three of the four factors using the same independent variables as with individual questions. It suggests that there *is* a set of underlying value dimensions that can be tapped and understood. Let's look at them in more detail for the period between 1952 and 1976.

Questionable Public Entitlements

Of the fourteen independent variables, two in particular are worth considering here: Race and Party Identification. Entitlements, as I've suggested before, reflect conservativism at its positive end. One would expect, therefore, Party Identification to have a strong positive coefficient (with Strong Republican = 7). It does, and it is significant in every year. One would also predict that Race (coded 0 = White, 1 = Black) would have a negative coefficient. It does, and this is also significant in every year. The data are displayed in table 6.

In addition to Race and Party Identification, Catholic and Jewish show consistency. With the exception of Catholic in 1972, they are generally negative, as one might expect, both groups being generally supportive of welfare state orientations.

Public Inadequacy

Public Inadequacy is a dimension made up essentially of two variables. One says, "People like me don't have any say in what the government does." The other asserts, "Voting is the only way that people like me can

Table 6
FACTOR: QUESTIONABLE PUBLIC ENTITLEMENTS

	1956	1960	1964	1968	1972	1976[5]	Median*
Analysis of Variance							
Multiple R	.48	.48	.63	.59	.51		
R Square	.23	.23	.39	.35	.26		
Significance	.00	.00	.00	.00	.00		
N (sample size)	951	1087	476	647	1279		
			Beta Weights[2] (Significance)[3]				
Independent Variable[1]							
Age	.00	-.03	-.07	-.02	$.24^{xx}$[4]		.07
Education	$.24^{xx}$	$.15^{xx}$	-.02	-.06	$-.07^{x}$		.07
Race	$-.19^{xx}$	$-.17^{xx}$	$-.44^{xx}$	$-.35^{xx}$	$-.23^{xx}$		.23
Region	.00	.10	$.24^{xx}$	$.12^{xx}$	$.20^{xx}$		.12
Income	$.08^{x}$	$.10^{xx}$	.07	.01	.02		.07
Marital Status	.04	-.01	.03	.06	$.08^{xx}$		.04
Party Identification	$.17^{xx}$	$.15^{xx}$	$.30^{xx}$	$.35^{xx}$	$.24^{xx}$		.24
Social Class	$.08^{x}$	$.12^{xx}$	.04	-.03	-.02		.04
Blue Collar Occupation	.03	-.04	-.00	-.04	-.05		.04
White Collar Occupation	.01	.02	.01	.05	-.03		.02
Farm Occupation	$.07^{x}$	-.02	.04	.06	-.02		.04
Sex	-.02	$.12^{xx}$	-.00	.03	$-.06^{x}$		.03
Catholic Religion	$-.10^{xx}$	$-.08^{xx}$	-.03	$-.08^{x}$	$.07^{xx}$		.08
Jewish Religion	$-.06^{x}$	$-.08^{xx}$	$-.11^{xx}$	$-.12^{xx}$	$-.11^{xx}$		.11

1. For scoring of variables, see Appendix A.

2. Rounded to the nearest .01.

3. $^{xx}p \leq .05$; $^{x}p \leq .01$.

4. The arbitrary factor solution produced by the computer program was rotated 180 degrees. This insured that the direction of the factor would be the same over time. By changing the signs of the factor scores, the signs on the beta coefficients will be consistent over the years and reflect the actual direction of the effects of the independent variables.

5. 1976 appears as 1976A on the Privatism Table (#8).

* Sign ignored.

have any say about how the government runs things." Those who feel positively on this dimension feel that the public system of democratic influence is inadequate; all people should have some sense of efficacy in making their wills felt in the public sphere; everyone should be able to feel that there are more ways to influence government than simply voting. Data are displayed in table 7.

One factor stands out above all others: Education. The more educated feel less sense of Public Inadequacy, i.e., that they do have some ways of influencing government besides voting. In all years but one, the educated show strong, significant, negative relationships on this dimension. No other variable comes close to Education for power and consistency.

The next two variables, however, are of interest. These are Subjective Social Class and Age. Subjective Social Class shows the same pattern as Education, with a mild reversal in the last year.

Age, with its change in sign, is different. While the beta levels are not as high as for Education, they reach significance in four out of six years. That they are of opposite sign suggests that elderly respondents feel distant from the political process and do not sense that they have much impact.

Other variables also behave like Education, except that they are also not very strong. Income, for example, is associated with greater feelings of adequacy. White Collar also presents this pattern. The beta weights, however, are generally so low that, with the exception of Education, they are worth noting only in passing. This observation also holds for the two variables that are generally among the most powerful: Race and Party Identification. Each is significant only once. Except for a change in 1976, Race is mildly associated with a sense of Public Inadequacy. It is curious that there is not more of a sense of Public Inadequacy because surely blacks can claim bad treatment on the part of the public weal. Whatever the reality, these questions do not seem to tap that particular sense among blacks.

There may be something about the nature of the question that attracts a positive answer from those who have more education. The nature of influence, as it is expressed in the dimension, is more amenable to manipulation by those who have more education. It may also be that, as society becomes more complex and issues more multi-faceted, information (particularly that contained within what we call "education") becomes increasingly more central to the understanding of political issues and their resolution. In other words, political issues are more and more educational in nature, involving the skills and characteristics of the educated class.

Privatism and Self-Reliance

Support for the private, self-reliant (i.e., non-governmental) system for handling problems has been one of the prime characteristics of the "American way." Despite this emphasis, however, U.S. society has "public" schools and "public" parks. In the human-service area especially,

Table 7
FACTOR: PUBLIC INADEQUACY

	1956	1960	1964	1968	1972	1976	Median*
Analysis of Variance							
Multiple R	.47	.46	.43	.50	.46	.43	
R Square	.22	.21	.18	.25	.21	.19	
Significance	.00	.00	.00	.00	.00	.00	
N (sample size)[1]	951	1087	476	647	1279	2821	
			Beta Weights[3] (Significance)[4]				
Independent Variable[2]							
Age	$.09^{xx}$ [5]	.06	$.16^{xx}$	$.12^{xx}$	$.07^{x}$	.04	.08
Education	$-.29^{xx}$	$-.23^{xx}$	$-.27^{xx}$	$-.28^{xx}$	$-.28^{xx}$	$-.36^{xx}$	.28
Race	.02	$.07^{x}$	-.07	.03	.01	-.05	.04
Region	$.08^{xx}$	-.00	$.10^{x}$	.05	$.07^{xx}$	$.06^{xx}$	.07
Income	$-.10^{xx}$	$-.07^{x}$	-.09	.00	-.03	-.06	.07
Marital Status	-.03	.01	$.11^{x}$	.00	-.00	.02	.01
Party Identification	-.05	$-.18^{xx}$	-.08	-.05	-.01	.05	.05
Social Class	$-.09^{x}$	$-.08^{x}$	-.05	$-.15^{xx}$	$-.13^{xx}$	.00	.09
Blue Collar Occupation	-.00	.02	.04	.03	-.03	.03	.03
White Collar Occupation	-.06	-.04	.06	-.07	$-.11^{xx}$	-.05	.06
Farm Occupation	-.06	.01	-.04	-.01	-.03	-.02	.04
Sex	-.04	-.02	-.03	-.02	.01	$-.07^{xx}$	.03
Catholic Religion	.05	-.01	.06	.03	.03	.02	.03
Jewish Religion	-.00	.01	.01	$.09^{x}$	-.04	-.01	.01

1. N is case replicated in 1976.

2. For scoring of variables, see Appendix A.

3. Rounded to the nearest .01.

4. $^{xx}p \leq .05$; $^{x}p \leq .01$.

5. The arbitrary factor solution produced by the computer program was rotated 180 degrees. This insured that the direction of the factor would be the same over time. By changing the signs of the factor scores, the signs on the beta coefficients will be consistent over the years and reflect the actual direction of the effects of the independent variables.

*Sign ignored.

the nation has made grants to "private" agencies to carry out "public" purposes. This has occurred to such an extent that some social agencies have much of their budget from "public" funds, yet they still call themselves (and consider themselves) "private" (Gilbert, 1983). There is, in fact, some question whether there really exists any private system at all.

In any event, there is now substantial confusion about just what "private" and "public" are, a confusion that is indicative of the tension I spoke of earlier. Rather than be in a society in which all is private, with public coming in only occasionally, our value system (very likely the social structure itself) is sharply mixed. Privatism and self-reliance dominates, but there is a strong sense of public purpose too.

This dualism is clearly revealed in the Privatism factor. In two of the reporting years, Privatism was stressed. Then Public seemed to be the essential element. Finally, in 1976, Public and Private emerged as separate factors, picking up that element that had appeared in the Questionable Public Entitlements factor. The data are displayed in table 8.

One variable stands out as a predictor: Party Identification. The result is not unexpected. Measured as this factor is against the thermometers, there is clearly a close similarity between the idea of Party Identification and feeling warmth or coolness toward Republican, Democrat, liberal, and conservative orientations. Furthermore, the power of Party Identification relates properly to the factor; i.e., it is positive when the factor includes public indicators, negative when it includes private indicators.

Equally interesting is the fact that Age is more strongly related to the private orientation than to the public. This may reflect the historical perspective of the aged, coming as they do from periods of greater privatism.

Catholics and Jews tend to be positive on public, negative on private. They are not completely consistent in this regard, however.

Public Inequity

This factor, the last one regularly appearing, deals with public perception of fairness in government: Does one trust the government to do what is right, and does one think that the government is run for the benefit of all or for a few big interests? This is the weakest factor of all, having an R^2 value not much larger than the two chief variables themselves. Overall, only Party Identification shows any vigor, with betas ranging from $-.17$ to $+.25$, as seen in table 9. Generally, the sense of Public Inequity for partisans increases when an administration of the opposite party takes office.[12]

What may be even more surprising and deserving of some speculation is the lack of power of some of the other variables in the package. Blacks, certainly, have reason to appear more strongly here. So, too, do some of the other ethnic groups. They do not. Apparently, this factor does not tap the issues as seen by these respondents.

Table 8
FACTOR: PRIVATISM AND SELF-RELIANCE

	1964	1968	1972[6]	1976(A)[7]	1976(B)[6,7]	
Analysis of Variance						
Multiple R	.67	.47	.43	.46	.57	
R Square	.45	.23	.19	.21	.33	
Significance	.00	.00	.00	.00	.00	
N (sample size)[1]	476	647	1279	2821	2821	

Beta Weights[3] (Significance)[4]

Independent Variable[2]	(Pvt)	(Pvt)	(Public)	(Pvt)	(Public)	Median*
Age	$.09^{x}$	$.12^{xx}$ [5]	.04	$.24^{xx}$	$.08^{xx}$	.12
Education	$.10^{x}$	$.14^{xx}$	.04	-.02	$-.08^{xx}$	.08
Race	-.06	.06	$.22^{xx}$	$-.14^{xx}$	$.22^{xx}$	.14
Region	.07	$.08^{x}$	-.04	$.09^{xx}$	.02	.07
Income	.06	-.02	-.05	.01	$-.09^{xx}$	.05
Marital Status	.06	.05	-.01	$.07^{xx}$	.01	.05
Party Identification	$.57^{xx}$	$.40^{xx}$	$-.29^{xx}$	$.28^{xx}$	$-.37^{xx}$	.40
Social Class	.02	$.09^{x}$	-.00	.00	.04	.02
Blue Collar Occupation	-.00	.06	.06	-.03	-.01	.03
White Collar Occupation	.03	.00	.01	-.01	-.01	.01
Farm Occupation	-.02	.03	.01	$.05^{xx}$	.02	.03
Sex	.08	-.07	$-.09^{xx}$	$-.10^{xx}$	$-.09^{xx}$	.09
Catholic Religion	-.02	$.10^{xx}$	.04	.04	.03	.04
Jewish Religion	-.05	$-.10^{xx}$	.03	-.06	$.06^{xx}$	.06
	Th Con	Th Con	Th Lib	Th Con	Th Dem	
	Th Rep	Th Rep	Th Dem	Th Rep	Th Lib	

1. N is case replicated in 1976.

2. For scoring of variables, see Appendix A.

3. Rounded to the nearest .01.

4. $^{xx}p \leq .05$; $^{x}p \leq .01$.

5. The arbitrary factor solution produced by the computer program was rotated 180 degrees. This insured that the direction of the factor would be the same over time. By changing the signs of the factor scores, the signs on the beta coefficients will be consistent over the years and reflect the actual direction of the effects of the independent variables.

6. Signs of large beta coefficients are reversed because the variables that load heavily on this factor are the Democrat and Liberal Thermometers, which reflect the opposite or public end of the Privatism factor.

7. In 1976, the factor was split into distinctive private and public dimensions.

* Sign ignored.

Table 9
FACTOR: PUBLIC INEQUITY

	1964	1968	1972	1976	
Analysis of Variance					
Multiple R	.33	.25	.25	.21	
R Square	.11	.06	.06	.04	
Significance	.00	.00	.00	.00	
N (sample size)[1]	476	647	1279	2821	
		Beta Weights[3] (Significance)[4]			
Independent Variable[2]					**Median***
Age	.03[5]	.02	.05	.04^x	.04
Education	-.09	-.01	.03	-.03	.03
Race	.02	.03	.06^x	-.07^{xx}	.05
Region	.06	-.00	-.07^x	-.04^x	.05
Income	-.11	.05	-.06^x	.02	.06
Marital Status	.00	-.04	.01	.03^x	.02
Party Identification	.25^{xx}	.16^{xx}	-.17^{xx}	-.14^{xx}	.17
Social Class	-.01	-.14^{xx}	-.08^x	-.05^{xx}	.17
Blue Collar Occupation	-.02	-.04	.02	-.08^{xx}	.03
White Collar Occupation	.10	-.01	-.02	-.01	.02
Farm Occupation	-.02	.01	.00	-.04^x	.02
Sex	-.05	.05	-.03	-.01	.04
Catholic Religion	-.12^x	-.13^{xx}	-.03	-.08^{xx}	.10
Jewish Religion	-.01	.01	.03	.02	.02

1. N is case replicated in 1976.

2. For scoring of variables, see Appendix A.

3. Rounded to the nearest .01.

4. $^{xx}p \leq .05$; $^{x}p \leq .01$.

5. The arbitrary factor solution produced by the computer program was rotated 180 degrees. This insured that the direction of the factor would be the same over time. By changing the signs of the factor scores, the signs on the beta coefficients will be consistent over the years and reflect the actual direction of the effects of the independent variables.

* Sign ignored.

Traditionalism

This factor, emerging in 1978 and consisting of reported Church Attendance and Women's Rights, implies traditional orientations. Traditionalism is an important factor because it contains two variables on which Age has important effects.[13]

Age is the single most powerful predictor in this factor, with a beta of .20. No other predictor is higher, which gives Age a unique status. While there are other factors in which the power of Age is as strong or stronger, its position is shared by other variables. Here, Age stands alone. Of lesser importance are White Collar, at −.16, and Party Identification, at .13.

CONCLUSION

What, then, *are* the roots of values? Many still lie deeply buried, but some variables do make a difference. The consistently powerful predictors are these five: Race, Party Identification, Education, Religion, and Age. (Zavalloni, 1980, has a model that helps one to examine interactions.) That is a substantial number, and they do explain some of the variance. But not much of it—not even for a significant portion of it. In spite of all the variables this study examined, the largest fraction of variance remains unexplained. This is both surprising and problematic, especially for policymakers.

In the end it is this lack of fit that creates problems for Marx and makes a politician's life hard. In more specific settings, values and structure interact in reinforcing ways. Mortimer and Lorence (1979) provide an example from the area of occupation (p. 1364). How much easier life would be if attitudes were a simple product of social positions and personal characteristics. In a more tightly structured society, this linkage may be present. Proof to any degree will have to await intensive comparative analysis. In this society there is a more open, more fluid situation. In spite of some ascribed statuses, the dominant theme is one of changeability, of "poorness of fit" between what people are and what they think. There is a substantial independence of thought—and where more appropriate than in a country that has celebrated independence from its beginning. The United States may well be a far more open society than anyone thought. This certainly appears to be true insofar as the fixed link between values and social position is concerned.

Given this "poorness of fit," how, then, is the policymaker to proceed? How can politicians chart their way in such independent waters? De Toqueville may have provided a clue: associations. In this modern day, one might add, committees.

U.S. society, it seems, has always emphasized process over result—the commitment to means over ends. U.S. pragmatism has stressed the equality of opportunity, not the equality of result—a chance to choose, not a sponsored sinecure. And, if things are bad in one place, you move on.

Still, a means-oriented, mobile society needs some mechanism to reach agreement. It needs some mechanism to find out what other people are thinking. It needs some mechanism through which policy alternatives can be developed. Associations/committees represent institutional mechanisms through which independent minds can, with an emphasis on process, handle these problems. Voluntary associations are substitutes for firm links among social-status values. The regression analysis presented here posits too simplistic a connection, too much of a one-step, linear relationship. It might be better to use social-status variables to predict association and committee memberships and move on from there to predict values. These member-ships, these networks, provide, I believe, a values filter and direction for the link between what people are, what statuses they have, and what people think. It is this fluidity in the system that provides opportunties, at least in the short run, for influences of specific periods to become manifest.

NOTES

1. An earlier exploration of some points in this chapter appeared in the *California Sociologist*. See John E. Tropman and John Strate (1983).

2. It is worthwhile stressing this point because of the great weight analysts put on particular questions without regard for their context or structure. The possibility of using several questions within a factor analytic scheme and then increasing the R^2 value in a regression model strongly suggests that the individual questions should be looked at with great care. Furthermore, the possibility that they simply represent part of a dimension to which people are sensitive should be seriously considered. The dependent variable may be more valid as a factor.

3. This statement may be a bit facile. What I am suggesting is that the low pro-portion of explained variance is consistent with a value structure of a contradictory nature in which the actions that might flow from such a structure are unclear. I am not suggesting that, even if the value structure were clear, there still could not be important and even patterned deviations from the structure. (Although, if one were to observe a pattern of structured deviations, one might assume that these deviations received support from a substructure of the value system.) Keep in mind, however, that there is a lot of random error in both Y and X that will lower the R^2. Opponents of such an interpretation could certainly argue that low R^2 levels mean only that the measurement is imprecise.

4. In many instances, of course, they are significant at probability levels con-siderably beyond .05. Reporting increasing numbers of significant results, however, adds little to understanding, as significance depends heavily on sample size relative to the size of the universe being sampled. Beta weights are a better measure for gaining an understanding of the strength of relationships.

5. A *beta weight* is a standardized statistical measure indicating the effect of an independent variable on a dependent variable, controlling the effects of other inde-pendent variables.

6. Note, also, that the Gallup data do not do much better in either of the two regression equations, the one that matches the independent variables as much as pos-sible and the other that uses what independent variables are available in each year.

7. Such ranges represent the folly of this grouping or "kitchen sink" approach. When there are such a large number of variables, however, and one wants to take a descriptive point of view, it is quite justified.

8. That income does not predict attitude is not all *that* surprising. Attitude does not predict income, either. Morgan (1974) comments: "Several self-rated attitudes were measured for each of the five years [of the Panel Study of Income Dynamics]. They included indexes of aspiration-ambition, trust-hostility, sense of personal efficacy, and perceived propensity to plan ahead. These attitudes affected almost none of the components of economic status and their changes over time. It is not merely that these measures failed to show up for the entire sample of families . . . they also failed to affect any of the important subgroups. . . . Insofar as we have segregated important subgroups, some of whom [sic] may have had some opportunities to make adjustments in their situation, the negative evidence is impressive" (p. 388).

9. One additional comparative point on these results needs to be mentioned. One might think that the low R^2 values might be due somehow to the particular questions or to the special nature of the approach I used. Fortunately, in 1976, the survey included a list of instrumental and terminal values developed by Milton Rokeach. Rokeach developed a set of five instrumental values and five terminal values, scores for which, and for each respondent, were available. I believed it would be appropriate to perform the same regression on his values and on my value questions. The R^2 values were similarly low. For this reason I concluded that there was nothing unique about my value results. For some studies of the Rokeach values with different ages of people, see Antonucci, Gillette, and Hoyer (1979). For a general analysis, see Davis (1982).

10. There are a few cases where the R^2 value of individual questions approaches those of the factors. Republican Thermometer is the closest case. In the main, however, they are below 10 percent.

11. Keep in mind, though, that the questions were not written with the idea of tapping a central policy-value system. Neither were they written with even a set of value dimensions in mind. With the information now available, fresh, more accurate questions could be designed.

12. This finding should probably be differentiated from support for government in general, as opposed to support for particular governmental actions.

13. No table is presented for this single year.

9
AMERICAN VALUES
AND THE ELDERLY

INTRODUCTION

Previous chapters have presented a large array of figures and a considerable quantity of data. It is now time to winnow out some conclusions from all of this information about U.S. values, public opinion, and the elderly adult. Because these topics are much too broad to consider as a single unit, I will proceed in three steps. First, I will examine the U.S. society itself as the milieu in which the elderly adult lives, an environment that he or she helped to shape. Certainly, changes in the policy values of elderly adults are to some extent responses to a world they made or substantially contributed to.

Second, I will look at elderly adult values specifically. That examination will be in the context of changing values, change in which the elderly adult has played a part.

Finally, I will review the impact of values change upon policy ideas and policy history. My principal effort here will be to see if there are causes and clues that can be derived from the data that may partially explain what has happened and what is now happening and to make some better informed predictions of what may happen in the future.

AMERICAN VALUES

The data reveal a considerable amount about American values, especially the context within which policy is made and within which all of us live our lives and take our meanings. A central theme must be change. The data show quite clearly that there are important changes in what the public believes and values over time. Lipset and Schneider (1983) saw this change, too. These changes are measurable, repeated, and patterned. This would seem to preclude the possibility that they are simply casual responses to recent events. This conclusion finds support in the analysis of responses to the particular questions and even stronger support in the factor analysis of all respondents. As Lipset and Schneider comment:

Our experience with poll data convinces us that no single survey can be taken as definitive or authoritative, and few specific survey results withstand the test of time. Indeed, much of the value of the information gathered by the pollsters lies in the fact that some of them have been reporting public attitudes on the same topics for decades. . . . The basic attitudes of the American public cannot be gauged from any single question. . . . Rather, various scraps of evidence must be assembled like a mosaic and reexamined over time. (Pp. xix-xx)

Several questions may be raised about values change and its overall meaning for U.S. society. One important inquiry concerns the direction of the change. Does it point to new and innovative orientations? Alternatively, does it represent a return by the American people to more traditonal values and commitments? Another question concerns the nature and meaning of the change. Is it a crisis of legitimacy for U.S. institutions, or does it represent something less dramatic? If the latter, then why is change so pervasive in the overall pattern of responses? If the former, then how does the society hang together in the face of such shifts? The most important question, and the one I shall answer first, deals with the causes of the change. Can it be explained, and, if so, why did it occur?

Sources of Values Change

There are no easy answers to the question: Why do values change? No one can state with absolute certainty why the policy opinions represented in these data have undergone such a large shift during the third quarter of the twentieth century. Most striking are the decline in trust in government, a decided conservative shift on civil rights, and the decline in ideal family size. Recall that Lipset and Schneider (1983), in reviewing similar data, come to the following conclusion, a portion of which was quoted in chapter 1:

We suggest that the increase in political dissatisfaction was not a cognitive or ideological change; it was rather a response to events, and to the perception of events, primarily in the political sphere. The vast majority of the population was not unhappy because government policy did not respond to their ideological predispositions. They were unhappy because political leadership was proving ineffective in dealing with massive social and political problems, like war, race relations, and the economy. (P. 399)

They go on to point out that the declines that they observed seem to begin around 1965 and proceed apace. To some extent, of course, they must surely be right. This is a more specific version of Hirschman's (1982) general explanation of why positions shift. In his book, *Shifting Involvements*, he talks about disappointment as a major factor generating change. In his case, he was dealing with a shift from a private life to a public life and back to a private life once again. The full sense of a phrase I cited previously is as follows:

Accordingly, the turn to the public life would not come about as a direct result of disappointments over any specific consumption experiences. Rather, these experiences are responsible for the deflation of an ideology that had presided over the quest for private happiness. To the extent that this ideology is resolutely "antipublic," its collapse is likely to lead to a search for meaningful participation in public affairs.

In the preceding account, ideology first buttresses a certain life-style and preference pattern, and then interacts with specific disappointment experiences so as to intensify the resulting changes in (*ed.* values) preferences. But why should ideology be confined to the role of merely magnifying the oscillations in preferences that originate in the sphere of consumption and consumption-related disappointment? Ideological alienation from "consumerism"—from the quest for happiness via the accumulation of consumer goods—could surely arise ahead of specific disappointment experiences, and the opposite sequence is also eminently realistic. If I have not dealt with such situations, it is because my reasoning has remained anchored in the conventional assumption of economic theory in general, and of consumption theory in particular, which conceives of its central actors as being "decked in the glory of their *one* all purpose preference ordering," as Amartya Sen put it ironically. . . . But the task I have set myself—the explanation of large-scale changes in life-style—can be eased by a substantial modification of the conventional postulates, leading to a more complex, but also more plausible, view of the process under study. (Pp. 67-68, emphasis in original)

Hirschman anticipated the explanation offered by Lipset and Schneider, though he was working in a substantively different area. If Hirschman's idea about alienation (or disappointment) at the ideological level interacting with specific disappointments were applied to the changes seen in the data I have presented here, it might be argued that some of the activities of the 1960s were as much a *result* of declines in confidence in the public weal as they were the cause of such declines. Once they occurred, of course, they further fueled additional decline. The perception of and attention to Watergate, for example, could have been produced in part by a rising consciousness of governmental nonfeasance, misfeasance, or malfeasance. Its discovery might then be taken as evidence of the initial postulate that the government was not to be trusted. Though he does not call it such, Hirschman is actually pointing us to a version of the classic self-fulfilling prophecy in which one begins with a particular idea of what one is to find;

expects it; begins acting, therefore, in ways that bring it about; and takes that finding as confirmation of the original hypothesis.

It is at this point where a dualistic or competitive theory of values provides a bit of help in the explanation. As Hirschman talked about it, quoting Sen, conventional perspectives suggest that values are in a hierarchical list with priorities clearly discernible. A dualistic theory suggests that there are competing values with conflicting orientations available and pressing for attention and use. Whatever disappointments occur, therefore, whatever specific difficulties develop within one value realm, there is a competing value realm to which one can turn. The pair that Hirschman uses—and that I also use here—public/private, is one historically validated pair of alternatives between which we are likely to swing. In a sense, after the spectacular rise in public activities that began in the 1930s, one might have begun to expect some of the pressure inherent in the public-private duality to begin to assert itself by the late 1950s and early 1960s. This pressure would not only be part of the stimulus for a loss of confidence in the public weal, but it also provided an alternative course of legitimate action to follow.

A sound engine of change, therefore, is the tension between conflicting values. This leads to a cyclical or adjustmental theory of history.[1] (Sorokin, 1957, also has a cyclical theory.) As a practical matter, of course, the more one does (i.e., the more actions that occur within a particular area), the more disappointments are likely to develop. It was unlikely, for example, that the United States federal government, after relative successes in the Depression and World War II, could keep up such a long string of positive actions. Failures, difficulties, actions that offended people were bound to occur. These were noticed, picked up, and began to fuel a process of cultural change.

My suggestion about cultural change is based, first, on the inherent tension between pair values to which we are committed and that conflict, each with the other. There are sets of these values, and I have mentioned a set of seven that I believe to be relevant.

Coughlin (1980) also has a set of seven conflicts on the specific dimension of pro-versus anti-welfare. He does not quite see the competing commitments concept, however, either along a specific dimension (dualism) or between any two dimensions (multiplicity). He comes very close, however. Neuman (1981) similarly comes close to this conception in his study of differentiation and integration of political thinking because these two concepts provide mechanisms through which conflicting values are present (differentiation) and at least one way that they are managed (integration).

A large point, though, transcends any particular set. Competing commitments must be honored whatever the time sequence. If one attends to one side of a competing commitment for a period of time, pressure builds up to pay attention to and honor the other side of that competing commitment. Part of this tension is within the cultural system itself. One may feel personal or national guilt over not attending to certain kinds of activities that demand recognition. Lack of equality for minorities is an example.

These cultural features are also linked to social ones. There are groups that demand attention based upon and within these various value realms. The endogenous pressure to attend to areas long ignored is matched in many instances by exogenous interest groups that point to this lack of attention and demand redress. Minority inequality demonstrates how these two pressures could work. Within the basic U.S. value system, the idea of "all men are created equal" is present and demands attention, however inadequate the attention to that value has been in the past. But the pressures for change do not simply rest on the presence of ignored values. Social protest from affected groups and civil liberties associations adds to the cultural discontent and draws strength from it.

Clearly, Lipset and Schneider are partially right. Events and specific disappointments did play a role in the decline of confidence in U.S. governmental institutions. Bad news causes negative reactions. One must remember, however, that there is *always* bad news. A question that demands attention is why we choose to emphasize a particular constellation or pattern of news at any particular time.

A Crisis of Legitimacy?

This perspective on change brings me back to the first question posed at the beginning of this section: Is there a crisis of legitimacy in U.S. institutions? I believe the answer would have to be no, and it derives from a competing theory of values. There is radical change in the specific sense that there is a shift to other commitments.

If one looks only at the declining confidence in public institutions then one might see a crisis looming. If one looks only at the confidence in big institutions (whether big government, big labor, or big business), then one might see declines in confidence there. If one takes a competing theory of values as a point of departure, however, then one would expect to see concomitant emphasis on privatism, for example, while seeing a decline in support for the public weal. One might expect to see a rise in equity-based programs and rewards on the one hand, concomitant with a decline in adequacy-based programs and rewards on the other. One might expect to see a rise in personal emphasis and commitments accompanied by a decline in family emphasis and commitments.

I point out, however, that value duality is linked importantly to value multiplicity. As a result, one does not necessarily expect to see each of these changes occurring at exactly the same time. One might see a shift from public to private at Time A. At some later time, one might see a shift from family to personal. At some later time still, a shift from adequacy to equity. Indeed, the situation is one of constant shifts, with different dimensions surfacing more prominently at particular periods of time and other dimensions being less prominent. Hence, a society such as U.S. society, pluralistic in structure as it is, might well be expected to have a pluralistic structure of values. The very multiplicity of values, changing as they do, provide a moving and altering picture of the texture of the cultural fabric. Focusing on one section of that fabric may lead one to a point of concern. For example, if one looks only at the "loss of confidence" data, then one might conclude that institutions are in trouble. But if one looks at commitment to the work ethic in these data, one sees stability. (Hendrickson and Axelson, 1985, report that 89.6 percent of Americans agreed with the statement, "I am a firm believer in the work ethic" p. 298.) Similarly, only modest change was seen in reported church attendance, another indication of stability.

Lipset and Schneider, for a somewhat different set of reasons, believe that the changes they detail do not represent a crisis in legitimacy. First, because they see the declining confidence in government as a specific response to events, they believe that Americans can remain committed to the government "in general" while expressing dissatisfaction "in particular." (For a discussion of differences between general and particular views, see Katz et al., 1975.) In addition, they see the public differentiating between the system itself and the individuals who perform in that system. It is the individuals who cause the problem, not the system. I share their conviction and agree with their reasoning. More important for me, however, than the reasons they offer, is the idea that the values changes we see here are part of a normal and expected swing among competing commitments, a repatterning to meet new conditions and disappointments with older modes of traditional value components. The changes described in this volume represent, as I have metaphorically suggested before, a turn in the kaleidoscope—a new pattern of old values. The old values remain. Only the pattern they present is different. Whether such a difference represents some kind of change that is more fundamental is at best problematic. There is no persuasive evidence to suggest that the change is more fundamental than simply one of patterning. Until such evidence can be marshaled, I believe that the change should not be regarded as anything more than that.

However, new patterns in themselves may certainly have significance. In discussing swings and shifts, it is understood that a reemphasis on older patterns does not mean that the picture is exactly the same as it was in that earlier period. Rather, an emergent combination may be manifest. At the time such a pattern develops, it is difficult to tell whether or not it will be a significant one or not. The perspective of history is needed for that judgment.

Pervasiveness

Indeed, it is precisely because of the pervasiveness of the change shared so broadly by almost all segments of the U.S. population represented in the interviews reported here that one can see it as a retargeting of legitimate values, rather than a fissure and breakup of values. It does represent new directions, but these new directions point toward places we have visited before, a refurbishment of neglected value realms. It is certainly true that, if over 65 and under 30 adults are taken into consideration, there are some differences. (More about this in the next section.) These differences are modest, however, compared to the overall uniformities revealed by age. One certainly would have expected, given the different experiences and perspectives that age can engender, to find substantial differences on many items. That was not the case. Hence, the very commonality of the change suggests an integrative rather than a disintegrative function of value change here. Holding values in common bonds people to each other, even if the values they hold are changing.

Stability

Much of the focus in this section has been on the decline of confidence with respect to governmental institutions. That was not the only thing that was measured, however. Besides this change, there was stability. Two areas are worth looking at in particular: preference for stability in the work week and reported church attendance. Both seem to remain relatively constant over the years, so it would be a mistake to assume that everything is changing. Some values (confidence) are changing and some (work week) are not. This, too, is part of the kaleidoscope.

U.S. society, then, shows both change and stability. The change, however, is not the sort that fractures bonds and separates people. Rather, it is a communal decision to move to values that have been held already and have remained latent in the society since before the Depression. Those are now returning to a greater ascendency, and the more recent value orientations are likely to recede to some extent. Still, it would be an error to think that this "return" is to things exactly as they were before. No turn of the kaleidoscope, however much the new pattern may look like one that came before it, is an exact replicate of the old. Instead, there is an enfolding or "re-traditionalizing" that incorporates new elements. Whatever the degree of loss in confidence in government—and it would appear to be substantial —it is unlikely that we will return to the extremely limited role of government that existed before the Depression. We, as a culture, are now changed. We are working through and incorporating these new patterns into the old culture.

Modification and homogeneity of change, relatively speaking, are more likely to be the rule than splintering and more fundamental change. It is the difference in the modes of change rather than change itself that makes the difference between growth and decay.

VALUES BY AGE

Within this constellation of culture, what can we learn about the differences by age? Is age fundamentally important or only somewhat important? How different are the elderly from the rest of the society and in what direction? What patterns of change have the elderly exhibited over the years?

With respect to loss of confidence in governmental bodies, the elderly are similar to but somewhat less trusting than younger (under 30) respondents. On the specific question of trusting government (figure 1), the elderly are ahead of the population in exhibiting greater mistrust. These older respondents show less of a sense of control or efficacy within the political process (figure 3), and they feel slightly more warmly toward conservatives (figure 6).

With respect to some aspects of civil rights, however, that same conclusion is not appropriate. On two questions in particular (protecting the Rights of the Accused and Women's Rights), the older adults were sharply and importantly different (figures 13 and 14). It is in these kinds of results that the closed-question survey often leaves the researcher wishing for more—if only the elderly adult could elaborate on why these positions were taken. At this point it is quite possible to say that, at least in the areas of criminal justice and gender equality, the older (over 65) adult takes a more traditional posture. Within certain limitations, too, this assertion is also true of family size (figure 17). The older adult respondent has always preferred a larger family size in every period surveyed since 1942. This is the most long-standing and consistent finding that exists in these data.

With respect to other social characteristics that might be used to explain policy opinion in the public function area, Age is of moderate strength. It ranks fourth, below Party Identification, Race, and Region. While important and significant, Age does not explain a great deal of variance. Neither do any of the other variables. Indeed, it is this independence of policy-value/policy-opinion responses from important social characteristics that forces one to look for sources of change that are independent of these characteristics. It is for this reason that a conflict perspective on policy values, one that suggests that there are inherent tensions built into the value system itself, has some appeal. This follows because it is not reasonable to think that such characteristics as Income, Occupation, Religion, and so on, would be completely independent of values.[2] And some research does, indeed, suggest that some areas of structure influence values. Goudy et al. (1980) showed that some occupational categories influenced attitudes toward retirement. Mortimer and Lorence (1979) found that work affected values independent of occupational selection: "Initial value differences, which constitute the basis for occupational selection, would be heightened by occupational socialization" (p. 1364). That study echoes similar conclusions reached by Kohn and Schooler (1973). Davis (1982) did a massive study of stratification and values using forty-nine dependent variables of which forty-two were value measures. Davis used the National Opinion Research

Center's General Social Survey, so his findings provide nice confirmation for those reported here. Overall, his conclusions were much like those I reported in chapter 7:

Despite broad and representative samples and a broad spectrum of dependent variable possibilities, we have failed to find a shred of support for the "obvious" propositions that Americans' attitudes and opinions are shaped by (1) intergenerational occupational mobility "sheer" or "score," (2) occupational return on educational "investment," (3) status consistency; (4) parental occupational stratum in a vertical sense. We did see some significant statistical effects for (1) farm vs. nonfarm origins, (2) current occupational stratum, (3) educational attainment. However, the statistical associations are seldom of impressive magnitude, and the occupational associations are centered on limited topics. (P. 585)

The issue may rest on a reformulation of the questions, which can enable a look at the social characteristics as affecting the balance and configuration of value structure rather than a single value alone. Unfortunately, these data do not permit a test of that idea directly, so it must await further research.

Age, then, as revealed in these data, is a marginal modifier, not a definitive determiner of the public's view.

To understand these conclusions more fully, it is necessary to go back to the set of ideas mentioned in chapter 1. First was the null hypothesis: there is no difference between the elderly and younger adults. This perspective receives a good bit of support. In many areas the elderly are much like their younger counterparts. There is then the matter of consistency. As we do not have data on the same individuals measured over time, it is not possible to assess accurately whether or not particular individuals remained consistent. Further, the breakdown for graphs (under thirty, thirty to sixty-four, over sixty-five) are not equal in year span, which makes them inappropriate for assessing cohort consistency. (Another study of these data is under way, looking at this very question.) What is clear, however, is that "period" effects—the influence of the period of time—is important. Elderly adults, generally speaking and consistent with the first point above, moved along with everyone else. Certainly, there is no evidence of age-based rigidity in any across-the-board sense. Neither is there any general evidence for conservatism except (if one defines this as conservatism) in the family area (Family Size and Women's Rights) and Civil Rights (Women's Rights and orientation toward the criminal justice system).

Some other hypotheses, though, might interpret these data differently. Perhaps one centering on self-interest could be a key:

(1) There could be an exploration of the self-interest hypothesis; i.e., elderly adults respond as other groups do in areas where their interest is high.

(2) There could be an exploration of a hypothesis centering on social consciousness, almost a reverse of the self-interest group hypothesis. The latter might suggest

that elderly respondents, each having a lifetime of experience, may see themselves as trustees of society and seek to express views that in their judgment
represent the overall best posture for the society and directly reflect no one's
particular interest, including their own.

(3) There could be an exploration of an alienation hypothesis, to some extent a
partial inversion of the trusteeship perspective in which the elderly adult sees
himself or herself as a societal trustee with influence and responsibility. Here the
elderly respondent sees himself or herself as removed from society and distant
from it, has neither direct interests in society nor any sense of trustee role.

(4) Finally, there could be an exploration of a continuity hypothesis, exploring
whether the values during the crucial imprinting period of adolescence are
retained lifelong and that what one sees are merely the replacement effects of one
cohort after another moving in.

Conclusions from these data with respect to the influence of age on
various policy-opinion measures over time remain, finally, contradictory.
There is no clear support for any of these hypotheses evident in the data,
but some support for most of them can be found. In many instances, as I
noted, the no-difference expectation would be sustained. On questions of
trust in government there does seem to be a movement toward conservatism,
but it is mild. Elderly adults seem partially attuned and partially out of
tune with their own political interests. Results on the questions on governmental support for medical care are ambiguous, partly because of changes
in wording over surveys. Unfortunately there are no questions that directly
assess social trusteeship or social consciousness, so nothing can be said here
about them. That focus will have to be set aside, without comment, for
purposes here. The voter's influence question, however, does suggest that
the elderly respondent feels apart from the body politic. In the Civil Rights
and Women's Rights questions, one can assume a certain continuity of perspectives. In short, there's a smorgasbord of findings that permits support
for a variety of theories and perspectives (if one reports selectively) and that
could sustain arguments either for similarity to younger respondents or for
differences from them.

Overall, the vast amount of data available here for inspection suggests
that only the most modest generalizations about the relationship between
age and policy opinion can be ventured. To those who would look for
evidence of widespread intergenerational conflict, however, results are disappointing. With the exception of substantial differences in particular areas
("rights of women" or "crime," for example), commonalities seem more
than sufficient to effect bonding across generations at least within policy-
value realms.

Part of the difficulty I noted was a theoretical one. As yet, we have no
particular reason to expect that age would exert a specific influence. Age is a
category, not a social mechanism. It lacks a social dynamic that would drive

policy opinions in a certain direction. A modest beginning for such theoretical considerations was suggested in chapter 8, where I focused on the
changeability or permanence of a particular status. In this case, it is status
rigidity (ascription) rather than psychological rigidity that might be of
importance. The mechanisms of this idea, though, need much further
exploration.[3]

Age, then, has a mixed influence on policy opinion. To some extent and
in some areas, one can observe relationships. Even when those relationships
are observed, one remains unclear about the reasons why it has the effect
that it does in some areas, while in others it has so little influence. On the
basis of these data, one can set aside simplistic generalizations at least and
begin to lay out the areas of further exploration.

POLICY OPINION AND SOCIAL POLICY

The lack of clear-cut relationships between age and policy opinion points
to some areas that require further investigation. One of these, as should
now be clear, is a theory that would indicate when age should have an
influence on policy opinion and policy action (or opinion and action in
general) and when it should not. (See Barbour et al., 1982, and Daneke,
Garcia, and Delli Priscoli, 1983 for value-conflict analyses of policy.)
Another is the self-interest hypothesis, which is particularly interesting
because of the curious lack of association found in these data. In general,
one would expect individuals, groups, and organizations to support the
entities that have provided them with important resources. Clearly, in the
third quarter of this century, the elderly were among the largest groups to
gain from social-policy innovation and development, but they seemed less
than enthusiastic about this (Estes, 1980; Estes, Newcomer and Associates,
1983; Kutza, 1981).

In addition, the gains of the elderly can be identified in very specific,
concrete terms. The government provided substantial and indexed increases
in Social Security income. It has embarked on a medical plan (Medicare) to
aid the elderly adult. The government has also provided substantial tax
benefits and set up programs on aging that provide a variety of practical,
useful services for the elderly throughout the country. It would be hard to
find another group that has benefited as much from policy initiatives at the
federal level than those over sixty years of age. State and local governments,
likewise, have joined with the federal government in providing benefits for
the elderly through property tax credits, local tax millages targeted for the
elderly, and so on.

If any single thing could be thought of as an essential component in a
theory of why the elderly should respond to policy-opinion questions in a
particular way, it would be that they, as a group in society, have benefited
immensely from governmental activity and have substantial interests to

protect and enhance. Thus, if the elderly respondents are viewed simply as a group of beneficiaries of governmental programs rather than as a group of a particular age or a particular gender, then one might expect them to differ sharply from non-beneficiaries.

One might further expect that elderly respondents would support governmental action enthusiastically and would feel a sense of efficacy and impact based upon the evidence of policy success at all levels of government. On the basis of political success, concrete benefits gained, specific changes and improvements in life-style, sharp differences between the young and the old should have been found. They were not.

While some analysts might take solace from the similarities exhibited here between the elderly and younger respondents and use these similarities as evidence for intergenerational bonding, it is hard to escape the idea that these findings are very curious, indeed, if not inexplicable, with respect to conventional political wisdom. The question on Government Medical Care (figure 7) is the most direct demonstration of this curiosity. Support for Government Medical Care, overall and by age, appears to be falling. Admittedly, the question wording changed; in the later years especially, the unfortunate introduction of language focusing on costs might have contributed to falling rates of support. Yet, even there, reason argues that when people are thinking of their own benefits to be paid for out of some large, collective fund, questions of cost should not be overwhelmingly important.

The data suggest that self-interest is not sufficient. Elderly adults show decreasing support for programs that have benefited them directly, importantly, and in a crucial area of concern. This curiosity requires additional, in-depth investigation where one can seek to understand the thinking and reasoning that leads to particular responses. If elderly adults actually have been taking positions over the years that have been contrary to their own interests, this discrepancy is most unsettling and needs to be explained.[4]

This curious gap between the conditions of one group of respondents and their responses over time prefigures another, larger issue of a similar sort. If one looks at society as a whole over the period from 1952 to 1978, one sees a truly steep curve of governmental activity and growth in almost every area. Social programs were among the largest areas, but other governmental areas at both federal and state levels grew, too. If one can imagine a curve of governmental activity, therefore, tracing number of employees, money, number of laws, and so on, that curve would show a sharp ascendancy over time. If one were to add to that graph a curve of the general findings presented here—a line that might be called "Support for Government"—it would clearly show a descent over time. The conundrum is this: governmental activity and support for its activity seem to be moving in generally opposite directions over the course of the 1950 to 1978 period.

It appears that there has been a discrepancy between what the society was doing and what it was thinking. There are a number of possible explanations. One of them, noted in chapter 1, is the inverse of William Fielding

Ogburn's (see Faris, 1968, vol. 3, p. 450) famous concept of "cultural lag." Ogburn argued that technological change proceeded more swiftly than cultural values could accommodate. Hence, culture lagged behind the social structure. In this particular case, we might think of a companion concept of social lag in which the government was acting in ways that did not have full support from the populace, including groups benefiting from governmental activity. But the lack of support took time to coalesce, mature, and express itself in some kind of structured way. One might argue, therefore, that the election of Ronald Reagan to the presidency in the 1980s was an electoral manifestation of attitudes that had been building throughout the 1950s, 1960s, and 1970s.

This approach suggests that the culture and the structure of any society may act in ways to counterbalance each other. In a sense the culture acted as a brake on even more governmental activity than we have already seen. However great the current kind of governmental activity, that level might well have been greater if there had been unequivocal and mounting support for it rather than questionable and eroding support.

The conflict theory of values provides some help here, as well. The "mechanical balance" theory I've just alluded to tends to assume one set of social actions and one set of cultural beliefs/opinions/values. In fact, there are multiple and conflicting activities on both sides of that equation. Clearly, governmental activity was drawing support from and building on some subset of values and attitudes within the American people. Government could not proceed at all without the consent of the governed in either informal or formal ways. At the same time, and doubtless in the same people in many cases, support was present and, perhaps, even building for adequacy values, public values, familial values. Countervailing tendencies were also developing within the value system, supporting privatism, personalism, and "equalitarian" approaches to social life. Unfortunately, the study questions used for this volume did not measure attitudes in ways reflective of this particular perspective. I can only offer, therefore, a speculation; namely, that whatever distrust for government was manifest, there was, at the same time, support for government. That support may have eroded over time, and the reigning political consensus may have inverted, i.e., turned from one prominent or dominant subset of values to another. These changes do not happen overnight. As the value system shifted, changed, turned around, so then might have the political system. Hirschman's point is germane here, as well. That turnaround was doubtless augmented and substantially enhanced by disappointment—the more one does, the more problems one may encounter.[5]

The problem to be investigated is one that lays out in more specific detail the statics and dynamics of the cultural system—the system of values, beliefs, and attitudes—within a perspective that sees these values, beliefs, and attitudes in constant conflict with each other within the same individuals, communities, organizations, and society itself. At crucial times, some subsets of values are waxing and others are waning. Once a clear picture of this very complex system is made available, it will be easier to map the relationships between what people think and what people do across a wide range of human thought and action.

NOTES

1. This idea of cycles has some similarity to the recent work of Harvey Wasserman in his book *American Born and Reborn*. He talks about cycles of history in terms of Phase One—Bursts of Energy; Phase Two—Awakening; Phase Three—War; Phase Four—Reaction; Phase Five—Aftermath. These are social rather than cultural cycles, and the relationship between social and cultural cycles remains to be explored. Nonetheless, the idea is present.

2. They may not be. There is doubtless a complex pattern of relationships among social characteristics and social values/social opinion. That we are not able to map these connections should not be taken as evidence that they do not exist. It is only that we have not had the wit, as yet, to discern the patterns. Neither should this point be taken to mean that the cultural structure is completely dependent on the social structure, a dependence to be revealed when the connections are better understood. Rather, some aspects of the cultural structure may be determined both by the other aspects of the cultural structure and by aspects of the social structure. Similarly, some aspects of the social structure may be determined by other aspects of the social structure and by the cultural structure. It is likely that the processes of influence are made up of long links of variables or long chains of relationships (see Gardner, 1983). It is far more likely that the model resembles A → B → C → D → E → F → G than the far more simplistic A → G, which we have used in this analysis. Another factor has to do with correctly understanding the role of time and then lagging variables appropriately to measure their influence. The simultaneity of the influence of events assumed here is likely to be wrong. It is certainly as probable that social characteristics influence events in the future as much as currently. The relationships need to be explored in much more detail.

3. In any event, Age is a category that has asymmetrical rigidity, like Education. One can go up; one cannot go down. Age is different, therefore, in a theoretical sense from Income or Occupation (where two-way change is possible) and from Race and Sex (where no change is normally possible). It is likely that the different social features of these status positions may, and almost certainly do, have different impacts on the individuals holding them. The nature of these impacts cries out for further exploration. There is one other point to make here. Over history, social designations and definitions of these categories may themselves change. Today, for example, it is understood that one may change jobs, even occupations, with relative ease. That has not always been the case. In the England of Karl Marx's time, occupation was for the most part a permanent, unchangeable status, *like race*. Marx's theory of revolution might well have been based on the unexamined assumption that both the classes and the people in those classes were fixed and unchangeable and would grind against each other until an inevitable explosion occurred. Time has refuted the assumption, but inherent in it is a point well worth considering; namely, there are actually two things that must be taken into consideration—the social designation and the persons occupying the designation. Whole classes can become more

open or more rigidly fixed. Individuals have relative freedom to move into and out of those classes. Indeed, both changes can occur simultaneously, which further complicates the social-structure picture.

4. One possible explanation for this discrepancy is contained in the idea of social trusteeship. One might argue that elderly adults have crucial interests, even in the medical area, to enhance the total health needs of society. They may believe, rightly or wrongly, that less governmental activity, even if that hurts them, may substantially aid societal health and, therefore, support it.

5. The problem of disappointment may be especially acute in the social-policy area. Dealing with those who are poor, unemployed, and handicapped has always presented an evocative and difficult set of problems surrounded by high affect and tumult. More significant for Hirschman's theory, however, is that the results are masked, uneven, and often difficult to point to. If one builds a bridge, it's there to be used. It either stands or falls. If one seeks to ameliorate social conflict, the success or failure of one's interventions may never be known. It's much easier to imagine what things may have been like without the bridge than it is to imagine what things would have been like without the mediator, counselor, or package of financial support that prevented even worse problems. Success is, thus, not easy to claim, and failure is easy to attribute.

APPENDICES

APPENDIX A
FREQUENCY DATA FOR
FLOATING BAR CHARTS

TABLES A1 THROUGH A5 AND A7 THROUGH A17

Table numbers correspond to figure numbers. Tables A1 to A15 are from the National Election Study, Inter-university Consortium for Social and Political Research, The University of Michigan, Ann Arbor, MI 48109. Data for tables A16 and A17 come from the Gallup Poll, Roper Center, Storrs, CT. 06268.

All Respondents

	1958	1964	1966	1968	1970	1972	1974	1976	1978
Always	16%	14%	17%	7%	7%	7%	3%	3%	3%
Most of the Time	57%	62%	48%	54%	47%	48%	34%	30%	27%
Depends	–	–	1%	–	–	–	–	–	–
Some of the Time	23%	22%	28%	36%	44%	44%	61%	62%	64%
Never	0%	0%	3%	0%	1%	0%	1%	2%	4%
Don't Know	4%	2%	3%	2%	2%	2%	2%	3%	3%
Total %	100%	100%	100%	99%	101%	101%	101%	100%	101%

Trust in Government
By Age

	Age	1958	1964	1966	1968	1970	1972	1974	1976	1978
Always	Under 30	19%	17%	20%	7%	6%	6%	4%	4%	2%
	30-64	15%	14%	16%	8%	7%	5%	2%	3%	2%
	Over 65	15%	12%	16%	7%	6%	4%	3%	3%	5%
Most of	Under 30	59%	65%	51%	63%	52%	50%	39%	34%	31%
the Time	30-64	59%	63%	49%	54%	48%	48%	33%	30%	27%
	Over 65	48%	59%	42%	44%	39%	42%	25%	25%	19%
Depends	Under 30	–	–	2%	29%	–	–	–	–	–
	30-64	–	–	1%	36%	–	–	–	–	–
	Over 65	–	–	2%	45%	–	–	–	–	–
Some of	Under 30	20%	18%	22%		40%	41%	55%	61%	62%
the Time	30-64	23%	22%	29%		44%	45%	64%	63%	64%
	Over 65	30%	25%	31%		51%	49%	60%	62%	67%
Never	Under 30	–	–	1%	–	–	1%	0%	0%	4%
	30-64	–	–	3%	–	–	0%	0%	1%	4%
	Over 65	–	–	3%	–	–	1%	2%	0%	2%
Don't Know	Under 30	3%	0%	4%	1%	2%	2%	2%	1%	2%
	30-64	3%	1%	2%	2%	1%	2%	1%	3%	3%
	Over 65	7%	5%	6%	4%	5%	4%	6%	10%	7%
Total %	Under 30	101%	100%	100%	100%	100%	100%	100%	100%	101%
	30-64	100%	100%	100%	100%	100%	100%	100%	100%	100%
	Over 65	100%	101%	100%	100%	101%	100%	100%	100%	100%

187

WHO IS THE GOVERNMENT RUN FOR THE BENEFIT OF?

All Respondents

	1958	1964	1966	1968	1970	1972	1974	1976	1978
Give Everyone a Fair Break	18%	64%	53%	51%	41%	38%	25%	24%	24%
Pro-Con Depends	1%	4%	6%	5%	5%	3%	2%	2%	1%
Few Big Interests	76%	29%	33%	40%	50%	53%	66%	66%	67%
Don't Know	5%	4%	7%	5%	4%	7%	7%	7%	8%
Total %	100%	101%	99%	101%	100%	101%	100%	99%	100%

Who Is the Government Run For the Benefit Of?

By Age

	Age	1958	1964	1966	1968	1970	1972	1974	1976	1978
Give	Under 30	16%	70%	61%	56%	50%	39%	30%	25%	26%
Everyone	30-64	18%	64%	54%	52%	41%	38%	24%	24%	25%
a Break	Over 65	20%	57%	42%	43%	30%	36%	20%	23%	21%
Pro-Con	Under 30	1%	3%	5%	7%	5%	2%	3%	2%	1%
Depends	30-64	1%	5%	7%	5%	6%	3%	3%	3%	1%
	Over 65	0%	2%	6%	3%	4%	2%	1%	2%	1%
Few Big	Under 30	79%	24%	28%	35%	43%	54%	61%	68%	64%
Interests	30-64	77%	29%	33%	39%	50%	53%	68%	67%	67%
	Over 65	71%	33%	41%	47%	59%	53%	68%	63%	68%
	Under 30	3%	2%	7%	2%	3%	5%	7%	5%	9%
Don't Know	30-64	5%	3%	6%	5%	3%	6%	5%	6%	7%
	Over 65	10%	8%	12%	7%	8%	9%	11%	13%	11%
	Under 30	99%	99%	101%	100%	101%	100%	101%	100%	100%
Total %	30-64	101%	101%	100%	101%	100%	100%	100%	100%	100%
	Over 65	101%	100%	101%	100%	101%	100%	100%	101%	101%

PEOPLE LIKE ME DON'T HAVE ANY SAY ABOUT WHAT THE GOVERNMENT DOES

All Respondents

	1952	1956	1960	1964	1966	1968	1970	1972	1974	1976	1978
Agree	31%	28%	27%	29%	34%	41%	36%	40%	40%	41%	45%
Depends	-	-	-	-	5%	-	-	-	-	-	-
Disagree	68%	71%	72%	70%	60%	59%	64%	59%	57%	56%	53%
Don't Know (Depends, 1974,76)	1%	1%	1%	1%	1%	0%	0%	1%	3%	3%	2%
Total %	100%	100%	100%	100%	100%	100%	100%	100%	100%	100%	100%

People Like Me Don't Have Any Say About What the Government Does
By Age

	Age	1952	1956	1960	1964	1966	1968	1970	1972	1974	1976	1978
Agree	Under 30	30%	26%	20%	23%	28%	32%	36%	40%	36%	44%	45%
	30-64	29%	27%	26%	29%	33%	41%	33%	38%	37%	38%	43%
	Over 65	42%	42%	37%	39%	44%	54%	44%	50%	54%	45%	52%
Depends	Under 30	-	-	-	-	5%	-	-	-	-	-	-
	30-64	-	-	-	-	5%	-	-	-	-	-	-
	Over 65	-	-	-	-	8%	-	-	-	-	-	-
Disagree	Under 30	69%	74%	79%	77%	67%	68%	64%	60%	62%	55%	54%
	30-64	70%	73%	73%	70%	63%	59%	67%	62%	61%	59%	55%
	Over 65	57%	56%	62%	59%	48%	45%	55%	49%	41%	50%	45%
Don't Know (Depends, 1974, 76)	Under 30	1%	1%	0%	0%	0%	0%	1%	0%	2%	1%	2%
	30-64	1%	1%	1%	1%	0%	0%	1%	1%	2%	3%	2%
	Over 65	2%	2%	1%	3%	1%	1%	2%	1%	4%	5%	3%
Total %	Under 30	100%	101%	99%	100%	100%	100%	101%	100%	100%	100%	101%
	30-64	100%	101%	100%	100%	101%	100%	101%	101%	100%	100%	100%
	Over 65	101%	100%	100%	101%	101%	100%	101%	100%	99%	100%	100%

VOTING IS THE ONLY WAY THAT PEOPLE LIKE ME CAN HAVE ANY SAY ABOUT HOW
THE GOVERNMENT RUNS THINGS

All Respondents

	1952	1956	1960	1964	1966	1968	1970	1972	1974	1976	1978
Agree	81%	73%	73%	73%	68%	57%	60%	62%	60%	55%	58%
Depends	-	-	-	-	4%	-	-	-	-	-	-
Disagree	17%	25%	25%	26%	27%	42%	39%	37%	37%	42%	40%
Don't Know (Depends 1974, 76)	2%	2%	2%	1%	1%	1%	1%	1%	3%	3%	2%
Total %	100%	100%	100%	100%	100%	100%	100%	100%	100%	100%	100%

Voting is the Only Way That People Like Me Can Have Any Say About How
The Government Runs Things

By Age

	Age	1952	1956	1960	1964	1966	1968	1970	1972	1974	1976	1978
Agree	Under 30	78%	70%	71%	66%	63%	42%	53%	54%	47%	50%	51%
	30-64	82%	73%	72%	73%	66%	56%	59%	61%	61%	52%	58%
	Over 65	85%	82%	81%	85%	83%	77%	74%	78%	76%	72%	70%
Depends	Under 30	-	-	-	-	3%	-	-	-	-	-	-
	30-64	-	-	-	-	4%	-	-	-	-	-	-
	Over 65	-	-	-	-	8%	-	-	-	-	-	-
Disagree	Under 30	20%	29%	29%	34%	34%	57%	47%	45%	49%	47%	47%
	30-64	17%	27%	26%	26%	30%	43%	41%	38%	37%	46%	40%
	Over 65	13%	13%	17%	14%	8%	21%	24%	21%	19%	24%	26%
Don't Know (Depends, 1974, 76)	Under 30	3%	2%	0%	0%	0%	1%	1%	0%	4%	3%	2%
	30-64	1%	1%	2%	1%	0%	1%	0%	1%	2%	2%	2%
	Over 65	2%	5%	2%	2%	1%	2%	2%	1%	5%	5%	5%
Total %	Under 30	101%	101%	100%	100%	100%	100%	101%	99%	100%	100%	100%
	30-64	100%	101%	100%	100%	100%	100%	100%	100%	100%	100%	100%
	Over 65	100%	100%	100%	101%	100%	100%	100%	100%	100%	101%	101%

Table A5
PUBLIC ATTITUDES TOWARDS GOVERNMENT ACTION TO INSURE EVERYONE A JOB
(AND A GOOD STANDARD OF LIVING)

All Respondents

	1956	1958	1960	1964	1968	1972	1974	1976	1978
Agree Strongly; Agree, But Not Very Strongly	57%	57%	58%	31%	31%	27%	25%	24%	17%
Not Sure; It Depends	7%	7%	8%	11%	11%	20%	20%	17%	19%
Disagree Strongly; Disagree, But Not Very Strongly	27%	26%	24%	43%	47%	38%	37%	38%	43%
Don't Know; No Opinion	10%	10%	10%	15%	11%	15%	18%	20%	21%
Total %	101%	100%	100%	100%	100%	100%	100%	99%	100%

Public Attitudes Towards Government Action to Insure Everyone a Job
(and a Good Standard of Living)

By Age

	Age	1956	1958	1960	1964	1968	1972	1974	1976	1978
Agree Strongly;	Under 30	57%	57%	66%	32%	34%	31%	33%	26%	21%
Agree, But Not	30-64	56%	56%	57%	31%	31%	24%	21%	23%	15%
Very Strongly	Over 65	62%	59%	64%	32%	31%	33%	23%	23%	18%
Not Sure;	Under 30	7%	11%	11%	12%	14%	19%	19%	20%	22%
It Depends	30-64	7%	7%	8%	11%	11%	22%	22%	17%	18%
	Over 65	4%	5%	5%	9%	8%	14%	19%	15%	18%
Disagree Strongly;	Under 30	28%	22%	20%	39%	45%	38%	28%	35%	41%
Disagree, But	30-64	28%	28%	26%	44%	49%	41%	42%	42%	46%
Not Very Strongly	Over 65	20%	24%	19%	42%	43%	31%	36%	34%	37%
	Under 30	9%	11%	4%	17%	7%	12%	20%	19%	17%
Don't Know; No Opinion	30-64	9%	10%	10%	14%	10%	13%	15%	18%	20%
	Over 65	15%	12%	13%	17%	18%	22%	23%	27%	28%
	Under 30	101%	101%	101%	100%	100%	100%	100%	100%	101%
Total %	30-64	100%	101%	101%	100%	101%	100%	100%	100%	99%
	Over 65	101%	100%	101%	100%	100%	100%	101%	99%	101%

PUBLIC SUPPORT FOR GOVERNMENT INVOLVEMENT IN HEALTH CARE

All Respondents

	1956	1960	1962	1964	1968	1970	1972	1976	1978
Favors Government Action	54%	60%	61%	50%	52%	39%	37%	35%	37%
Not Sure; Depends; Neutral	8%	12%	0%	6%	6%	13%	12%	10%	11%
Opposes Government Action	26%	20%	24%	28%	27%	35%	33%	34%	35%
Don't Know; No Opinion	12%	9%	15%	16%	16%	14%	18%	21%	17%
Total %	100%	101%	100%	100%	101%	101%	100%	100%	100%

Public Support for Government Involvement in Health Care
By Age

	Age	1956	1960	1962	1964	1968	1970	1972	1976	1978
Favors	Under 30	52%	60%	55%	49%	45%	38%	39%	38%	34%
Government	30-64	53%	57%	62%	49%	52%	38%	36%	34%	37%
Action	Over 65	63%	74%	66%	58%	60%	46%	41%	35%	45%
Not Sure;	Under 30	12%	12%	–	4%	5%	12%	11%	7%	12%
Depends;	30-64	8%	12%	–	7%	6%	12%	12%	11%	11%
Neutral	Over 65	4%	9%	–	4%	3%	15%	13%	12%	8%
Opposes	Under 30	25%	20%	27%	27%	29%	35%	32%	33%	33%
Government	30-64	28%	22%	23%	30%	27%	39%	37%	37%	37%
Action	Over 65	15%	11%	20%	23%	23%	20%	20%	26%	26%
	Under 30	12%	9%	18%	21%	21%	16%	19%	22%	21%
Don't Know;	30-64	11%	9%	15%	15%	15%	11%	15%	19%	15%
No Opinion	Over 65	18%	7%	14%	16%	14%	20%	26%	27%	21%
	Under 30	101%	101%	100%	101%	100%	101%	101%	100%	100%
Total %	30-64	100%	100%	100%	101%	100%	100%	100%	101%	100%
	Over 65	100%	101%	100%	101%	100%	101%	100%	100%	100%

OPINION ON GOVERNMENT INVOLVEMENT IN ELECTRIC POWER AND HOUSING

All Respondents

	1956	1958	1960	1964
Agree. Leave for Private Businessmen to Handle.	42%	44%	48%	39%
Not Sure; It Depends.	7%	6%	6%	4%
Disagree. Government Should Be Involved.	23%	23%	22%	19%
Don't Know; No Opinion.	29%	27%	23%	37%
Total %	101%	100%	99%	99%

Opinion on Government Involvement in Electric Power and Housing
By Age

	Age	1956	1958	1960	1964
Agree. Leave for	Under 30	37%	33%	47%	33%
Private Businessmen	30-64	42%	46%	49%	41%
To Handle.	Over 65	42%	44%	48%	40%
Not Sure;	Under 30	6%	7%	2%	4%
It Depends.	30-64	8%	6%	8%	4%
	Over 65	4%	5%	3%	4%
Disagree.	Under 30	27%	25%	20%	18%
Government Should	30-64	23%	24%	24%	20%
Be Involved.	Over 65	16%	18%	15%	16%
Don't Know;	Under 30	30%	34%	32%	46%
No Opinion.	30-64	27%	24%	19%	34%
	Over 65	38%	33%	34%	41%
	Under 30	100%	99%	101%	101%
Total %	30-64	100%	100%	100%	99%
	Over 65	100%	100%	100%	101%

IS THE GOVERNMENT IN WASHINGTON GETTING TOO POWERFUL?

All Respondents

	1964	1966	1968	1970	1972	1976	1978
The Government Is Getting Too Powerful.	30%	39%	41%	31%	41%	49%	43%
Other; Depends.	3%	4%	3%	6%	4%	3%	2%
The Government Is Not Getting Too Powerful.	36%	27%	30%	33%	27%	20%	14%
Don't Know; No Opinion.	31%	31%	27%	30%	28%	28%	42%
Total %	100%	101%	101%	100%	100%	100%	101%

Is the Government In Washington Getting Too Powerful?
By Age

	Age	1964	1966	1968	1970	1972	1976	1978
The Government Is Getting Too Powerful.	Under 30	26%	35%	40%	25%	41%	47%	37%
	30-64	31%	37%	42%	33%	42%	54%	46%
	Over 65	33%	48%	35%	31%	38%	40%	42%
Other; Depends.	Under 30	5%	6%	5%	8%	5%	4%	2%
	30-64	3%	3%	2%	5%	3%	3%	1%
	Over 65	2%	1%	2%	5%	3%	1%	2%
The Government Is Not Getting Too Powerful.	Under 30	38%	29%	28%	37%	25%	20%	13%
	30-64	35%	29%	31%	34%	28%	20%	14%
	Over 65	36%	16%	30%	28%	28%	19%	15%
Don't Know; No Opinion.	Under 30	32%	29%	27%	31%	29%	29%	48%
	30-64	31%	30%	25%	28%	27%	24%	39%
	Over 65	30%	35%	33%	37%	31%	40%	42%
Total %	Under 30	101%	99%	100%	101%	100%	100%	100%
	30-64	100%	99%	100%	100%	100%	101%	100%
	Over 65	101%	100%	100%	101%	100%	100%	101%

Table A10

SHOULD GOVERNMENT SEE TO IT THAT BLACKS GET FAIR TREATMENT IN JOBS AND HOUSING?

All Respondents

	1952	1956	1958	1960	1964	1968	1972
National Government Should Take Action[a]	23%	61%	64%	64%	39%	38%	42%
Government Should Take Action[b]	14%	7%	6%	7%	7%	6%	6%
State Government Should Take Action[c]	31%	19%	18%	18%	40%	43%	35%
Government Should Stay Out Entirely[d]	20%	–	–	–	–	–	–
Favors Restrictive Legislation	5%	–	–	–	–	–	–
Don't Know	6%	13%	12%	11%	14%	13%	17%
Total %	99%	100%	100%	100%	100%	100%	100%

Should Government See To It That Blacks Get Fair Treatment in Jobs and Housing?

By Age

	Age	1956	1958	1960	1964	1968	1972
National Government Should Take Action[a]	Under 30	60%	68%	66%	44%	42%	48%
	30-64	61%	63%	65%	39%	38%	40%
	Over 65	64%	62%	60%	35%	34%	38%
Government Should Take Action[b]	Under 30	7%	6%	7%	7%	10%	5%
	30-64	7%	6%	8%	7%	6%	7%
	Over 65	4%	6%	6%	8%	3%	5%
State Government Should Take Action[c]	Under 30	22%	14%	21%	37%	40%	32%
	30-64	19%	19%	18%	41%	44%	37%
	Over 65	16%	19%	16%	40%	40%	35%
Government Should Stay Out Entirely[d]	Under 30	11%	13%	7%	13%	9%	15%
	30-64	13%	12%	9%	13%	11%	17%
	Over 65	17%	13%	18%	17%	23%	22%
Total %	Under 30	101%	101%	101%	101%	101%	100%
	30-64	100%	100%	100%	100%	99%	101%
	Over 65	101%	100%	100%	100%	100%	100%

a   Answer in 1952. In 1956-1960, answer was "Agree." In 1964-1972, answer was "National Government Should Get Involved."
b   Answer used in 1952. In 1958-1960, answer was "Not Sure." In 1964-1972, answer was "Other; Depends."
c   Answer used in 1952. In 1958-1956, answer was "Disagree." In 1964-1972, answer was "State and Local Communities."
d   Answer used in 1952. In 1956-1972, answer was "Don't Know; No Opinion."

PUBLIC ATTITUDES TOWARD THE SPEED OF THE CIVIL RIGHTS MOVEMENT

All Respondents

	1964	1966	1968	1972	1976
Too Fast; Somewhat Too Fast	63%	65%	63%	46%	39%
Depends	–	–	–	–	–
About Right	25%	19%	28%	41%	47%
Too Slow; Somewhat Too Slow	5%	5%	7%	8%	8%
Don't Know	6%	11%	3%	5%	5%
Total %	99%	100%	101%	100%	99%

Public Attitudes Toward the Speed of the Civil Rights Movement
By Age

	Age	1964	1966	1968	1972	1976
Too Fast; Somewhat Too Fast	Under 30	63%	62%	59%	39%	34%
	30-64	64%	65%	65%	49%	41%
	Over 65	61%	67%	57%	47%	43%
Depends	Under 30	–	1%	–	–	–
	30-64	–	1%	–	–	–
	Over 65	–	0%	–	–	–
About Right	Under 30	24%	22%	29%	45%	51%
	30-64	26%	20%	28%	40%	46%
	Over 65	24%	13%	26%	39%	44%
Too Slow; Somewhat Too Slow	Under 30	8%	8%	10%	13%	11%
	30-64	5%	4%	5%	7%	8%
	Over 65	5%	3%	8%	5%	5%
Don't Know	Under 30	5%	7%	2%	3%	4%
	30-64	6%	10%	2%	4%	5%
	Over 65	10%	17%	8%	9%	9%
Total %	Under 30	100%	100%	100%	100%	100%
	30-64	101%	100%	100%	100%	100%
	Over 65	100%	100%	99%	100%	101%

Table A12

PUBLIC ATTITUDE TOWARDS CHANGE IN THE POSITION OF NEGROES (BLACKS)

All Respondents

	1964	1966	1968	1972	1976
A Lot of Progress	41%	39%	50%	55%	59%
Some Progress	38%	39%	35%	35%	32%
Not Much Progress	19%	18%	14%	8%	7%
Don't Know	2%	4%	1%	2%	2%
Total %	100%	100%	100%	100%	100%

Public Attitude Towards Change in the Position of Negroes (Blacks)
By Age

	Age	1964	1966	1968	1972	1976
A Lot of Progress	Under 30	42%	41%	50%	52%	51%
	30-64	40%	40%	52%	57%	61%
	Over 65	39%	36%	44%	53%	64%
Some Progress	Under 30	33%	40%	34%	39%	41%
	30-64	40%	38%	34%	34%	30%
	Over 65	35%	40%	37%	33%	25%
Not Much Progress	Under 30	23%	16%	15%	8%	8%
	30-64	18%	18%	13%	7%	7%
	Over 65	22%	17%	16%	10%	6%
Don't Know	Under 30	2%	3%	0%	1%	
	30-64	2%	4%	1%	1%	2%
	Over 65	4%	7%	4%	4%	4%
Total %	Under 30	100%	100%	99%	100%	100%
	30-64	100%	100%	100%	99%	100%
	Over 65	100%	100%	101%	100%	99%

197

Table A13

PUBLIC ATTITUDE TOWARDS PROTECTING THE RIGHTS OF THE ACCUSED

All Respondents

	1970	1972	1974	1976	1978
Protect Rights of Accused (1-3)	29%	30%	33%	28%	23%
Neutral (4)	15%	16%	16%	14%	16%
Stop Crime (5-7)	42%	40%	34%	40%	46%
Don't Know; No Opinion	13%	14%	17%	18%	15%
Total %	99%	100%	100%	100%	100%

Public Attitude Towards Protecting the Rights of the Accused
By Age

	Age	1970	1972	1974	1976	1978
Protect Rights	Under 30	39%	40%	45%	37%	33%
of Accused	30-64	30%	31%	30%	27%	20%
(1 - 3)	Over 65	16%	14%	19%	18%	18%
	Under 30	17%	17%	14%	14%	18%
Neutral (4)	30-64	15%	17%	17%	16%	16%
	Over 65	13%	11%	15%	9%	10%
	Under 30	34%	33%	22%	36%	39%
Stop Crime	30-64	43%	40%	39%	41%	48%
(5 - 7)	Over 65	48%	50%	41%	44%	51%
Don't Know;	Under 30	10%	9%	19%	13%	11%
No Opinion	30-64	12%	9%	14%	15%	16%
	Over 65	23%	17%	24%	30%	23%
	Under 30	100%	99%	100%	100%	101%
Total %	30-64	100%	97%	100%	99%	100%
	Over 65	100%	92%	99%	101%	102%

PUBLIC ATTITUDES TOWARDS WOMEN'S RIGHTS

All Respondents

	1972	1974	1976	1978
Women Should Have Equal Rights	46%	50%	50%	57%
Neutral	19%	18%	18%	16%
Women's Place Is In The Home	29%	26%	23%	21%
Don't Know; No Opinion	5%	6%	9%	6%
Total %	99%	100%	100%	100%

Public Attitudes Towards Women's Rights
By Age

	Age	1972	1974	1976	1978
Women Should	Under 30	55%	66%	61%	67%
Have Equal	30-64	45%	46%	51%	56%
Rights	Over 65	37%	38%	33%	40%
Neutral	Under 30	18%	15%	18%	16%
	30-64	21%	20%	17%	17%
	Over 65	17%	17%	20%	17%
Women's Place	Under 30	24%	16%	16%	14%
Is In The Home	30-64	30%	29%	24%	22%
	Over 65	34%	34%	31%	35%
Don't Know;	Under 30	4%	3%	6%	3%
No Opinion	30-64	4%	5%	8%	6%
	Over 65	11%	12%	16%	9%
	Under 30	101%	100%	101%	100%
Total %	30-64	100%	100%	100%	101%
	Over 65	99%	101%	100%	101%

Table A15
FREQUENCY OF CHURCH ATTENDANCE

All Respondents

	1952	1956	1958	1960	1962	1964	1966	1968	1970	1972	1974	1976	1978
Regularly[1]	38%	42%	42%	40%	44%	42%	40%	37%	37%	37%	37%	37%	39%
Often[2]	18%	18%	18%	16%	16%	16%	18%	15%	15%	12%	12%	14%	13%
Seldom[3]	35%	33%	32%	30%	31%	30%	31%	35%	29%	32%	30%	28%	33%
Never; Inapplicable	8%	6%	8%	12%	9%	12%	11%	13%	18%	20%	21%	21%	16%
Total %	99%	99%	100%	98%	100%	100%	100%	100%	99%	101%	100%	100%	101%

1   (52, 56, 58, 60, 62, 64, 66, 68) Would you say you go to church regularly, often, seldom or never?
2   (70) Would you say you go to church -- every week, several times a month, a few times a year, or never?
3   (72, 74, 76, 78) Would you say you go to (church/synagogue) every week, almost every week, several times a month, a few times a year, or never?

Frequency of Church Attendence
By Age

		1952	1956	1958	1960	1962	1964	1966	1968	1970	1972	1974	1976	1978
Regularly[1]	Under 30	35%	43%	36%	43%	38%	31%	34%	32%	29%	27%	25%	27%	29%
	16-64	39%	43%	45%	45%	44%	43%	40%	39%	38%	41%	40%	39%	41%
	Over 65	37%	41%	37%	37%	51%	51%	44%	39%	45%	43%	46%	45%	48%
Often[2]	Under 30	18%	20%	17%	19%	16%	18%	17%	16%	20%	14%	11%	16%	16%
	16-64	18%	18%	18%	18%	17%	17%	19%	15%	15%	11%	12%	13%	12%
	Over 65	18%	18%	20%	12%	14%	14%	15%	14%	12%	10%	13%	13%	11%
Seldom[3]	Under 30	40%	33%	40%	32%	38%	37%	40%	41%	30%	37%	36%	31%	39%
	30-64	35%	34%	30%	32%	31%	29%	31%	35%	31%	31%	31%	29%	31%
	Over 65	32%	29%	32%	37%	24%	24%	23%	29%	22%	26%	21%	23%	27%
Never; Inapplicable	Under 30	7%	4%	8%	7%	7%	14%	10%	11%	22%	23%	28%	25%	17%
	30-64	8%	5%	7%	5%	8%	12%	10%	11%	16%	17%	17%	19%	16%
	Over 65	14%	13%	12%	13%	12%	11%	18%	19%	20%	21%	21%	19%	14%
Total %	Under 30	100%	100%	101%	101%	99%	100%	101%	100%	101%	101%	100%	99%	101%
	16-64	100%	100%	100%	100%	100%	101%	100%	100%	100%	100%	100%	100%	100%
	Over 65	101%	101%	101%	99%	101%	100%	100%	101%	99%	100%	101%	100%	100%

1   1952-1968: regularly; 1970: every week; 1972-1976: every week; almost every week
2   1952-1968: often; 1972-1976: several time a month
3   1952-1968: seldom; 1970-1976: few times a year

PUBLIC ATTITUDES TOWARDS THE ISSUE OF REDUCING THE HOURS IN A WORK WEEK

All Respondents

	1953	1959	1962	1965
Should	21%	26%	31%	28%
Should Not	73%	67%	61%	65%
No Opinion	6%	7%	8%	7%
Total %	100%	100%	100%	100%

Public Attitudes Towards the Issue of Reducing the Hours in a Work Week
By Age

	Age	1953	1959	1962	1965
	Under 30	23%	22%	33%	29%
Should	30-64	20%	28%	32%	30%
	Over 65	23%	22%	21%	20%
	Under 30	73%	74%	62%	68%
Should Not	30-64	74%	65%	60%	63%
	Over 65	71%	67%	66%	69%
	Under 30	4%	4%	5%	4%
No Opinion	30-64	6%	7%	8%	7%
	Over 65	7%	12%	13%	11%
	Under 30	100%	100%	100%	101%
Total %	30-64	100%	100%	100%	100%
	Over 65	101%	101%	100%	100%

PUBLIC ATTITUDES ABOUT THE IDEAL NUMBER OF CHILDREN IN A FAMILY

All Respondents

	1941	1953	1963	1968	1971	1974 [3]	1978
As Many As You Like, Up to Family[2]	2%	2%	7%	1%	5%	0%	6%
Five or More	12%	12%	13%	9%	4%	5%	4%
Four	26%	28%	35%	32%	19%	13%	13%
Three	30%	28%	26%	32%	29%	23%	24%
Two	27%	27%	18%	25%	41%	48%	51%
None to One	2%	1%	1%	1%	1%	2%	2%
Total %	99%	98%	100%	100%	99%	91%	100%

Public Attitudes About the Ideal Number of Children in a Family
By Age

	Age	1941	1953	1963	1968	1971	1974	1978[4]
As Many As You Like, Up to Family[2]	Under 30	2%	1%	7%	%	3%	-%	
	30-64	2%	3%	7%	2%	6%	-%	
	Over 65	6%	4%	7%	1%	5%	-%	
Five or More	Under 30	7%	9%	10%	6%	2%	3%	
	30-64	12%	12%	13%	9%	5%	6%	
	Over 65	21%	18%	21%	13%	7%	9%	
Four	Under 30	18%	24%	32%	30%	13%	9%	
	30-64	27%	28%	35%	32%	20%	15%	
	Over 65	36%	34%	41%	35%	22%	20%	
Three	Under 30	31%	29%	28%	33%	28%	25%	
	30-64	32%	29%	26%	33%	29%	25%	
	Over 65	18%	24%	24%	30%	32%	28%	
Two	Under 30	40%	36%	23%	31%	51%	57%	
	30-64	25%	26%	19%	24%	39%	52%	
	Over 65	17%	19%	6%	18%	33%	41%	
None to One	Under 30	3%	2%	0%	0%	2%	3%	
	30-64	2%	2%	0%	1%	1%	2%	
	Over 65	3%	2%	0%	0%	0%	2%	
Total %	Under 30	101%	101%	100%	100%	99%	97%	
	30-64	100%	100%	100%	101%	100%	100%	
	Over 65	101%	101%	99%	97%	99%	100%	

1   Exact coding categories are unclear for this question in reputed documents because of the long number of years involved. Interested scholars should check with the Roper Center or the Gallup Organization. Dates sometimes vary between questionnaire administration and reporting.

2   Asked in 1971, 74. Other, undesignated in 1978.

3   10 percent expressed no opinion in 1974.

4   Data are not available for 1978.

APPENDIX B
INTERNATIONAL COMPARISONS—
GERMANY AND JAPAN

COMPARATIVE ANALYSIS: GERMANY—1972, 1976; JAPAN—1967, 1972

There is always a suspicion that the kinds of results reported here, regardless of how extensive these results might be, are culture-specific and that the same questions asked in different types of cultural settings would produce vastly different responses. Through the Inter-university Consortium of Social and Political Research, I was able to secure information from the 1972 and 1976 German Election Panel Study and from the 1967 Japanese National Election Study. These results provided a rare opportunity for cross-cultural comparison, as, in a few instances at least, questions were asked in these studies that matched those of the U.S. surveys. The data were, therefore, directly comparable, although "comparable" must be considered carefully in an international context.* (See Davidson and Thompson, 1980; and Zavalloni, 1980.)

FINDINGS

Say in Government

The first question available for analysis is "say in government"; i.e., "People like me don't have any say about what the government does." During that period of

---

*The 1967 Japanese National Election Study was ICPSR #7294. Principal investigators were Robert E. Ward and Akira Kubota. The 1972 and 1976 German Election Panel Studies were ICPSR #7102 and ICPSR #7513, respectively. I express my deep appreciation to ICPSR for their support. The countries were selected both because the data is comparable and because of my familiarity with both nations. I have traveled somewhat in Germany and lectured for four months in Japan as a Fulbright scholar. An early version of these results was given at a meeting of the North Central Sociological Association, Detroit, 1982.

time, the older American respondents appeared fairly constant at about a 46 percent "agree" proportion (table A3). This ranged over the years from a high of 54 percent to a low of 37 percent* and suggests a rather high degree of intertemporal stability. It is important to point out, however, that the over 65 respondent over all those years is somewhat more likely to agree than the under 30 respondent. This is not always greatly so, but it is always so.

On this question, comparable data exists for Germany in 1972 and 1976. These data are presented in tables B1 and B2.

Data from those years reveal markedly higher agreements with this statement by older (65 +) respondents than was true of the American respondents over sixty-five. In 1972, 74 percent of the elderly German respondents agreed with this statement, and a similar result occurs in 1976. In 1976 data are available for a "strongly agree/disagree" breakdown, and 41 percent of the elderly German population falls into the "strongly agree" category.

Thus, in both the United States and Germany, the elderly adult is more likely to agree with the proposition "people like me do not have much influence on what the government does," though it is higher in Germany than in the United States. In the United States, an average of about 46 percent of elderly adults agree with the statement over the years. In Germany, at least for the two years sampled, 74 percent of elderly adults agree.

A similar situation emerges from the 1967 Japanese survey. This is clear from the data presented in table B3.

About 80 percent of the elderly Japanese respondents gave an affirmative answer. This result suggests that the Japanese were much closer to Germans than to Americans. Let me stress, however, that cultural influence surely plays a more important role than age. This conclusion is suggested by the overall responses to this question for both nations.

Table B1

PEOPLE LIKE ME DO NOT HAVE ANY SAY ABOUT
HOW GOVERNMENT DOES THINGS, GERMANY, 1972

		Age of Respondents			Totals	
		18–29	30–64	65+	Row %	N
Agree	Row %	16	61	23		
	Column %	47 [40]*	60 [38]*	74 [50]*	100	874
Disagree	Row %	27	61	12		
	Column %	53	40	26	100	578
Totals	Column % =	100	100	100		
	N =	296	882	274		1452

Source: *USA%; Table A3, 1972 (USA% is the proportion of Americans answering the same question in the same year who agreed.)

Table B2

PEOPLE LIKE ME DO NOT HAVE ANY SAY ABOUT
WHAT GOVERNMENT DOES, GERMANY, 1976

		Age of Respondents			Totals	
		18-29	30-64	65+	Row %	N
Strongly Agree	Row %	12	65	23	100	634
	Column %	19	31	41		
Agree	Row %	22	59	19	100	634
	Column %	36 [44]*	29 [38]*	33 [45]*		
Disagree	Row %	18	69	13	100	529
	Column %	24	28	19		
Strongly Disagree	Row %	29	61	10	100	266
	Column %	20	12	7		
Totals	Column % =	100**	100	100		
	N =	384	1320	359		2063

Source: *USA%; Table A3, 1976
**Column sums to 99 because of rounding.

Table B3

PEOPLE LIKE ME DO NOT HAVE ANY SAY ABOUT
WHAT GOVERNMENT DOES, JAPAN, 1967

		Age of Respondents			Totals	
		18-29	30-64	65+	Row %	N
Agree	Row %	22	66	12	100	10,096
	Column %	[28]* 58 [32]**	[33]* 69 [41]*	[44]* 80 [54]**		
Disagree	Row %	32	61	6	100	4,917
	Column %	42	31	20		
Totals	Column % =	100	100	100		
	N =	3854	9686	1473		15,013

Source: *USA%; Table A3, 1966
**USA%; Table A3, 1968

Overall, 61 percent of the 1972 and 63 percent of the 1976 German respondents and 67 percent of the 1967 Japanese respondents expressed agreement with the question. These results contrast with about 40 percent for the United States in 1974 and 1976 and 34 percent in 1966 (table A3). This means that there is generally a higher level of agreement in these two countries than in the United States.

The pattern of the elderly being at the upper end of these distributions is one also found in the U.S. data. (See figure 3.) It seems reasonable to conclude, therefore, that in all three countries, using a variety of measures and a variety of times, the elderly are expressing fairly high levels of feeling lack of influence over what government does.

Voter's Influence

"Voting is the only way people like me can have any say about how the government runs things" is another statement that can assess the degree of policy efficacy the elderly adult feels. United States data from 1952 to 1978 (figure 4, table A4) reveal a high degree of agreement with this statement. That agreement suggests a theme that people do not feel linked to informal processes of influence. It is interesting to note, however, that the proportion of elderly adults who have affirmed this statement has been dropping in recent years. It was above 80 percent between 1952 and 1966. In 1968, it dropped to 77 percent; in 1978, to 70 percent. In fact, the entire U.S. population appears to be following this same general pattern.

In Germany in 1972, as table B4 shows, 69 percent of the respondents overall and 79 percent of elderly respondents expressed agreement with this statement.

In Japan, as table B5 demonstrates, 77 percent of respondents overall and 86 percent of the elderly group expressed agreement. We see, therefore, a pattern, similar to that of the last question, emerging, with the elderly adult showing higher agreement with this statement than the younger adult.

Table B4

VOTING IS THE ONLY WAY PEOPLE LIKE ME CAN HAVE ANY SAY
ABOUT HOW THE GOVERNMENT RUNS THINGS, GERMANY, 1972

| | | Age of Respondents | | | Totals | |
		18-29	30-64	65+	Row %	N
Agree	Row %	18	61	21	100	963
	Column %	59 [54]*	69 [61]*	79 [78]*		
Disagree	Row %	29	59	12	100	435
	Column %	41	31	21		
Totals	Column% =	100	100	100		
	N =	301	841	256		1398

Source: *USA%; Table A4, 1972

Table B5

VOTING IS THE ONLY WAY PEOPLE LIKE ME CAN HAVE ANY SAY
ABOUT HOW THE GOVERNMENT RUNS THINGS, JAPAN, 1967

| | | Age of Respondents | | | Totals | |
		18-29	30-64	65+	Row %	N
Agree	Row %	24	68	8	100	11,567
	Column %	[63]* 73 [42]**	[66] 78 [56]	[83] 86 [77]		
Disagree	Row %	30	66	4	100	3410
	Column %	27	22	14		
	Column % =	100	100	100		
	N =	3763	10,106	1108		14,977

Source: *USA%; Table A4, 1966
** USA%, Table A4, 1968

Officials' Concern

In three instances information is available from abroad that is not directly available from the U.S. surveys. It does permit, however, assessment of the same general topic area. One statement has to do with the concern of public officials: "I don't think public officials care much about what people like me think." Data from 1972 and 1976 German studies are presented in tables B6 and B7. Data from the 1967 Japanese study are presented in table B8.

In 1972, 53 percent of German respondents agreed with that statement. The percentage rose to 59 percent in 1976. About 84 percent of Japanese respondents agreed, revealing a higher perceived lack of caring in Japan than in Germany. Once again, the elderly adult is higher in agreement than the overall population. In 1972, 65 percent of elderly German adults agreed. In 1976, 68 percent agreed. In Japan, an astounding 95 percent of the elderly adults felt that public officials did not care much about them. Both German and Japanese adults, therefore, seem to feel some disaffection with the political process.

Government Complications

The process of government, obviously, is complicated. There is also no persuasive evidence that its complexity is decreasing as years go by. One might expect, therefore, that adults in general and elderly adults in particular perceive it as too complicated to deal with. A statement in the German and Japanese surveys examines that dimension: "Sometimes politics and government seem so complicated that a person like me cannot really understand what is going on." Data from these studies are presented in tables B9, B10, and B11.

Table B6

I DON'T THINK PUBLIC OFFICIALS CARE MUCH
ABOUT WHAT PEOPLE LIKE ME THINK, GERMANY, 1972

| | | Age of Respondents | | | Totals | |
		18-29	30-64	65+	Row %	N
Agree	Row %	17	60	23	100	723
	Column %	43	53	65		
Disagree	Row %	25	61	14	100	641
	Column %	57	47	35		
Totals	Column % =	100	100	100		
	N =	287	825	252		1364

Table B7

I DO NOT THINK PUBLIC OFFICIALS CARE MUCH ABOUT
WHAT PEOPLE LIKE ME THINK, GERMANY, 1976

| | | Age of Respondents | | | Totals | |
		18-29	30-64	65+	Row %	N
Strongly Agree	Row %	13	63	24	100	581
	Column %	20	28	38		
Agree	Row %	21	61	18	100	598
	Column %	33	27	30		
Disagree	Row %	19	67	14	100	606
	Column %	30	31	24		
Strongly Disagree	Row %	24	66	10	100	276
	Column %	17	14	8		
Totals	Column % =	100	100	100		
	N =	384	1319	358		2061

Table B8

I DON'T THINK DIET MEMBERS AND PUBLIC OFFICIALS CARE MUCH
ABOUT WHAT PEOPLE LIKE ME ARE THINKING, JAPAN, 1972

| | | Age of Respondents | | | Totals | |
		18-29	30-64	65+	Row %	N
Agree	Row %	24	68	8	100	12,247
	Column %	74	83	95		
Disagree	Row %	37	61	2	100	2732
	Column %	26	17	5		
Totals	Column % =	100	100	100		
	N =	3936	10,005	1038		14,979

Table B9

SOMETIMES POLITICS AND GOVERNMENT SEEM SO COMPLICATED THAT A PERSON
LIKE ME CANNOT REALLY UNDERSTAND WHAT IS GOING ON, GERMANY, 1972

| | | Age of Respondents | | | Totals | |
		18-29	30-64	65+	Row %	N
Agree	Row %	17	61	22	100	891
	Column %	49	61	74		
Disagree	Row %	27	61	12	100	572
	Column %	51	39	26		
Totals	Column % =	100	100	100		
	N =	305	888	270		1463

Table B10

SOMETIMES POLITICS AND GOVERNMENT SEEM SO COMPLICATED THAT A PERSON
LIKE ME CANNOT REALLY UNDERSTAND WHAT IS GOING ON, GERMANY, 1976

| | Age of Respondents | | | Totals | |
	18-29	30-64	65+	Row %	N
Row % Strongly Agree	13	63	24	100	584
Column %	20	28	39		
Row % Agree	21	62	17	100	675
Column %	36	32	32		
Row % Disagree	20	66	14	100	482
Column %	25	24	18		
Row % Strongly Disagree	23	65	12	100	322
Column %	19	16	11		
Totals Column % =	100	100	100		
N =	384	1320	359		2063

Table B11

SOMETIMES POLITICS AND GOVERNMENT SEEM SO COMPLICATED THAT A PERSON
LIKE ME CANNOT REALLY UNDERSTAND WHAT IS GOING ON, JAPAN, 1976

| | Age of Respondents | | | Totals | |
	18-29	30-64	65+	Row %	N
Row % Agree	26	66	8	100	12,907
Column %	80	81	95		
Row % Disagree	28	70	2	100	2903
Column %	20	19	5		
Totals Column % =	100	100	100		
N =	4135	10,564	1111		15,810

It is certainly possible that perceived lack of influence of "people like me" stems as much from feelings of befuddlement as from feelings of exclusion. In 1972 and 1976, about 61 percent of the German respondents felt that this was so; 85 percent of Japanese respondents agreed. As with the other questions, elderly adults were higher in agreement in 1972: 74 percent of the German over-sixty-five group agreed with the statement. In 1976, 62 percent of German adults overall and 71 percent of elderly adults agreed or strongly agreed with the statement. In Japan, 95 percent of older respondents agreed with the statement.

DISCUSSION AND IMPLICATIONS

In all cases examined, the null hypothesis would have to be modified, if not rejected. The elderly adult did reveal pattern differences from the younger respondent. I hasten to add a cautionary note not to make too much of these differences. Age *appears* to make something of a difference. It does so, presumably, *along with* a number of other relatively unimportant variables (such as class and job) that have not been considered here.

While it is not appropriate to conclude from these data that elderly adults are more conservative than younger adults, the elderly of Germany and Japan do seem to feel a greater degree of distance from influence over governmental process, at least as expressed in policy opinion. In this respect, it is very important to have the Japanese data available. Without them, it would be tempting to conclude that a process of disengagement in Western industrialized countries was taking place. That argument might then be followed quickly with a comment that if one had the opportunity to look at Oriental countries, where traditions were more intact and the elderly had a more respected position than in Western societies, one would see a very different finding. Tentative as the data presented here are, they do permit a modest assessment of that assertion. Given the evidence here, at least, it must be rejected out of hand. Elderly adults in Japan look very much like elderly adults in Germany and in the United States. Indeed, in at least two instances, the data reveal greater rather than lesser distance from the social structure as measured by policy opinion. Any conclusions, therefore, about what elderly adults may think in countries where "age is more respected" should be carefully and cautiously anayzed and considered.

Questions available to us for comparative analysis do not permit even a rudimentary assessment of the interest-group hypothesis that people's support relates to areas of gain for them. There do seem to be some commonalities with respect to elderly respondents. Whether these reflect commonalities of condition or commonalities of interest cannot be ascertained at this time. Indeed, a great deal more assessment is imperative. Would the elderly adult, for example, be different from the younger adult? Are the age breaks (such as sixty-five) entirely appropriate for defining the elderly populations in different nations, and would the results be significantly altered if different age breaks were used? No one knows at this point, but the matter cries out for further and more intensive study.

Historically, both Germany and Japan had in the recent past governments of a more authoritarian sort, with smaller ruling cliques exerting relatively great influence. While there has been great debate in this country about elites, ours has always seemed a relatively more open society than either of these two nations. It is heartening, then, to see in these data tendencies that support such a general assumption, at least with respect to a greater perceived sense of influence by all groups in the United States than in those other countries. It is problematic how much real comfort can be drawn from these tendencies, though, and it is at this point that one feels the need for more. There must be additional cross-tabulations, regressions, and other assessments of what it is that influences an individual's policy opinion. There must also be more qualitative, in-depth, extensive assessments of what people understand by the particular questions they are being asked—how they interpret them and what they mean by their answers.

The culture or national climate, then, appears to make a difference in the pattern of responses. This could be due to the nature of the questions as they appear in the native language; to a variety of differences in interviewer training; or to any number of other reasons, including actual cultural differences. It is not possible, therefore, to be sure that national culture is the single variable of importance here. We do have, however, two Western countries and one Oriental country; and the findings seem close enough to each other to suggest that, while culture may affect the direction of the responses, it does not necessarily do so with these questions. Culture may, of course, affect the magnitude of the responses, as well. That finding is present here. More data points would be needed to assess this point fully.

This brief exploration into the distribution of policy opinion by age in other countries is meant to provide only a glimpse of what further analyses might suggest. It does show, however, that the elderly in these two countries are alike in ways that can compare to American respondents—and this kind of comparison is all too infrequently available.

APPENDIX C
A LIST OF QUESTIONS FROM THE NATIONAL ELECTION STUDY, UNIVERSITY OF MICHIGAN, AND THE GALLUP POLL

A LIST OF QUESTIONS*

A. National Election Study—University of Michigan

1. TRUST IN GOVERNMENT (GOVERNMENT TRUST/GV TRUST)

YEARS: 1958, 1964, 1968, 1970, 1972, 1974, 1976, 1978

QUESTION: How much of the time do you think you can trust the government in Washington to do what is right—just about always, most of the time, or some of the time?

CODING: 1 = JUST ABOUT ALWAYS
           3 = MOST OF THE TIME
           5 = ONLY SOME OF THE TIME
           7 = NONE OF THE TIME

YEAR: 1966

QUESTION: How much do you think we can trust the government in Washington to do what is right: just about always, most of the time, some of the time, or almost never?

CODING: 1 = JUST ABOUT ALWAYS
           2 = MOST OF THE TIME
           3 = ONLY SOME OF THE TIME
           5 = NONE OF THE TIME

*Simplified and condensed somewhat for ease of reading. A full set with complete text for each is available from the author (University of Michigan, Ann Arbor, MI 48109) or the National Election Study Codebooks (ICPSR, University of Michigan, Ann Arbor MI 48109).

2. WHO IS THE GOVERNMENT RUN FOR THE BENEFIT OF? (GOVERNMENT BENEFIT/GV BEN)

YEAR: 1958

QUESTION: Do you think that the high-up people in government give everyone a fair break whether they are big shots or just ordinary people, or do you think some of them pay attention to what the big interests want?

CODING: 1 = GIVE EVERYONE A FAIR BREAK
           3 = PRO-CON, IT DEPENDS
           5 = FEW BIG INTERESTS

YEARS: 1964, 1966, 1968, 1970, 1972, 1974, 1976, 1978

QUESTION: Would you say the government is pretty much run by a few big interests looking out for themselves or that it is run for the benefit of all the people?

CODING: 1 = FOR BENEFIT OF ALL
           3 OR 7 = OTHER, DEPENDS, BOTH BOXES CHECKED
           5 = FEW BIG INTERESTS

3. PEOPLE LIKE ME DON'T HAVE ANY SAY ABOUT WHAT THE GOVERNMENT DOES (SAY IN GOVERNMENT/SAY GV)

YEARS: 1952, 1956, 1960, 1964, 1966, 1968, 1970, 1972, 1974, 1976, 1978

QUESTION: People like me don't have any say about what the government does.

CODING: (ALL YEARS EXCEPT 1966)
           1 = AGREE
           5 = DISAGREE
           (1966)
           1 = STRONGLY AGREE
           2 = AGREE
           3 = NOT SURE, IT DEPENDS
           4 = DISAGREE
           5 = STRONGLY DISAGREE

4. VOTING IS THE ONLY WAY THAT PEOPLE LIKE ME CAN HAVE ANY SAY ABOUT HOW THE GOVERNMENT RUNS THINGS (VOTER INFLUENCE/VOTE INF)

YEARS: 1952, 1956, 1960, 1964, 1966, 1968, 1970, 1972, 1974, 1976, 1978

QUESTION: Voting is the ony way that people like me can have any say about how the government runs things.

CODING: (ALL YEARS EXCEPT 1966)
           1 = AGREE
           5 = DISAGREE
             (1966)
           1 = STRONGLY AGREE
           2 = AGREE
           3 = NOT SURE, IT DEPENDS
           4 = DISAGREE
           5 = STRONGLY DISAGREE

5. PUBLIC ATTITUDES TOWARDS GOVERNMENT ACTION TO INSURE EVERYONE A JOB AND A GOOD STANDARD OF LIVING (GOVERNMENT JOB/GV JOB/GV WORK)

YEAR: 1956

QUESTION: The government in Washington ought to see to it that everybody who wants to work can find a job.

CODING: 1 = AGREE STRONGLY
            2 = AGREE BUT NOT VERY STRONGLY
            3 = NOT SURE, IT DEPENDS
            4 = DISAGREE BUT NOT VERY STRONGLY
            5 = DISAGREE STRONGLY

YEAR: 1958

QUESTION: The government in Washington ought to see to it that everybody who wants work can find a job. Now would you have an opinion on this or not. (IF YES) Do you think the government should do this?

CODING: 1 = AGREE STRONGLY
            2 = AGREE BUT NOT VERY STRONGLY
            3 = NOT SURE, IT DEPENDS
            4 = DISAGREE BUT NOT VERY STRONGLY
            5 = DISAGREE STRONGLY

YEAR: 1960

QUESTION: Around election time people talk about different things that our government in Washington is doing or should be doing. Now I would like to talk to you about some of the things that our government might do. Of course, different things are important to different people, so we don't expect everyone to have an opinion about all of these. . . . The government in Washington ought to see to it that everybody who wants to work can find a job.

CODING: 1 = AGREE STRONGLY
            2 = AGREE BUT NOT VERY STRONGLY
            3 = NOT SURE, IT DEPENDS
            4 = DISAGREE BUT NOT VERY STRONGLY
            5 = DISAGREE STRONGLY

YEARS: 1964, 1968

QUESTION: "In general, some people feel that the government in Washington should see to it that every person has a job and a good standard of living. Others think the government should just let each person get ahead on his own." Have you been interested enough in this to favor one side or the other? (IF YES) Do you think that the government:

CODING: 1 = (YES) SHOULD SEE TO IT THAT EVERY PERSON HAS
                A JOB AND A GOOD STANDARD OF LIVING
            3 = (YES) OTHER, DEPENDS, BOTH BOXES CHECKED
            5 = (YES) SHOULD LET EACH PERSON GET AHEAD ON
                HIS OWN

YEAR: 1972

QUESTION: Some people feel that the government in Washington should see to it that every person has a job and a good standard of living. Others think the government should just let each person get ahead on his own. And, of course, other people have opinions somewhere in between. Suppose people who believe that the government should see to it that every person has a job and a good standard of living are at one end of the scale—at point number 1. And suppose that the people who believe that the government should let each person get ahead on his own are at the other end—at point number 7. Where would you place yourself on this scale, or haven't you thought much about this?

CODING: SCALE OF 1 TO 7
            1 = GOVERNMENT
            4 = MIDPOINT
            7 = LEAVE IT UP TO THE INDIVIDUAL

YEARS: 1974, 1976, 1978

QUESTION: Some people feel that the government in Washington should see to it that every person has a job and a good standard of living. Suppose that these people are at one end of this scale—at point number 1. Others think the government should just let each person get ahead on his own. Suppose that these people are at the other end—at point number 7. And, of course, some other people have their opinions somewhere in between. Where would you place yourself on this scale, or haven't you thought much about this?

CODING: SCALE OF 1 TO 7
            1 = GOVERNMENT
            4 = MIDPOINT
            7 = LEAVE IT UP TO THE INDIVIDUAL

6. FEELING THERMOMETERS (FOUR QUESTIONS) (LIBERAL THERMOMETER/TH LIB; CONSERVATIVE THERMOMETER/TH CON; REPUBLICAN THERMOMETER/TH REP; DEMOCRAT THERMOMETER/TH DEM)

YEARS: 1964, 1966, 1968, 1970, 1972, 1974, 1976, 1978

QUESTION: [Respondents were asked how warmly or coldly they felt towards a particular group. The four groups of interest in this study are liberals, conservatives, Republicans, and Democrats.]

CODING: SCALE OF 0 to 97, 98 OR 100 DEGREES
            97, 98 OR 100 DEGREES = VERY WARMLY
            50 DEGREES = NEUTRAL
            0 DEGREES = VERY COLDLY
            FROM 1964 THROUGH 1968, THOSE RESPONDENTS WHO REPLIED "don't know" WERE CODED BY SRC AS 50 DEGREES. ALSO, DUE TO LIMITATIONS OF COMPUTER SOFTWARE, ALL RESPONSES OF ZERO DEGREES WERE RECODED AS ONE DEGREE.

7. PUBLIC SUPPORT FOR GOVERNMENT INVOLVEMENT IN HEALTH CARE (GOVERNMENT HEALTH/GV HEALTH/GV MED)

YEARS: 1956, 1960

QUESTION: The government ought to help people get doctors and hospital care at low cost.

CODING: 1 = AGREE STRONGLY
            2 = AGREE BUT NOT VERY STRONGLY
            3 = NOT SURE, IT DEPENDS
            4 = DISAGREE BUT NOT VERY STRONGLY
            5 = DISAGREE STRONGLY

YEAR: 1962

QUESTION: Now on a different problem. The government ought to help people get doctors and hospital care at low cost. Do you have an opinion on this or not?

CODING: 1 = YES
            2 = YES, BUT QUALIFIED
            3 = YES, FOR THE AGED
            4 = NO, BUT QUALIFIED
            5 = NO
            6 = NO, EXCEPT FOR THE AGED
            7 = YES, FOR THE NEEDY

YEARS: 1964, 1968

QUESTION: Some say the government in Washington ought to help people get doctors and hospital care at low cost; others say the government should not get into this. Have you been interested enough in this to favor one side over the other. (IF YES) What is your position? Should the government in Washington:

CODING: 1 = (YES) HELP PEOPLE GET DOCTORS AND HOSPITAL
                CARE AT LOW COST
            3 = (YES) OTHER, DEPENDS, BOTH BOXES CHECKED
            5 = (YES) STAY OUT OF THIS

YEARS: 1970, 1972, 1976, 1978

QUESTION: There is much concern about the rise in medical and hospital costs. Some feel there should be a government health ["HEALTH" OMITTED 1972] insurance plan which would cover all medical and hospital expenses. Others feel that medical expenses should be paid by individuals and through private insurance like Blue Cross. (SHOW CARD TO R.) Where would you place yourself on this scale or haven't you thought much about this?

CODING: SCALE OF 1 TO 7
            1 = GOVERNMENT INSURANCE PLAN
            4 = MIDPOINT
            7 = PRIVATE INSURANCE PLAN/INDIVIDUAL SHOULD PAY

8. OPINION ON GOVERNMENT INVOLVEMENT IN ELECTRIC POWER AND HOUSING (GOVERNMENT POWER/GV POW)

YEAR: 1956

QUESTION: The government should leave things like electric power and housing for private businessmen to handle.

CODING: 1 = AGREE STRONGLY
              2 = AGREE BUT NOT VERY STRONGLY
              3 = NOT SURE, IT DEPENDS
              4 = DISAGREE BUT NOT VERY STRONGLY
              5 = DISAGREE STRONGLY

YEARS: 1958, 1960

QUESTION: The government should leave things like electric power and housing for private businessmen to handle. Do you have an opinion on this or not? (IF YES) Do you think the government should leave things like this to private business?

CODING: 1 = AGREE STRONGLY
              2 = AGREE BUT NOT VERY STRONGLY
              3 = NOT SURE, IT DEPENDS
              4 = DISAGREE BUT NOT VERY STRONGLY
              5 = DISAGREE STRONGLY
              9 = NO OPINION

YEAR: 1964

QUESTION: Some people think it's all right for the government to own some power plants while others think the production of electricity should be left to private business. Have you been interested enough in this to favor one side over the other? (IF YES) Which position is more like yours, having the:

CODING: 1 = (YES) GOVERNMENT OWN POWER PLANTS
              3 = (YES) OTHER, DEPENDS, BOTH BOXES CHECKED
              5 = (YES) LEAVING THIS TO PRIVATE BUSINESS

9. IS THE GOVERNMENT IN WASHINGTON GETTING TOO POWERFUL? (TOO POWERFUL/TOO POW)

YEARS: 1964, 1966, 1968

QUESTION: Some people are afraid the government in Washington is getting too powerful for the good of the country and the individual person. Others feel that the government [ADD "in Washington" 1966, 1968] has not gotten too strong for the good of the country. Have you been interested enough in this to favor one side over the other? (IF YES) What is your feeling, do you think:

CODING: 1 = (YES) THE GOVERNMENT IS GETTING TOO POWERFUL
              3 = (YES) OTHER, DEPENDS, BOTH BOXES CHECKED
              5 = (YES) THE GOVERNMENT HAS NOT GOTTEN TOO
                   STRONG

YEARS: 1970, 1972, 1976, 1978

QUESTION: Some people are afraid the government in Washington is getting too powerful for the good of the country and the individual person. Others feel that the government in Washington has not gotten [SUBSTITUTE "is not getting" for 1972, 1976] too strong [OMIT "for the good of the country." in 1972]. Have you been interested enough in this to favor one side over the other? [SUBSTITUTE "Do you have an opinion on this?" for 1976.] (IF YES) What is your feeling, do you think the government is getting too powerful or do you think the government has not gotten [SUBSTITUTE "is not getting" for 1972, 1976] too strong?

CODING: 1 = THE GOVERNMENT IS GETTING TOO POWERFUL
5 = THE GOVERNMENT HAS NOT GOTTEN TOO STRONG (SUBSTITUTE "IS NOT GETTING" FOR 1972, 1976, 1978)
7 = OTHER, DEPENDS, BOTH BOXES CHECKED

10. SHOULD GOVERNMENT SEE TO IT THAT BLACKS GET FAIR TREATMENT IN JOBS AND HOUSING? (NEGRO JOBS/NGR JOB)

YEAR: 1952

QUESTION: There is a lot of talk these days about discrimination, that is, people having trouble getting jobs because of their race. Do you think the government ought to take an interest in whether Negroes have trouble getting jobs or do you think the government should stay out of this problem? (IF GOVERNMENT SHOULD TAKE AN INTEREST) Do you think we need laws to deal with this problem or are there other ways that will handle it better? . . . What do you have in mind? . . . Do you think the national government should handle this or do you think it should be left for each state to handle in its own way? (IF GOVERNMENT SHOULD STAY OUT) Do you think the state governments should do something about this problem or should they stay out of it also?

CODING: 00 = NATIONAL GOVERNMENT SHOULD PASS LAWS AND DO OTHER THINGS TOO
10 = NATIONAL GOVERNMENT SHOULD PASS LAWS, OR N.A. FOR NATIONAL OR STATE
20 = STATE GOVERNMENT SHOULD PASS LAWS AND DO OTHER THINGS TOO
30 = STATE GOVERNMENT SHOULD PASS LAWS
40 = GOVERNMENT SHOULD DO OTHER THINGS ONLY
50 = GOVERNMENT SHOULD TAKE AN INTEREST, N.A. HOW
60 = NATIONAL GOVERNMENT SHOULD STAY OUT BUT STATE GOVERNMENT SHOULD TAKE ACTION
70 = GOVERNMENT (NATIONAL AND STATE) SHOULD STAY OUT ENTIRELY
80 = RESPONDENT FAVORS RESTRICTIVE LEGISLATION (INCLUDE HERE CLEAR ANTI-NEGRO STATEMENTS)

YEARS: 1956, 1960

QUESTION: If Negroes are not getting fair treatment in jobs and housing, the
government should see to it that they do.

CODING: 1 = AGREE STRONGLY
             2 = AGREE BUT NOT VERY STRONGLY
             3 = NOT SURE, IT DEPENDS
             4 = DISAGREE BUT NOT VERY STRONGLY
             5 = DISAGREE STRONGLY

YEAR: 1958

QUESTION: If Negroes are not getting fair treatment in jobs and housing, the
government should see to it that they do. Do you have an opinion on
this or not. (IF YES) Do you think the government should do this?

CODING: 1 = AGREE STRONGLY
             2 = AGREE BUT NOT VERY STRONGLY
             3 = NOT SURE, IT DEPENDS
             4 = DISAGREE BUT NOT VERY STRONGLY
             5 = DISAGREE STRONGLY

YEARS: 1964, 1968, 1972

QUESTION: Some people feel that if Negroes (colored people) [OMIT "(colored
people)" in 1968; SUBSTITUTE "black people" FOR "Negroes
(colored people)" in 1972] are not getting fair treatment in jobs, the
government in Washington should see to it that they do. Others feel
that this is not the federal government's business. Have you had
enough interest in this question to favor one side over the other? (IF
YES) How do you feel?

CODING: 1 = (YES) SEE TO IT THAT BLACK PEOPLE GET FAIR
                 TREATMENT IN JOBS
             3 = [1964, 1968] OTHER, DEPENDS
             5 = LEAVE IT TO STATE AND LOCAL COMMUNITIES
             7 = [1972] OTHER, DEPENDS

11. PUBLIC ATTITUDE TOWARDS THE SPEED OF THE CIVIL RIGHTS MOVEMENT (CIVIL RIGHTS/CV RTS)

YEARS: 1964, 1966, 1968, 1972, 1976

QUESTION: Some say that the civil rights people have been trying to push too fast.
Others feel they haven't pushed fast enough. How about you: Do you
think that civil rights leaders are trying to push too fast, are they
[OMIT "they" 1972, 1976] going too slowly, or are they moving
about the right speed?

CODING: 1 = TOO FAST
             3 = ABOUT RIGHT
             5 = TOO SLOWLY

12. PUBLIC ATTITUDES TOWARDS CHANGE IN THE POSITION OF NEGROES (BLACKS) (NEGRO POSITION/NGR POS)

YEARS: 1964, 1966, 1968, 1972

QUESTION: In the past few years we have heard a lot about civil rights groups working to improve the position of the Negro (colored people) [SUBSTITUTE "blacks" FOR "Negro" (colored people) 1972] in this country. How much real change do you think there has been in the position of the Negro (colored people) [SUBSTITUTE "black" FOR "Negro (colored people)" 1972] in the past few years: a lot, some, or not much at all?

CODING: 1 = A LOT
              3 = SOME
              5 = NOT MUCH

YEAR: 1976

QUESTION: In the past few years we have heard a lot about working to improve the position of black people in this country. How much real change do you think there has been in the position of black people in the past few years: a lot, some, or not much at all?

CODING: 1 = A LOT
              3 = SOME
              5 = NOT MUCH

13. PUBLIC ATTITUDES TOWARDS PROTECTING THE RIGHTS OF THE ACCUSED (RIGHTS OF THE ACCUSED/RTS ACC)

YEARS: 1970, 1972, 1974, 1976, 1978

QUESTION: Some people are primarily concerned with doing everything possible to protect the legal rights of those accused of committing crimes. Others feel that it is more important to stop criminal activity even at the risk of reducing the rights of the accused. . . . Where would you place yourself on this scale, or haven't you thought much about this?

CODING: SCALE OF 1 TO 7
              1 = PROTECT THE LEGAL RIGHTS OF THOSE ACCUSED OF COMMITTING CRIMES
              4 = MIDPOINT
              7 = STOP CRIMINAL ACTIVITY EVEN AT THE RISK OF REDUCING THE RIGHTS OF THE ACCUSED— "STOP CRIME"

14. PUBLIC ATTITUDES TOWARDS WOMEN'S RIGHTS (WOMEN'S RIGHTS/WOMEN RTS)

YEARS: 1972, 1974, 1976, 1978

QUESTION; Recently there has been a lot of talk about women's rights. Some people feel that women should have a role with men in running business, industry, and government. Others feel that women's place is in the home. . . . Where would you place yourself on this scale, or haven't you thought much about this?

CODING: SCALE OF 1 TO 7
              1 = WOMEN SHOULD HAVE EQUAL ROLE
              4 = MIDPOINT
               7 = WOMEN'S PLACE IS IN THE HOME

15. FREQUENCY OF CHURCH ATTENDANCE (CHURCH ATTENDANCE/CH ATT)

YEARS: 1952, 1956, 1958, 1960, 1962, 1964, 1966, 1968

QUESTION: Would you say you go to church regularly, often, seldom, or never.

CODING: 1 = REGULARLY
          2 = OFTEN
          4 = SELDOM
          5 = NEVER

YEAR: 1970

QUESTION: Would you say you go to church—almost every week, several times a month, a few times a year, or never?

CODING: 1 = EVERY WEEK
          2 = ONCE OR TWICE A MONTH
          3 = A FEW TIMES A YEAR
          4 = NEVER

YEARS: 1972, 1974, 1976, 1978

QUESTION: Would you say you go to (church/synagogue) every week, almost every week, once or twice a month, a few times a year, or never?

CODING: 1 = EVERY WEEK
          2 = ALMOST EVERY WEEK
          3 = ONCE OR TWICE A MONTH
          4 = A FEW TIMES A YEAR
          5 = NEVER

B. Questions from the Gallup Poll, Roper Center, Storrs, CT. 06268.

1. PUBLIC ATTITUDES TOWARDS THE ISSUE OF REDUCING THE HOURS IN A WORK WEEK

YEARS: 1953, 1959, 1962, 1965

QUESTION: Do you think the work week in most industries should or should not be reduced from 40 hours to 35 hours?

CODING: YES
          NO

2. PUBLIC ATTITUDES ABOUT THE IDEAL NUMBER OF CHILDREN IN A FAMILY

YEARS: 1941, 1953

QUESTION: What do you consider is the ideal size of family—husband and wife and how many children?

YEARS: 1962-1963, 1967-1968, 1970-1971, 1974, 1978

QUESTION: What do you think is the ideal number of children for a family to have?

CODING: NUMBER OF CHILDREN

APPENDIX D
DATA AND METHOD

Data for this study came from two sources: the Inter-university Consortium for Political and Social Research (ICPSR) and the Roper Center (Gallup Poll). Of the seventeen questions analyzed here, fifteen came from ICPSR and two (Work Week and Ideal Number of Children in the Family) from Roper. In selecting the questions, a variety of continuing surveys conducted by the Institute of Social Research at The University of Michigan were considered. The ICPSR, as a data archive, stores the original data on computer tape for just the purposes we wished to use them, i.e., for secondary analysis where various kinds of comparative analysis can be performed. For such review, the National Election Study seemed the most appropriate choice. Not only was it one of the longest running, continuous social surveys in the United States (begun in a preliminary fashion in 1948), but it permitted good access to data beginning in 1952.

Those researchers who have sought to use data collected by others for secondary analysis will know of the time that is often spent and difficulties encountered due to problems in recording, coding, and so on. In this case, the data had been cleaned and checked by the ICPSR and Roper staff.*

Since the National Election Study was adminsitered every congressional election year (i.e., every second year since 1952), there were a number of iterations to review and a large chance for repeated questions. We found fifteen repeated questions that had policy-relevant content, which had been repeated three or more times, and where the repetition was of a sufficiently similar nature as to make comparison over

---

*Technical details concerning the administration of any particular study are available from ICPSR, The Unviersity of Michigan, Ann Arbor, MI 48109 and the Roper Center, University of Connecticut, Storrs, CT 06268.

time viable. The only case where we violated that self-imposed guideline was with the question on medical care. Because of the importance of that issue to elderly Americans (and to policy-interested persons), we included it.

As national probability samples of the U.S. population, these surveys provide a "snapshot" of U.S. society at the time (usually in November, before the election in question, though sometimes post-election as well). Hence, the ability to look at responses over time, using these questions, provides an amazing peek at the policy-value structure of the United States in the third quarter of the twentieth century.

The Gallup questions were also probability samples of the nation. We did not use more questions from Gallup because that organization tends not to repeat questions. In the case of work orientation and ideal family size, however, questions were repeated and, thus, were available for selection.

In all cases, of course, it was important to have social characteristics available for each respondent for each year so that the respondents and their answers could be examined. These characteristics were available for each respondent, for each variable, for each time we used the question. As one can understand, it became a substantial data set.

The strategy for data analysis was reasonably straightforward. First, the dependent variables were considered in some detail over the years. These are the seventeen questions that became the object of analysis. They were grouped into theoretically relevant areas to aid in comprehension and understanding. Basic presentation of the variable and the trends it exhibits became the initial order of business.

The second step in the analysis was to see if there were any patterns of relationship within the group of dependent variables. This process, essentially, is what the factor analysis accomplished. Variables were compared, and those factors that summarized their interrelationships were established.

The process of naming factors is always tricky because the addition of a name to a factor gives a reality and concreteness that may be unwarranted. Thus, the variables that are most strongly related to the factor (heavily loaded) play an important part in suggesting what the conceptual center of the factor might be. The names here followed this precedent, but also took advantage of the conceptual touchstones that provided the initial organizational framework.

The third step was to consider relationships between important social characteristics and the dependent variables, both individually and as factors. Personal characteristics (demographics) become independent variables in this approach. One seeks to explain and/or predict expressed beliefs and belief patterns through the personal characteristics of the respondent. Theoretically speaking, one would say that the underlying hypothesis here is that the expressed value is a function of the social characteristic in question. In other words, were one to know the social characteristic, then one would know what the person's opinion would be on this or that question. As you, the reader, know by now (or will if you're reading this part first), a tight connection between personal characteristics and at least these measures of policy opinion was not found. While some explanations for the patterns we did find were offered, much further research will be needed to explore these findings and relationships between social characteristics and social values.

A number of cautions and caveats relevant to the interpretation of these data have been mentioned throughout the text at the points where they were most relevant. It is necessary, however, to note some of the most important ones here. First, the time span of these data means that questionnaire administration varied over the course of many years. Sampling error did, too, in each iteration. The effect of these problems on the data cannot be known, but should induce caution in interpretation of the results. The stability and patterning of the findings over the years, however, suggest that the data were not seriously skewed.

Question wording is a second area for concern. Changes in wording do seem to have an effect upon the overall rates of response, suggesting that different kinds of wording evoke different aspects of a policy-value package in the respondent. By the same token, one should not assume that the same wording means that the question was the same. Because times change, identical wording may become anachronistic. Again, this issue needs to be studied separately. Here, consistent wording was sought but with the understanding that there might be some problems involved in interpretation. In each case the question text is available below the data figure.

A third issue is the presentation of data. After consultation, I selected floating bar charts without numbers. I do not believe that the actual numbers in this case mean as much as the slope of the graphs, especially when presenting multi-year findings. Presenting numbers in the graphs would have created a disharmonious display. Presenting numbers would have given only the usual "square" table (in shape, with the changing values represented in the different values of the numbers rather than changes in the length of the bars). Presenting numbers also seemed inelegant. Admittedly, this presentation is unusual and could cause problems for some readers. The numbers are available, however, in appendix A.

In these presentations I did lay out all of the responses, even when the "inappropriate" and "don't know" categories were large. As suggested in the text, at some points (the "rights of criminals/stop crime" question, for example) these reponses may have substantive implications.

A fourth issue has to do with the extent to which various competing forces influence response. Behavior or values at any moment in time may be the result of several such competing forces. One of these is a *cohort effect*, or the influence upon the group of people, including the researcher or reader, who share some important temporal commonality; i.e., who were born at the same time or who were in the same high school class or who started college at the same time, etc.

A closely related effect results from that definable segment of history during which one was born; e.g., born in the Depression years of the thirties or the war years of the forties or the conservative period of the fifties. It recognizes that what is going on during one's formative years affects to some extent one's developing attitudes.

There is also a period effect, which deals with influences of the here and now. In our case, that "here and now" refers to the time the questionnaire was administered.

Yet another force is the potential influence of commonalities or universalities occurring at specific stages of life regardless of age or background. Parents of young children, for example, might be expected to have similar issues to face regardless of parental ages.

One final force I will mention here—the importance of which is not yet fully explored—is the generation-of-parent effect. One may feel comfortable in defining a particular cohort (all people born in 1920, for example), but there is an immediate confounding factor introduced because the ages of their parents will vary considerably. The generation-of-parent effect introduces a heterogeneity of influence into the commonality cohort. (See Bengston et al., 1985.)

A fifth issue centers on comparative analysis. In appendix B, I have provided some data on Japan and Germany, where surveys were taken containing some of the same questions asked on the U.S. schedules. Cross-cultural comparison is difficult and fraught with problems. These problems are particularly sticky in the areas of values and attitudes, as Davidson and Thompson (1980) and Zavalloni (1980) point out. In spite of the difficulties and cautions, however, I wished at the least to lay out the results for thought and consideration. I, too, warn readers that the meaning of these data is even less clear than in the U.S. context.

Finally, in the matter of interpretation, I have sought to provide suggestions, explanations, and hypotheses consistent with the data. In such a preliminary analysis, however, these suggestions should be regarded as speculative and initial, awaiting further research and investigation.

APPENDIX E
FACTOR ANALYSIS
TECHNIQUES

The following strategy was used in the factor analysis for each year. A matrix of product-moment correlations was computed for the indicators on those cases with complete data. A principal components solution was then computed on this matrix with the elements of the principal diagonal (or communalities) being estimated iteratively. Their initial values were set at a level equal to the maximum correlation of the indicator in question with any of the other indicators. This was done because the hypothesis was that the indicators fell into distinctive values arenas and would cluster with some of the other indicators but not all of them. Otherwise, it might have been preferable to use the multiple correlation coefficients as initial estimates of the communalities. In general, nine iterations proved sufficient for the communalities to converge so that the maximum percentage change in communality estimates was 2 percent or less. The largest percentage change, in 1960, was 5.43 percent. In 1964, thirteen iterations were performed. In determining the number of factors presented in the initial solution, first, the number was restricted so that it would be no higher than our expectation as to the number represented in any given set of indicators. In 1956, 1960, 1964, 1972, and 1976, this was four. In 1968, it was five. The number was also restricted by the Kaiser criterion, which was set arbitrarily at .25. The rationale for setting the criterion at this level, rather than at the frequently suggested level of 1.0, is that there were likely to be very few indicators loading on each factor. Each factor would thus have a very low eigenvalue; i.e., it would account for little of the variation in the indicators. The idea was to give as much chance as possible for the hypothesized factor structure to emerge.

The factor solutions from this principal components analysis were rotated using the varimax method. The rotations were accomplished simultaneously through an interactive method. The maximum number of iterations was set at eight or nine. In most cases, however, convergence was achieved with a fewer number. The rotations were accomplished on the factors that appeared from the principal components solutions. In 1956 and 1960, a two-factor solution was rotated. In all other years a four-factor solution was rotated. The number of factors present in 1956, 1960, and 1968 was overestimated.

BIBLIOGRAPHY

Abramson, Paul R. "Developing Party Identification: A Further Examination of Life-Cycle, Generational, and Period Effects." *American Journal of Political Science*, 23, 1 (February 1979): 79-96.

Abramson, Paul R. "Generational Change and the Decline of Party Identification in America, 1952-1974." *American Political Science Review*, 70 (June 1976): 469-478.

Achenbaum, W. Andrew. *Old Age in the New Land: The American Experience Since 1790.* Baltimore: Johns Hopkins University Press, 1978.

Achenbaum, W. Andrew. *Shades of Grey.* Boston: Little, Brown, 1983.

Ahlstrom, Sydney E. *A Religious History of the American People.* New Haven: Yale University Press, 1972.

Alves, Wayne M. and Peter H. Rossi. "Who Should Get What? Fairness Judgements of the Distribution of Earnings." *American Journal of Sociology*, 84, 3 (November 1978): 541-564.

Alwin, Duane. "Trends in Parental Socialization Values: Detroit, 1958-1983." *American Journal of Sociology*, 90, 2 (September 1984): 359-382.

Alwin, Duane. "Religion and Parental Child Rearing Orientations: Evidence of a Catholic-Protestant Convergence." *American Journal of Sociology*, 92, 2 (September 1986): 412-440.

Andersen, Bent Rold. *Creating a Coherent Public Policy for the Elderly in a Welfare State.* Ann Arbor: The University of Michigan School of Social Work, 1982.

Andrews, K. and D. B. Kandel. "Attitude and Behavior." *American Sociological Review*, 44, 2 (April 1979); 298-310.

Antonucci, Toni, Nancy Gillett, and Frances Hoyer. "Values and Self-Esteem in Three Generations of Men and Women." *Journal of Gerontology*, 34, 3 (May 1979): 415-422.

Attneave, Carolyn. "American Indians and Alaska Native Families: Emigrants in Their Own Homeland." In Monica McGoldrick, John K. Pearce, and Joseph Gordiano (Eds.), *Ethnicity and Family Therapy*. New York: The Guilford Press, 1982.

Austin, David R. "Attitudes Toward Old Age: A Hierarchical Study." *The Gerontologist*, 25, 4 (August 1985): 431-434.

Baier, Kurt and Nicholas Rescher (Eds.). *Values and the Future: The Impact of Technological Change on American Values*. New York: The Free Press, 1969.

Bane, Frank. "The Social Security Act Expands." *Social Service Review*, 13, 4 (December 1939): 602-610.

Banfield, Edward C. and James Q. Wilson. *City Politics*. Cambridge: Harvard University Press, 1963.

Barbour, Ian, Harvey Brooks, Sanford Lakeoff, and John Opie. *Energy and American Values*. New York: Praeger, 1982.

Beauchamp, Dan E. "Public-Health and Individual Liberty." *Annual Review of Public Health*, 1 (1980): 121-136.

Bell, Daniel. *The Cultural Contradictions of Capitalism*. New York: Basic Books, 1976.

Bell, Daniel. *The End of Ideology: On the Exhaustion of Political Ideas in the Fifties*. Glencoe, Illinois: The Free Press, 1960.

Benedict, Robert C. "Trends in the Development of Services for the Aging Under the Older Americans Act." In Barbara R. Herzog (Ed.), *Aging and Income: Programs and Prospects for the Elderly*. New York: Human Sciences Press, 1978.

Bengtson, Vern L. and Mary Christine Lovejoy. "Values, Personality, and Social Structure: An Intergenerational Analysis." *American Behavioral Scientist*, 16, 6 (August 1973): 880-912.

Bengston, Vern L. et al. "Generations, Cohorts and Relations Between Age Groups." In Robert H. Binstock and Ethel Shanas (Eds.), *Handbook of Aging and the Social Services*. 2nd ed. New York: Van Nostrand Reinhold, 1985.

Benjamin, Albert J., Jr., et al. "Elders and Children: Patterns of Public Policy in the Fifty States." *Journal of Gerontology*, 35, 6 (November 1980): 928-954.

Berger, Bennett M. *The Survival of a Counter Culture: Ideological Work and Everyday Life Among Rural Communards*. Berkeley: The University of California Press, 1981.

Binstock, Robert H. "Aging and the Future of American Politics." *The Annals of the American Academy of Political and Social Science*, 415 (September 1974): 199-212.

Bishop, George D., David A. Hamilton, and John B. McConahay. *Attitudes and Non-Attitudes in Belief Systems of Mass Public: A Field Study*. Working paper. Center for Policy Analysis, Institute of Policy Sciences and Public Affairs, Duke University, 1977.

Bougart, Leo. "No Opinion, Don't Know, and Maybe No Answer." *Public Opinion Quarterly*, 31, 3 (Fall 1967): 331-345.

Boulding, Kenneth E. "Decision Making in the Modern World." In Lyman Bryson

(Ed.), *An Outline of Man's Knowledge of the Modern World*. New York: McGraw-Hill, 1960.

Briar, Scott et al. (Eds.), *1983-84, Supplement to the Encyclopedia of Social Work*. 17th ed. Silver Spring, Maryland: NASW, 1983.

Brickman, Philip. "A Social Psychology of Human Concerns." In Robin Gilmour and Steve Duck (Eds.), *The Development of Social Psychology*. London, New York: Academic Press, 1980.

Brickman, Philip, Robert Folger, Erica Goode, and Yaacov Schul. "Micro and Macro Justice." In Melvin J. Lerner and Sally C. Lerner (Eds.), *The Justice Motive in Social Behavior: Adapting to Times of Scarcity and Change*. New York: Plenum Press, 1981.

Brody, Charles J. "Things Are Rarely Black and White: Admitting Grey into the Converse Model of Attitude Stability." *American Journal of Sociology*, 92, 3 (November 1986): 657-677.

Brody, Elaine M. "Aging." In John B. Turner et al. (Eds.), *Encyclopedia of Social Work*. 17th ed. Vol. 1. Washington, D.C.: NASW, 1977.

Brown, Lawrence. "The Scope and Limits of Equality as a Normative Guide to Federal Health Care Policy." *Public Policy*, 26, 4 (Fall 1978): 481-532.

Burke, Vincent J. and Vee Burke. *Nixon's Good Deed: Welfare Reform*. New York: Columbia University Press, 1974.

Butler, Robert N. *Why Survive? Being Old in America*. 1st ed. New York: Harper and Row, 1975.

Calhoun, Richard B. *In Search of the New Old*. New York: Elsevier, 1978.

Campbell, Angus. "Politics Through the Life Cycle." *The Gerontologist*, 11, 2 (Summer 1971): 112-117.

Campbell, John Creighton and John Strate. "Are Old People Conservative?" *The Gerontologist*, 21, 6 (December 1981): 580-591.

Christensen, Harold T. *Handbook of Marriage and the Family*. Chicago: Rand-McNally, 1964.

Clark, Ruth and Greg Martire. "Americans, Still in a Family Way." *Public Opinion*, 2, 5 (October-November 1979): 16-19.

Cohen, Wilbur J. Personal communication, 1978.

Cohen, Wilbur J. "Social Insurance." In John B. Turner et al. (Eds.), *Encyclopedia of Social Work*. 17th ed. Vol. 2. Washington, D.C.: NASW, 1977.

Conkin, Paul K. *The New Deal*. New York: Thomas Y. Crowell Co., 1967.

Converse, Philip E. *The Dynamics of Party Support: Cohort-Analyzing Party Identification*. Beverly Hills: Sage Publications, 1976.

Converse, Philip E. "The Nature of Belief Systems in Mass Publics." In David Ernest Apter (Ed.), *Ideology and Discontent*. New York: The Free Press, 1964.

Converse, Philip E. "Rejoinder to Judd and Milburn." *American Sociological Review* 45, 4 (August 1980): 644-646.

Coser, Lewis, "Conflict." In David L. Sills (Ed.), *International Encyclopedia of the Social Sciences*. Vol. 3. New York: Crowell Collier and Macmillan, 1968.

Coughlin, Richard M. *Ideology, Public Opinion and Welfare Policy*. Berkeley: Institute of International Studies, 1980.

Cowill, Donald. *Aging Around the World*. Belmont, California: Wadsworth, 1986.

Cox, Harold. *Later Life: The Realities of Aging*. Englewood Cliffs, New Jersey: Prentice-Hall, 1984.

Cumming, Elaine. "Allocation of Care to the Mentally Ill, American Style." In Mayer Zald (Ed.), *Organizing for Community Welfare*. Chicago: Quadrangle Books, 1967.

Cutler, Neal. "Aging and Public Policy: The Politics of Agenda-Setting." *Policy Studies Journal*, 13, 1 (September 1984): 1-13.

Cutler, Stephen. "Perceived Prestige Loss and Political-Attitudes Among Aged." *The Gerontologist*, 13, 1 (Spring 1973): 69-75.

Cutler, Stephen J. et al. "Aging and Conservatism: Cohort Changes in Attitudes About Legalized Abortion." *Journal of Gerontology*, 35, 1 (January 1980): 115-123.

Dahrendorf, R. *Life Chances: Approaches to Social and Political Theory*. Chicago: The University of Chicago Press, 1979.

Daneke, G. A., M. Garcia, and J. Delli Priscoli (Eds.). *Public Involvement and Social Impact Assessment*. Boulder: Westview Press, 1983.

Davidson, Andrew R. and Elizabeth Thompson. "Cross Cultural Studies of Attitudes and Beliefs." In Harry C. Triandis and Richard W. Breslin (Eds.), *Handbook of Cross Cultural Psychology: Vol. 5, Social Psychology*. Boston: Allyn and Bacon, 1980.

Davis, James A. "Achievement Variables and Class Cultures." *American Sociological Review*, 47 (October 1982): 569-586.

Davison, W. Phillips. "The Public Opinion Process." In Reo M. Christenson and Robert O. McWilliams (Eds.), *Voice of the People: Readings in Public Opinion and Propaganda*. New York: McGraw-Hill, 1962.

Dawes, Robyn M. and Tom L. Smith. "Attitude and Opinion Measurement." In G. Lindzey and E. Aronson (Eds.), *The Handbook of Social Psychology*, Vol. 1. New York: Random House, 1985.

Degler, Carl N. *Affluence and Anxiety: America Since 1945*. 2nd ed. Glenview, Illinois: Scott Foresman, 1975.

De Schweinitz, Karl. *England's Road to Social Security from the Statute of Laborers in 1349 to the Beveridge Report of 1942*. New York: Barnes, 1943. [A Perpetual Edition published in 1961]

Detroit Free Press. February 20, 1979.

Dickstein, Morris. *Gates of Eden: American Culture in the Sixties*. New York: Basic Books, 1977.

DiRenzo, Gordon J. (Ed.). *We, the People: American Character and Social Change*. Westport, Connecticut: Greenwood Press, 1977.

Dollar, Charles M. et al. *America: Changing Times*. New York: John Wiley and Sons, 1979.

Dos Passos, John. *State of the Nation*. Houghton Mifflin, 1944.

Drucker, Peter F. *The Unseen Revolution: How Pension Fund Socialism Came to America*. 1st ed. New York: Harper and Row, 1976.

Dubin, Robert and Joseph E. Champoux. "Workers Central Life Interests and Personality Characteristics." *Journal of Vocational Behavior*, 6, 2 (April 1975): 165-174.

Dubin, Robert, Joseph E. Champoux, and Lyman W. Porter. "Central Life Interests and Organizational Commitment of Blue-Collar and Clerical Workers."

Administrative Science Quarterly, 20, 3 (September 1975): 411-421.

Dumazedier, Joffre. "Leisure." In David L. Sills (Ed.), *International Encylopedia of the Social Sciences*. Vol. 9 New York: The Free Press, 1968.

Dunn, William N. (Ed.). *Values, Ethics, and the Practice of Policy Analysis*. Lexington, Kentucky: Lexington Books, 1983.

Dye, Thomas R. (Co-Ed.). "Symposium on Determinants of Public Policy: Cities, States, and Nations." *Policy Studies Journal*, 7, 4 (Summer 1979).

Edelman, Murray. *Political Language: Words That Succeed and Policies That Fail*. New York: Academic Press, 1977.

Ehrenreich, Barbara. *The Hearts of Men: American Dreams and the Flight from Commitment*. 1st ed. Garden City, New York: Anchor Press, 1983.

Ehrlich, Howard J. "Attitudes, Behavior, and the Intervening Variables." *American Sociologist*, 4, 1 (February 1969): 29-34.

Elder, Glenn H. *Children of the Great Depression: Social Change in Life Experience*. Chicago: University of Chicago Press, 1974.

Eliot, T. S. "The Love Song of J. Alfred Prufrock." In T. S. Eliot, *The Poems and Plays of T. S. Eliot*. 1st ed. New York: Harcourt, Brace, 1952.

Erickson, Robert S. and Norman R. Luttbeg. *American Public Opinion: Its Origins, Content, and Impact*. New York: John Wiley, 1973.

Erikson, Kai T. *Everything in Its Path: Destruction of Community in the Buffalo Creek Flood*. New York: Simon & Schuster, 1976.

Estes, Carroll Lynn. *The Aging Enterprise: A Critical Examination of Social Policies and Services for the Aged*. San Francisco: Jossey-Bass, 1980.

Estes, Carroll Lynn, Robert J. Newcomer, and Associates. *Fiscal Austerity and Aging: Shifting Government Responsibility for the Elderly*. Beverly Hills: Sage Publications, 1983.

Etzioni Amitai and C. O. Atkinson. *Sociological Implications of Alternative Income Transfer Systems*. New York: Bureau of Social Science Research, Columbia University, 1969.

Eustis, Nancy N., Jay N. Greenberg, and Sharon K. Patten. *Long Term Care for Older Persons: A Policy Perspective*. Monterey: Brooks, Cole Pub. Co., 1984.

Fallows, James J. "Entitlements." *Atlantic Monthly* 250 (November 1982): 51-59.

Faris, Robert E. L. "Creativity: Genius and Ability." In David L. Sills (Ed.), *International Encyclopedia of the Social Sciences*., Vol. 3. New York: Crowell Collier & Macmillan, 1968.

Fischer, David Hackett. *Growing Old in America*. Expanded ed. New York: Oxford University Press, 1978.

Fischer, Frank. *Politics, Values and Public Policy: The Problem of Methodology*. Boulder: Westview Press, 1980.

Fishbein, Martin and Bertram H. Raven. "The AB Scales—An Operational Definition of Belief and Attitude." *Human Relations*, 15, 1 (February 1962): 35-44.

Fogel, Richard W., Elaine Hatfield, Sara B. Kiesler, and Ethel Shanas (Eds.). *Aging, Stability and Change in the Family*. New York: Academic Press, 1981.

Free, Lloyd A. and Hadley Cantril. *The Political Beliefs of Americans: A Study of Public Opinion*. New Brunswick, New Jersey: Rutgers University Press, 1967.

Freud, Sigmund. *The Future of an Illusion*. New York: Anchor, n.d.

Friedmann, Eugene A. and Robert J. Havighurst et al. *The Meaning of Work and Retirement*. Chicago: University of Chicago Press, 1954.

Fromm, Erich. *Escape from Freedom*. New York: Holt, Rinehart and Winston, 1961.

Galbraith, John Kenneth. *The Affluent Society*. Boston: Houghton Mifflin, 1958.

Gardner, Howard. *Frames of Mind: The Theory of Mulitple Intelligences*. New York: Basic Books, 1983.

Garraty, John Arthur. *The American Nation: A History of the United States*. 3rd ed. New York: Harper and Row, 1975.

Gilbert, Neil. *Capitalism and the Welfare State: Dilemmas of Social Benevolence*. New Haven: Yale University Press, 1983.

Glasser, Lois N. and Paul H. Glasser. "Hedonism and the Family: Conflict in Values?" *Journal of Marriage and Family Counseling*, 3, 4 (October 1977): 11-18.

Glazer, Nathan and Daniel Patrick Moynihan. *Beyond the Melting Pot: The Negroes, Puerto Ricans, Jews, Italians, and Irish of New York City*. Cambridge: MIT Press, 1963.

Gold, Byron, Elizabeth Kutza, and Theodore R. Marmor. "United States Social Policy on Old Age: Present Patterns and Predictions." In Bernice L. Neugarten and Robert Havighurst (Eds.), *Social Policy, Social Ethics, and the Aging Society*. Committee on Human Development, University of Chicago. Washington, D.C.: Government Printing Office, 1976.

Goodman, Ellen. *Turning Points*. New York: Doubleday, 1979.

Goudy, Willis J. et al. "Changes in Attitudes Toward Retirement: Evidence from a Panel Study of Older Males." *Journal of Gerontology*, 59, 2 (November 1980): 942-948.

Green, G. G. et al. "What's Happening to the American Family? Results of a Questionnaire." *Bettter Homes and Gardens*, 56 (June 1978): 23-24ff.

Grichting, Wolfgang. *Security vs. Liberty: Analyzing Social Structure and Social Policy*. Lanham, Maryland: University Press of America, 1984.

Handel, W. "Normative Expectations and the Emergence of Meaning as Solutions to Problems: Convergence of Structural and Interactionist Views." *American Journal of Sociology*, 84, 4 (January 1979): 855-881.

Hardy, Jean. *Values in Social Policy: Nine Contradictions*. London: Routledge & Kegan Paul, 1981.

Harootyan, Robert A. *Annotated Index of Federal Legislation Impacting on the Elderly*. Los Angeles, California: Social Policy Laboratory, Andrus Gerontology Center, University of Southern California, Fall 1977.

Harrington, Michael. *The Other America*. New York: Macmillan, 1962.

Hayworth, J. T. and M. A. Smith (Eds.). *Work and Leisure: An Interdisciplinary Study in Theory Education and Planning*. Princeton: Princeton Book Co., 1975.

Heidenheimer, Arnold J. et al. *Comparative Public Policy: The Politics of Social Choice in Europe and America*. New York: St. Martin's Press, 1975.

Hendrickson, Robert M. and L. J. Axelson. "Middle Class Attitudes Toward the Poor: Are They Changing?" *Social Service Review*, 59, 2 (June 1985): 295-304.

Herberg, Will. *Protestant, Catholic, Jew: An Essay in American Religious Sociology*.

Garden City, New York: Anchor Books, 1960.

Himmelfarb, Gertrude. *The Idea of Poverty: England in the Early Industrial Age.* 1st ed. New York: Knopf, 1984.

Hirschman, Albert O. *Shifting Involvements: Private Intrest and Public Action.* Princeton: Princeton University Press, 1982.

Hobart, Charles W. "Commitment, Value Conflict and the Future of the American Family." *Marriage and Family Living,* 25, 4 (November 1963): 405-414.

Howe, Irving. *World of Our Fathers.* New York: Harcourt Brace Jovanovich, 1976.

Jablonski, Sharon. Personal Communication, 1986.

Janowitz, Morris. *The Last Half-Century.* Chicago: The University of Chicago Press, 1978.

Jansson, Bruce S. *Theory and Practice of Social Welfare Policy: Analysis, Processes, and Current Issues.* Belmont, California: Wadsworth Publishing Co., 1984.

Johnson, A. Sidney III. "Interim Conclusions of the Family Impact Seminar." In John E. Tropman et al. (Eds.), *New Strategic Perspectives on Social Policy.* New York: Pergamon Press, 1981.

Judd, Charles M. and Michael A. Milburn. "The Structure of Attitude Systems in the General Public: Comparisons of a Structural Equation Model." *American Sociological Review,* 45, 4 (August 1980): 627-643.

Katz, Daniel. "The Functional Approach to the Study of Attitudes." *Public Opinion Quarterly,* 34, 2 (Summer 1960): 163-209.

Katz, Daniel et al. *Bureaucratic Encounters: A Pilot Study in the Evaluation of Government Services.* Ann Arbor: Survey Research Center, Institute for Social Research, University of Michigan, 1975.

Keach, William R. "Review of Seymour Martin Lipset and William Schneider, 'The Confidence Gap Business: Labor and Government in the Public Mind.' " *Science,* 223 (January 6, 1984): 43-44.

Kelso, Robert Wilson. *Poverty.* New York: Longmans, Green and Co., 1929.

Kiesler, Sara B., James N. Morgan, Valerie Kincade Oppenheimer (Eds.). *Aging, Social Change.* New York: Academic Press, 1981.

Kim, Jae-on and Charles W. Mueller. *Introduction to Factor Analysis: What It Is and How to Do It.* Beverly Hills: Sage Publications, 1978.

Kinder, Donald R. and David O. Sears. "Public Opinion and Political Action." In G. Lindzey and E. Aronson (Eds.), *The Handbook of Social Psychology.* Vol. 2. New York: Random House, 1985.

Kirkpatrick, Clifford. *The Family as Process and Institution.* 2nd ed. New York: Ronald Press, 1963.

Kirkpatrick, Samuel A. "Aging Effects and Generational-Differences in Social-Welfare Attitude Constraint in the Mass Public." *Western Political Quarterly,* 29, 1 (1976): 43-58.

Knoke, David. "In Confidence We Trust." *Contemporary Sociology,* 43, 3 (May 1984): 275-276.

Kohn, Melvin and Carmi Schooler. "Occupational Experience and Psychological Functioning: An Assessment of Reciprocal Effects." *American Sociological Review,* 38 (February 1973): 97-118.

Kornhauser, William. *The Politics of Mass Society.* Glencoe, Illinois: The Free Press, 1959.

Kreps, Juanita M. *Lifetime Allocation of Work and Leisure*. U.S. Department of H.E.W., Social Security Administration Office of Research and Statistics, Research Report No. 22, 1968.

Kutza, Elizabeth Ann. *The Benefits of Old Age: Social-Welfare Policy for the Elderly*. Chicago: University of Chicago Press, 1981.

Ladd, Everett Carll, Jr. "Traditional Values Regnant." *Public Opinion*, 1, 1 (March-April 1978): 45-49.

LaFrance, Arthur B. *Welfare Law: Structure and Entitlement in a Nutshell*. St. Paul, Minnesota: West Publishing Co., 1979.

Lammers, William W. *Public Policy and the Aging*. Washington, D.C.: C.Q. Press, 1983.

Lammers, William W. and David Klingman. *Explanations of Changing State Policy Efforts for the Aging*. Los Angeles, California: Andrus Gerontology Center, University of Southern California, n.d.

Lasch, Christopher. *Haven in a Heartless World: The Family Besieged*. New York: Basic Books, 1977.

Lemon, Nigel. *Attitudes and Their Measurement*. New York: Wiley, 1973.

Lenski, Gerhard Emmanuel. *The Religious Factor: A Sociological Study of Religion's Impact on Politics, Economics, and Family Life*. Rev. ed. Garden City, New York: Doubleday, 1963.

Levinson, Daniel J. et al. *The Seasons of a Man's Life*. New York: Knopf, 1978.

Lipset, Seymour Martin. *The First New Nation*. New York: Basic Books, 1963.

Lipset, Seymour Martin and William Schneider. *The Confidence Gap: Business, Labor, and Government in the Public Mind*. New York: The Free Press, 1983.

Longman, Phillip. "From Calhoun to Sister Boom Boom: The Dubious Legacy of Interest Group Politics." *The Washington Monthly*, 15, 4 (June 1983): 11-22.

Louis Harris and Associates. *The Myth and Reality of Aging in America*. Washington, D.C.: National Council on Aging, 1975.

Lowenthal, Marjorie Fiske, Majda Thurnher, and David Chiriboga. *Four Stages of Life*. 1st ed. San Francisco: Jossey-Bass, 1975.

Luttbeg, Norman R. (Ed.). *Public Opinion and Public Policy: Models of Political Linkage*. 3rd ed. Itasca, Illinois: F. E. Peacock, 1981.

Lynd, Robert S. *Knowledge for What? The Place of Social Science in American Culture*. Princeton: Princeton University Press, 1939.

Machlowitz, Marilyn M. *Workaholics, Living with Them, Working with Them*. Reading, Massachusetts: Addison-Wesley, 1980.

Maddox, George L. "Retirement as a Social Event in the United States." In Bernice L. Neugarten (Ed.), *Middle Age and Aging: A Reader in Social Psychology*. Chicago: The University of Chicago Press, 1968.

Maeda, Daisaku et al. "Japan/U.S. Cross Cultural Study on the Knowledge of Aging, the Attitudes Toward Old People and the Sense of Responsibility for Aged Parent." Unpublished. Tokyo, Japan: Tokyo Metropolitan Institute of Gerontology, n.d.

Mannheim, Karl. *Ideology and Utopia: An Introduction to the Sociology of Knowledge*. Translated by Louis Wirth and Edward Shils. New York: Harcourt, Brace, 1955.

Marmor, Theodore R. (Ed.). *Poverty Policy: A Compendium of Cash Transfer Proposals*. Chicago: Aldine Atherton, 1971.

Martin, George T., Jr. and Mayer N. Zald (Eds.). *Social Welfare in Society*. New York: Columbia University Press, 1981.

McConnell, James. Personal Communication, 1985.

McCormick, James M. *American Foreign Policy and American Values*. Itasca, Illinois: F. E. Peacock, 1985.

McCuskey, Neal G. and Edgar F. Borgatta. *Aging and Retirement: Prospects, Planning and Policy*. Beverly Hills: Sage Publications, 1981.

McGuire, W. "Attitudes and Attitude Change." In G. Lindzey and E. Aronson (Eds.), *The Handbook of Social Psychology*. Vol. 2. New York: Random House, 1985.

McKeon, Richard. *Introduction to Aristotle*. New York: The Modern Library, 1947.

Merton, Robert King. "Bureaucratic Structure and Personality." In Robert K. Merton, *Social Theory and Social Structure*. Rev. ed. Glencoe, Illinois: The Free Press, 1957.

Merton, Robert and Elinore Barber. "Sociological Ambivalence." In Edward A. Tiryakian (Ed.), *Sociological Theory, Values, and Sociocultural Change*. New York: The Free Press of Glencoe, 1963.

Michelon, L. C. "The New Leisure Class." *American Journal of Sociology*, 59, 4 January 1954): 371-378.

Miller, Arthur H., Patricia Gurin, and Gerald Gurin. "Age Consciousness and Political Mobilization of Older Americans." *The Gerontologist*, 20, 6 (December 1980): 691-700.

Miller, Douglas T. and Marion Nowak. *The Fifties: The Way We Really Were*. 1st ed. Garden City, New York: Doubleday, 1977.

Miller, S. M. "Criteria for Anti-Poverty Policies: A Paradigm for Choice." *Poverty and Human Resources Abstracts*. Sept.-Oct., 1968: 3-11.

Miller, W. Lee. *Welfare and Values in America: A Review of Attitudes Towards Welfare and Welfare Policies in the Light of American History and Culture*. Durham, North Carolina: Duke University, Welfare Policy Project, 1977.

Monroe, Alan D. "Public Opinion as a Factor in Public Policy Formation." *Policy Studies Journal*, 6, 4 (Summer 1978): 542-548.

Morgan, James N. *Five Thousand American Families*. Ann Arbor: Institute for Social Research, 1974.

Morgan, James N. et al. *Income and Welfare in the United States*. New York: McGraw-Hill, 1962.

Mortimer, J. T. and J. Lorence. "Work Experience and Occupational Value Socialization: A Longitudinal Study." *American Journal of Sociology*, 84, 6 (May 1979): 1361-1385.

Myles, John F. *Old Age in the Welfare State: The Political Economy of Public Pensions*. Boston: Little, Brown, 1984.

Myrdal, Gunnar. *An American Dilemma: The Negro Problem and Modern Democracy*. 2 vols. New York: Harper and Row, 1944; reprint, 1962.

Naisbett, John. *Megatrends*. New York: Warner, 1982.

Neuberger, Richard L. and Kelley Loe. *An Army of the Aged: A History and Analysis of the Townsend Old Age Pension Plan*. New York: Da Capo Press, 1936; reprint, 1973.

Neugarten, Bernice L. "Age Groups in American Society and the Rise of the Young-Old." *The Annals of the American Academy of Political and Social Science*,

415 (September 1974): 187-198.

Neugarten, Bernice Levin (Ed.). *Middle Age and Aging: A Reader in Social Psychology*. Chicago: The University of Chicago Press, 1968.

Neugarten, Bernice Levin and Robert Havighurst (Eds.). *Conference on Social Policy, Social Ethics and the Aging Society*. Washington, D.C.: U.S. Government Printing Office, 1977.

Neuman, W. R. "Differentiation and Integration in Political Thinking." *American Journal of Sociology*, 86, 6 (May 1981): 1236-1268.

Nie, Norman H., Sidney Verba, and John R. Petrocik. *The Changing American Voter*. Cambridge: Harvard University Press, 1976.

Olber, Jeffrey. "The Odd Compartmentalization: Public Opinion Aggregate Data and Policy Analysis." *Policy Studies Journal*, 7, 3 (Spring 1979): 524-540.

Organization for Economic Cooperation and Development. *The Welfare State in Crisis*. Paris: Organization for Economic Cooperation and Development, 1981.

Ozawa, Martha N. "Individual Equity versus Social Adequacy in Federal Old-Age Insurance." *Social Service Review*, 48, 1 (March 1974): 24-38.

Palmore, Erdman. *Social Patterns in Normal Aging: Findings from the Duke Longitudinal Study*. Durham, North Carolina: Duke University Press, 1981.

Parsons, Talcott. Personal correspondence, 1978.

Parsons, Talcott. *Social Structure and Personality*. New York: The Free Press of Glencoe, 1964.

Patterson, James T. *America's Struggle Against Poverty, 1900-1980*. Cambridge: Harvard University Press, 1981.

Pierce, Dean. *Policy for the Social Work Practitioner*. New York: Longmans, 1984.

Piven, Frances Fox and Richard A. Cloward. *Regulating the Poor: The Functions of Public Welfare*. New York: Random House, 1971.

Plath, David W. *Long Engagements: Maturity in Modern Japan*. Stanford: Stanford University Press, 1980.

Pole, J. R. *The Pursuit of Equality in American History*. Berkeley: The University of California Press, 1978.

Pratt, Henry J. *The Gray Lobby*. Chicago: The University of Chicago Press, 1976.

Rajecki, D. W. *Attitudes, Themes and Advances*. Sunderland, Massachusetts: Sinauer Associates, 1982.

Reamer, Frederic G. "The Concept of Paternalism in Social Work." *Social Service Review*, 57, 2 (June 1983): 254-271.

Reid, William J. "Sectarian Agencies." In John B. Turner et al. (Eds.), *Encyclopedia of Social Work*. 17th ed. Vol. 2. Washington, D.C.: NASW, 1977.

Riesman, David. "Some Clinical and Cultural Aspects of Aging." *American Journal of Sociology*, 59, 4 (January 1954): 379-383.

Riesman, David et al. *The Lonely Crowd: A Study of the Changing American Character*. New Haven: Yale University Press, 1950.

Riley, Matilda White, M. Johnson, and Anne Foner. *Aging and Society*. Vol. III. New York: Russell Sage, 1972.

Robinson, Robert V. and W. Bell. "Equality, Success and Social Justice in England and the United States." *American Sociological Review*, 43, 2 (April 1978): 125-143.

Rokeach, Milton. *Beliefs, Attitudes and Values: A Theory of Organization and*

Change. San Francisco: Jossey-Bass, 1968.

Rokeach, Milton. *The Nature of Human Values*. New York: The Free Press, 1973.

Rokeach, Milton (Ed.). *Understanding Human Values: Individual and Societal*. New York: The Free Press, 1979.

Rosenthal, Peggy. *Words and Values: Some Leading Words and Where They Lead Us*. New York: Oxford University Press, 1984.

Rothman, David J. and Stanton Wheeler (Eds.). *Social History and Social Policy*. New York: Academic Press, 1981.

Rotter, Julian G. "Generalized Expectancies for Internal versus External Control of Reinforcement." *Psychological Monographs: General and Applied*, 80, 1 (Whole #609).

Ryan, William. *Equality*. New York: Pantheon Books, 1981.

Salamon, Lester. "The Results Are Coming In." *The Foundation News* (July-August, 1984): 16-23.

Schlitz, Michael E. *Public Attitudes Toward Social Security 1935-1965*. USDHEW, SSA Research Report #33; Washington, D.C.: U.S. Social Security Administration, Office of Research and Statistics, 1970.

Schorr, Alvin L. *Explorations in Social Policy*. New York: Basic Books, 1968.

Schrag, Peter. *The Decline of the Wasp*. New York: Simon & Schuster, 1971.

Schreiber, E. M. and Lorna R. Marsden. "Age and Opinions on a Government Program of Medical Aid." *Journal of Gerontology*, 27, 1 (1972): 95-101.

Schuman, H. and M. Johnson. "Attitudes and Behavior." *Annual Review of Sociology* (1976): 161-207.

Sennett, Richard. *The Fall of Public Man*. New York: Random House, 1978.

Sessoms, Hanson Douglas. "Recreation in Environmental Planning." In John B. Turner et al. (Eds.), *Encyclopedia of Social Work*. 17th ed., vol. 2. Washington, D.C.: NASW, 1977.

Shils, Edward. *Center and Periphery: Essays in Macrosociology*. Chicago: University of Chicago Press, 1975.

Shils, Edward. "Tradition and the Generations." *American Scholar* (Winter 1983-1984): 27-40.

Shock, Nathan Wetheril. *Trends in Gerontology*. 2nd ed. Stanford: Stanford University Press, 1957.

"Should You Be Forced to Retire at 65?" *U.S. News and World Report*, 43 (September 13, 1957): 94-97.

Simmel, Arnold. "Privacy." In David L. Sills (Ed.), *The International Encyclopedia of the Social Sciences*. Vol. 12. New York: Crowell Collier and Macmillan, 1968.

Skidmore, Felicity (Ed.). *Social Security Financing*. Cambridge: MIT Press, 1981.

Sorokin, Pitrim. *The Crisis of Our Age*. New York: Dutton, 1957.

Stack, Carol B. *All Our Kin: Strategies for Survival in a Black Community*. New York: Harper & Row, 1974.

Starr, Jerold M. "Mass or Public? The American People as Revealed Through the Polls." 73rd Annual Meeting of the American Sociological Association, San Francisco, September 1978. For a more recent discussion, see Jerold M. Starr (Ed.). *Cultural Politics*. New York: Praeger, 1985.

Stavrianos, Leften Stavros. *The Promise of the Coming Dark Age*. San Francisco: W. H. Freeman, 1976.

Stone, Deborah A. "Diagnosis and the Dole: The Functions of Illness in American Distributive Politics." *Journal of Health Politics Policy and Law*, 4, 3 (Fall 1979): 507-521.

Tallman, I. and M. Ihinger-Tallman. "Values, Distributive Justice and Social Change." *American Sociological Review*, 44, 2 (April 1979): 216-233.

Talmon, Yonina. "Aging: Social Aspects." In David L. Sills (Ed.), *International Encyclopedia of the Social Sciences*. Vol. 1. New York: Crowell Collier and Macmillan, 1968.

Tax, Sol and Larry S. Krucoff. "Social Darwinism." In David L. Sills (Ed.), *The International Encyclopedia of the Social Sciences*. Vol. 14. New York: Crowell Collier and Macmillan, 1968.

The Myth and Reality of Aging in America. Washington, D.C.: The National Council on Aging, 1977.

Tobin, Sheldon S., Steven M. Davidson, and Ann Sack. *Effective Social Service for Older Americans*. Ann Arbor: Institute of Gerontology, The University of Michigan/Wayne State University, 1976.

Trattner, Walter I. *From Poor Law to Welfare State: A History of Social Welfare in America*. 2nd ed. New York: The Free Press, 1974.

Tropman, John E. "Societal Values and Social Policy." In J. E. Tropman et al. (Eds.), *Strategic Perspectives on Social Policy*. New York: Pergamon Press, 1976.

Tropman, John E. *Policy Management in the Human Services*. New York: Columbia University Press, 1984.

Tropman, John E. "The Constant Crisis: Social Welfare and the American Cultural Structure." *California Sociologist*, 2 (Winter 1978): 61-87.

Tropman, John E. and Jane K. McClure. "Policy Analysis and Older People: A Conceptual Framework." *Journal of Sociology and Social Welfare*, 5, 6 (November 1978): 808-822.

Tropman, John E. and Jane K. McClure. "Values Dualism and Social Policy Affecting the Elderly." *Policy Studies Journal*, 9, 4 (Special Issue #2, 1980-1981): 604-613.

Tropman, John E. and John Strate, "Social Characteristics and Personal Opinion: Notes Toward a Theory." *California Sociologist*, 6, 1 (Winter 1983): 23-38.

Turner, John B. et al. (Eds.). *Encyclopedia of Social Work*. 17th ed. Washington, D.C.: NASW, 1977.

Turner, Ralph H. "Modes of Ascent Through Education: Sponsored and Contest Mobility." In Reinhard Bendix and Seymour Martin Lipset (Eds.), *Class, Status, and Power: Social Stratification in Comparative Perspective*. 2nd ed. New York: The Free Press, 1966.

U.S. Bureau of the Census. *Historical Statistics of the United States, Colonial Times to 1957*. Washington, D.C.: Government Printing Office, 1960.

Vaillant, George. *Adaptation to Life*. Boston: Little, Brown, 1977.

Vickers, Geoffrey. "Values, Norms and Policies." *Policy Sciences*, 4, 1 (1973): 103-111.

Vickery, Clair. "The Changing Household: Implications for Devising an Income Support Program." *Public Policy*, 26 (Winter 1978): 121-151.

Vidich, Arthur J. and Joseph Bensman. *Small Town in Mass Society: Class, Power and Religion in a Rural Community*. Princeton: Princeton University Press, 1968.

Vladeck, Bruce C. *Unloving Care: The Nursing Home Tragedy*. New York: Basic Books, 1980.

Wall Street Journal. June 4, 1986.

Walster, Elaine, G. William Walster, and Ellen Berscheid. *Equity: Theory and Research*. Boston: Allyn and Bacon, 1978.

Wasserman, Harvey. *America Born and Reborn*. New York: Macmillan, 1983.

Weber, Max. *The Protestant Ethic and the Spirit of Capitalism*. Translated by Talcott Parsons. New York: Scribner, 1956.

Webster, Murray, Jr. and James E. Driskell, Jr. "Status Generalization: A Review and Some New Data." *American Sociological Review*, 43 (April 1978): 220-236.

Welford, Alan Traviss et al. *Skill and Age, An Experimental Approach*. London, New York: Oxford University Press, 1951.

White, Ronald Cedric and C. Howard Hopkins. *The Social Gospel: Religion and Reform in Changing America*. Philadelphia: Temple University Press, 1976.

Wilensky, Harold L. and Charles N. Lebeaux. *Industrial Society and Social Welfare*. New York: The Free Press, 1956.

Williams, Robin M., Jr. *American Society*. 2nd ed. New York: 1960.

Williams, Robin M., Jr. "Values: The Concept of Values." In David L. Sills (Ed.), *The International Encyclopedia of the Social Sciences*. Vol. 16. New York: Crowell Collier and Macmillan, and The Free Press, 1968.

Williams, Robin M., Jr. "Individual and Group Values." In Bertram M. Gross (Ed.), *Social Intelligence for America's Future: Explorations in Societal Problems*. Boston: Allyn and Bacon, 1969.

Willits, Fern K., Robert C. Bealer, and Donald M. Crider. "Changes in Individual Attitudes Toward Traditional Morality: A 24-Year Follow-Up Study." *Journal of Gerontology*, 32, 6 (November 1977): 681-688.

Wilson, Albert J. E. III. *Social Services for Older Persons*. Boston: Little, Brown, 1984.

Wilson, Robert N. "The Courage to Be Leisured." *Social Forces*, 60, 2 (November 1981): 282-303.

Wohlenberg, Ernest H. "A Regional Approach to Public Attitudes and Public Assistance." *Social Service Review*, 50 (September 1976): 491-505.

Wolfensberger, Wolf et al. *The Principle of Normalization in Human Services*. Toronto: Leonard/Crainford/National Institute of Mental Retardation, 1972.

Yankelovich, Daniel. *New Rules: Searching for Self-Fulfillment in a World Turned Upside Down*. New York: Random House, 1981.

Yankelovich, Daniel. "The Work Ethic Is Underemployed." *Psychology Today*, 16 (May 1982): 5-6ff.

Yeric, Jerry L. and John R. Todd. *Public Opinion: The Visible Politics*. Itasca, Illinois: F. E. Peacock, 1983.

Yinger, J. Milton. *Countercultures: The Promise and Peril of a World Turned Upside Down*. New York: The Free Press, 1982.

Zavalloni, M. "Values." In Harry Triandis and R. W. Brislin (Eds.), *Handbook of Cross Cultural Social Psychology*. Vol. 5. Boston: Allyn and Bacon, 1980.

Zelizer, Viviana A. "Human Values and the Market: The Case of Life Insurance and Death in 19th Century America." *American Journal of Sociology*, 84, 3 (November 1978): 591-610.

INDEX

Accused, rights of, 104, 105(figure), 106
Adequacy, versus equity, 37-40, 62, 68, 91-92, 109 n.1
Age: and public opinion, 10, 12, 14-15; and values, 154
Alves, Wayne M., 38, 39
Alwin, Duane, 52
American Born and Reborn (Wasserman), 182 n.1
Association of Benevolent Societies (Boston), 41
Associations, and values, 166-67
Attitudes, over time, 127-28

Barber, Elinore, 27
Bengston, Vern L., 26
Bishop, George D., 15-16
Blacks: and government help, 96-99; progress of, 101, 102(figure), 103
Boy Scouts, 48
Brown v. The Topeka Board of Education, 8, 95

Calvin, John, 46, 47-48
Catholicism, orientations of, 50-52, 56-57 n.11
Champoux, Joseph E., 48
Change: of 1960s, 5; pervasiveness of, 174-75; and values, 120-22
Children, ideal number of, 117, 118(figure), 119-20
Christensen, Harold T., 52
Church: attendance, 112, 113(figure), 114; versus state, 56 n.3, 62
Civil rights, 7-8, 178; cost of, 110 n.4; declining support for, 109, 170; progress of, 101, 102(figure), 103; questions on, 13(chart); speed of, 99, 100(figure), 101
Civil rights movement, 5, 73, 95
Class action suits, 95
Cohen, Wilbur J., 39, 40, 41-42, 46, 54
Collective, versus individual, 32-33
Commitments, 5; competing, 76, 172; decline by age, 8; measuring, 37; questions on, 13(chart); strength of, 122. *See also* Values

Confidence Gap, The (Lipset and Schneider), 19
Conflict: functioning of, 31-32; of 1960s, 5
Conflict theory of values, 26-31
Conservatism, 11(chart), 15, 65, 135; and feeling thermometers, 79, 80(figure), 81
Coser, Lewis, 43-44
Coughlin, Richard M., 172
Counterculture, 5
Countercultures: The Promise and Peril of a World Turned Upside Down (Yinger), 5, 29
Cultural structure, 21 n.3

Davis, James A., 176-77
Democrats, 135; and feeling thermometers, 79, 80(figure), 81
Depression (1930s), 61, 86, 103, 175
De Schweinitz, Karl, 47, 49
Differentiation, 28
Division of labor, 108
Dualism, of values, 31, 34, 92-93, 128, 137, 172, 173
Dubin, Robert, 48
Dumazedier, Joffre, 46-47

Edelman, Murray, 28, 33
Education, 46; and values, 154
Elderly: as children, 49; compared to other age groups, 93; as conservative, 15; differences over time, 139; as powerless, 70, 71, 106; as public policy beneficiaries, 7; studies of, 6
Electric power, provision of, 84-86, 90, 92
Employment, 74-78, 91, 96, 97(figure), 98
English Poor Law, 44
Entitlement: conflict over, 131; versus struggle, 43-46, 76, 96, 104, 109 n.1
Equity, versus adequacy, 37-40, 62, 68, 91-92, 109 n.1
Erikson, Kai T., 20, 26, 27-28, 34

Fairness, principle of, 37-40
Factor analysis: by age, 140-41(chart);

distribution of variables in 130(chart); policy opinion in, 132-33(chart)
Factors: over time, 138-43; privatism, 135, 161-63, 164(table); public inadequacy, 134-35, 159-61, 162(table); public inequity, 136, 163, 165(table); questionable public entitlements, 131-34, 159, 160(table); self-reliance, 135, 161-63, 164(table); public inadeism, 136-37, 166; as value groupings, 158-59
Family: extended vs. nuclear, 52, 122 n.1; ideal number of children, 117, 118(figure), 119-20; life-cycle of, 123 n.3; versus personal development, 52-55
Family Impact Seminar (George Washington University), 53-54
Fischer, David Hackett, 6, 42
Four Freedoms, 44

Gallup Poll, 1, 12; questions from, 13(chart)
Gerontology, 6
Gerontophobia, to gerontofratria, 6
Gilbert, Neil, 42
Girl Scouts, 48
Glasser, Lois, 54
Glasser, Paul, 54
Goodman, Ellen, *Turning Points*, 29
Goudy, Willis J., 176
Government: benefits from, 67(figure); criticism of, 65; and electric power provision, 84, 85(figure), 86, 90; and fair treatment, 96, 97(figure), 98-99; and health care, 81, 82(figure), 83-84, 90, 180; and housing, 84, 85(figure), 86, 90; individual's role in, 68, 69(figure), 70-71; and job assurance, 74-76, 77-78(figure), 91; limitations on, 135; as moral model, 62; role of, 5, 6-7, 61; and self-reliance, 62; and special interests, 66, 68; as too powerful, 86-87, 88(figure), 89; trust in, 63, 64(figure), 65-66, 70, 90, 170. *See also* Public function

Gray Panthers, 46
Greeley, Andrew, 57 n.12

Hamilton, David A., 15-16
Health care, 81, 82(figure), 83-84, 90, 180
Hirschman, Albert O., 26, 183 n.5; *Shifting Involvements*, 171-72
Hobart, Charles W., 52
Home for Little Wanderers, 41
Housing, provision of, 84-86, 90, 92 96, 97(figure), 98
Howe, Irving, 154

Income, and values, 155
Independence, versus interdependence, 42-43, 75, 92
Individual, versus collective, 32-33
Industrialization, 48, 52
Institutions, legitimacy of, 173-74
Interdependence, 122; versus independence, 42-43, 75, 92
Inter-university Consortium on Political and Social Research (ICPSR), 1

Jablonski, Sharon, 42
Janowitz, Morris, 65
Johnson, M., 74
Judd, Charles M., 16

Keach, William R., 19
Kennedy administration, 68
Kim, Jae-on, 128
King, Martin Luther, Jr., 8
Kirkpatrick, Clifford, 53
Knowledge for What? (Lynd), 27

LaFrance, Arthur B., 44, 45-46
Legitimacy, crisis of, 173-74
Leisure, 115, 117; versus work, 46-49
Lenski, Gerhard Emmanuel, 50-51
Liberalism, 11(chart), 135; and feeling thermometers, 79, 80(figure), 81
Lipset, Seymour Martin, 6, 7, 74, 170-71, 173, 174; *The Confidence Gap*, 19
Lorence, J., 176
Lovejoy, Mary Christine, 26

Luther, Martin, 48
Lynd, Robert S., 10; *Knowledge for What?*, 27

McCarthy, Eugene, 73
McConahay, John B., 15-16
McConnell, James V., 137
Maddox, George L., 48
Marx, Karl, 46, 48, 145
Medicare, 7, 81
Merit, and work, 56 n.1
Merton, Robert, 27
Methodology, factor analysis for, 128-29
Milburn, Michael A., 16
Miller, S. M., 28-29
Miller, William Lee, 25
Monroe, Alan D., 17, 18
Mortimer, J. T., 176
Mueller, Charles, 128

Narcissism, 42, 111, 114
National Election Study, 1, 12, 106, 112; questions from, 13(chart)
National Opinion Research Center, General Social Survey, 176-77
New Narcissism, 9, 53
New Rules (Yankelovich), 5
Nursing homes, 54

Occupation, and values, 155
Ogburn, William, 18, 180-81
Ozawa, Martha N., 39

Parsons, Talcott, 47
Personal development, versus family, 52, 55
Personal policy, 21 n.5
Plessy v. *Ferguson*, 95, 103
Pole, J. R., *The Pursuit of Equality in American History*, 53
Policy opinion, 21 n.4; ambivalence in, 74; change factors, 55; defined, 16-17; and policy value dilemmas, 36(chart); and public opinion, 15-18, 20; roots and structure of, 19-20; and social policy, 179-82; and values, 25

Policy-value conflicts, areas of, 37-55
Politics of disenchantment, 89
Poverty, 28
Private, versus public, 40-42, 56 n.5, 68, 90-91, 109 n.1
Privatism, 6, 7, 54, 81, 86
Protestantism, orientations of, 50-52, 56-57 n.11
Public, versus private, 40-42, 56 n.5, 68, 90-91, 109 n.1
Public function, 6-7; eclipse of, 19; limitation of, 90; questions on, 13(chart), 35, 37; values encompassed by, 62-63. See also Government
Public opinion, 10, 12, 14-15; and policy opinion, 15-18, 20; and polls, 83-84; trends, 11(chart)
Public Opinion magazine, 10
Pursuit of Equality in American History, The (Pole), 53

Race, and values, 154
Racial discrimination, 95
Reagan, Ronald, 181
Regression analysis: independent variables, 147(chart), 152-53(table), 157(table); median beta weights, 156(table); results, 148-50
Religion: and church attendance, 112, 113(figure), 114; and values, 154
Religious, versus secular, 49-52
Republican, 135; and feeling thermometers, 79, 80(figure), 81
Retirement, 48
Rokeach, Milton, 26, 168 n.9
Roper Center, 1
Rosenthal, Peggy, 9, 17-18
Rossi, Peter H., 38, 39

Schlitz, Michael, 76
Schneider, William, 6, 7, 74, 170-71, 173, 174; The Confidence Gap, 19
Schumann, H., 74
Secular, versus religious, 49-52
Self-development, 9
Self-reliance, 62, 122
Sen, Amartya, 26
Sennett, Richard, 112

Separate-but-equal, 95
Sessoms, Hanson Douglas, 48
Shelley v. Kraemer, 95
Shifting Involvements (Hirschman), 171-72
Shils, Edward, 7, 8-9
Simmel, Arnold, 40, 41
Slavery, 95
Social Darwinism, 44-45
Social Gospel movement, 45, 49
Socialization, formative, 20-21 n.2
Social lag, 18
Social policy, and policy opinion, 179-82
Social programs, 7; and subdominant values, 32; and taxation, 65
Social Security Act, 7, 37, 39, 44, 45, 54, 56 n.4
Social structure, 21 n.3
Social system, 21 n.3
Social welfare, institutional vs. residual, 61
Specialization, 48, 108
Standard of living, 74-78, 91
Status, ascribed, 158
Struggle, versus entitlement, 43-46, 76, 96, 104, 109 n.1
Sumner, William Graham, 44

Talmon, Yonina, 123 n.3
Taxation, 65
Turning Points (Goodman), 29

University of Michigan, Institute for Social Research, 12
Urbanization, 48, 52

Vaillant, George, 48
Value indicators: clustering of, 129-30; factor analysis of, 128-29; structure to, 127
Values: by age, 138-43, 176-79; ambivalence in, 28; change vs. stability in, 120-22; conflict theory of, 26-31; defined, 25-26; dominant/subdominant, 32-33; dualism in, 31, 34, 92-93, 128, 137, 172, 173; juxtaposition of, 28, 31, 34; maintaining,

5; multiple regression approach to, 146, 148; predictors of, 151-58, 166; questioning origins of, 145-46; social vs. personal, 28; sources of change in, 170-73; staiblity in, 175. *See also* Commitments
Value structure, indicators of, 150
Vickers, Geoffrey, 28
Vietnam War, 7, 65, 73, 89, 103
Voluntarism, 7, 110 n.4
Voting, value of, 71, 72(figure), 73-74

War on Poverty, 7, 20 n.1, 86
Wasserman, Harvey, *American Born and Reborn*, 182 n.1
Watergate, 65, 89, 171
Weber, Max, 145, 146
Welfare state, 62, 110 n.4
White House Conference on the Aging, 6

White House Conference on the Family, 53
Williams, Robin M., Jr., 26, 32-33
Witmer, Helen, 61
Wohlenberg, Ernest H., 17
Women's movement, 29
Women's rights, 7, 8, 178; attitudes toward, 106, 107(figure), 108
Work: hours reduction for, 114-15, 116(figure), 117; versus leisure, 46-49; and merit, 56 n.1
World War II, 86

Yankelovich, Daniel, 9, 10, 16, 43; *New Rules*, 5
Yinger, J. M., *Countercultures: The Promise and Peril of a World Turned Upside Down*, 5, 29
Youth culture, 70

About the Author

JOHN E. TROPMAN is a Professor in the School of Social Work and in the School of Business at the University of Michigan. He has been Acting Director of the Institute of Gerontology at the university and is doing research on American values and social policy. His published works include *Meetings: How to Make Them Work for You, Policy Management in the Human Services, New Strategic Perspectives on Social Policy*, and *Conflict in Culture*.